Rethinking
Global Sisterhood

Rethinking Global Sisterhood
WESTERN FEMINISM AND IRAN

Nima Naghibi

UNIVERSITY OF MINNESOTA PRESS

MINNEAPOLIS

LONDON

Material in chapter 2 previously appeared as "Bad Feminist or Bad-Hejabi? Moving outside the Hejab Debate," *Interventions: International Journal of Postcolonial Studies* 1, no. 4 (1999); published by Routledge; reprinted with permission.

Material in chapter 3 previously appeared as "Five Minutes of Silence: Voices of Iranian Feminists in the Post-Revolutionary Age," in *Postcolonizing the Commonwealth: Studies in Literature,* ed. Rowland Smith (Waterloo: Wilfrid Laurier University Press, 2000); reprinted with permission.

Copyright 2007 by the Regents of the University of Minnesota

Published by the University of Minnesota Press
111 Third Avenue South, Suite 290
Minneapolis, MN 55401-2520
http://www.upress.umn.edu

Library of Congress Cataloging-in-Publication Data

Naghibi, Nima.
    Rethinking global sisterhood : western feminism and Iran / Nima Naghibi.
        p. cm.
    Includes bibliographical references and index.
    ISBN 978-0-8166-4759-0 (hc)
    ISBN 978-0-8166-4760-7 (pb)
    1. Feminism—Iran. 2. Feminism—International cooperation.
3. Women—Iran—Social conditions. 4. Women—Iran—Public opinion. 5. Muslim women—Iran. 6. Women in motion pictures—Iran.
7. East and West. 8. Other (Philosophy). I. Title.
HQ1735.2.N34 2007
305.48'89155—dc22

                                            2006101635

Printed in the United States of America on acid-free paper

12 11 10 09 08 07   10 9 8 7 6 5 4 3 2 1

For my parents
whose sacrifices were my gain

and

for Andrew, Safianna, and Cyrus
who bring me joy

Contents

Preface

I N THE COURSE OF WRITING A BOOK that argues for self-reflexivity in scholarship in feminist, postcolonial, and Middle East studies, I have been necessarily faced with my own motivations for pursuing this project, as well as my own various subject positions. (As an Iranian feminist with a conventionally male first name, for instance, I have experienced many a confusing first encounter!)

More significantly, though, like other Iranians of my generation who were old enough to feel the impact of the revolution in 1979, but too young to participate actively in the intellectual and political fervor of those heady days, my life was nevertheless irrevocably changed by those events. As an adolescent I filled many journals with purple prose, pondering the whys and wherefores of these changes. Like other diasporic subjects in the postrevolutionary age, I have literally felt the effects of the discursive shift in the West from "exotic Persian" to "fundamentalist Islamist" and, more specifically, to "oppressed Muslim woman."

Attending school in Paris shortly after the revolution, I was inevitably subjected to bigoted statements about the character flaws of *ces gens*. *Ces gens* were irrevocably uncivilized; these people veiled, in other words, oppressed their women; these people were unshaven and dirty; these people were religious fundamentalists; and so on. These representations did not, in my mind, correspond with what I knew of my family, my friends, my culture. I did not know it at the time, but I was experiencing the power of discourse to shape my subjectivity and the power of ideology to hail me as its subject.

The shame I felt in the face of these remarks was a personal one, but it was also part of a larger shame, one born out of a fear of confirming suspicions about the backwardness of all Iranians at a time when they were regularly vilified in Western popular discourses. Having experienced the palpable racism of the French during the early postrevolutionary period, I felt the double burden of representation: I was the Muslim Other, but at the same time I felt the pressure of having to represent the "true" or "accurate" picture of what "these people/my people" were like. This was rather a heavy responsibility to bear for a young girl, but one that I felt compelled to assume in the politically charged atmosphere of the time. I no longer feel bound to represent all Iranians, nor do I think it a necessary or desirable impulse, but the impact of the discursive violence that divided the world into "us" and "them," "progressive women" and "oppressed women," has remained with me, and undoubtedly fuels my work as a postcolonial feminist scholar.

My work is informed by my training in the discipline of English, which is committed to the view that representations do matter and that they do have material effects. My understanding of discourse is influenced by the work of Michel Foucault, who has written about the production of the "real" and the imbrication of power and knowledge through discursive representations. What I am most interested in is how particular kinds of (often contradictory) representations of the Persian woman as abject, as repressed, and, paradoxically, as licentious become consolidated as unquestioned "truths" in dominant Western and Iranian feminist discourses. Because this field has a certain fraught history, I feel I must clarify again that I am *not* suggesting that there were no active and agential Iranian feminists during the late nineteenth and twentieth centuries. I am *not* suggesting that all Iranian women passively "fit" into the category of the abject Other. Rather, I am interested in exploring the ways in which such discursive representations *become* dominant and consolidated in certain "mainstream" or dominant feminist discourses. In Foucault's words:

Each society has its régime of truth, its "general politics" of truth: that is, the types of discourse which it accepts and makes function as true; the mechanisms and instances which enable one to distinguish true and false statements, the means by which each is sanctioned; the techniques and procedures accorded value in the acquisition of truth; the status of those who are charged with saying what counts as true. (1980, 131)

It is this "régime of truth" that I am interested in exploring and uncovering. By doing so, I do not intend to deny the agency of "real" Iranian women but instead to study the effects of discourse and representations on the material lives of these women.

Indeed, an examination of representations and self-representations of Iranian women serves a critical function, especially at this historical juncture, when the language of regime change is being applied to Iran. Shortly after September 11, 2001, the United States invaded and "liberated" Afghanistan in the name of its women. The fiasco of the American occupation of Iraq was structured around similar discursive representations of its oppressed and long-suffering people, including and especially its women and children. My research here attempts to provide an examination of the complex social, cultural, and historical relations that have been occluded in contemporary analyses of the tensions between Middle Eastern and Western nations.

My training in postcolonial and feminist theories from within an English department offers me, I believe, a different lens through which to view these issues. There remains an unfortunate suspicion of postcolonial and poststructuralist theories among historians and scholars of the Middle East, and it is my hope here to make a case for the inclusion of the postcolonial in these disciplines. Minoo Moallem has argued:

New scholarly paradigms are needed to study Muslims in the West, since neither modernist notions of identity nor taken-for-granted notions of area studies are able to grasp the complexity of an unstable and contested world of meanings, identities and subjectivities. As a field of knowledge production, Middle Eastern studies is marked by the absence of a certain postmodern scholarship that could potentially equip it to meet these challenges—in particular, colonial and postcolonial studies, transnational feminist theories, and transnational cultural studies. . . . In recent years, new forms of Orientalism, along with racism vis-à-vis Middle Eastern peoples and cultures, have found currency in a reinvestment in the civilizational tropes of Islam and the West.

> However, the inability of Middle Eastern studies to catch up with
> the transnational nature of such transformations has kept it in a
> space/time where it is protected from the risk of its own disciplinary
> undoing. (2005, 19)

Too often, postcolonial and poststructuralist theories are casually dismissed as "culturally relativist" positions by otherwise estimable scholars whose work I generally admire. This regrettable position only further demonstrates Foucault's argument about the production of "truth" through regulating and regulatory divisions between various disciplines. Disciplinary distinctions are themselves "facts of discourse that deserve to be analyzed beside others" (Foucault 1972, 22). Thus, different disciplines have their own regimes of truth and bestow upon representatives of a particular discipline the status of authority and truth while denying legitimacy to those who speak from outside that discipline. It is my hope that this work can, in some small way, work toward breaking down some of these disciplinary tensions in the interest of producing useful ways of understanding historical and contemporary East/West relations.

My work is equally committed to bringing the Middle East into postcolonial debates. Although Edward Said's groundbreaking work *Orientalism* (1978) focuses on the ways in which the Middle East, or the Orient, is produced by the West through academic scholarship, literary texts, and military and government documents, much of the postcolonial scholarship that has followed Said has tended to overlook the Middle East in favor of other geographic areas, such as Africa, Australasia, the Caribbean, North America, and South Asia.

The absence of the Middle East in postcolonial scholarship is paradoxically offset by its excess of presence in the media. Since the late 1970s and particularly, I would suggest, since the 1979 Iranian revolution, the Middle East and Islam have garnered tremendous negative attention in the Western popular imagination: in the media and in literature. The events of 9/11 in particular have led to the increased visibility of Middle Easterners and Muslims in North American media. Visually, the Middle East is marked as "Other" in the popular media by a concentration of images of bearded and turbaned men in robes who are construed as potential terrorist threats to "homeland security." Middle Eastern Muslim women are depicted as voiceless and abject, suffering behind the folds of the veil. These representations have been circulating with particular vigor since September 11, but as this book demonstrates, they did not emerge suddenly out of a vacuum; they have a long history in Western intellectual, literary, popular, and (liberal) feminist discourses.

In *Covering Islam,* Said writes: "Underlying every interpretation of other cultures—especially of Islam—is the choice facing the individual scholar or intellectual: whether to put intellect at the service of power or at the service of criticism, community and moral sense" (1981, 64). It seems to me that particularly in the aftermath of the events of 9/11, it is more urgent than ever to include the Middle East in postcolonial scholarship and to include the postcolonial in scholarship about the Middle East. There is, I believe, a sense of political urgency here to contextualize events so that it will no longer be possible for the question "Why do they hate us so much?" to circulate so prominently and uncritically in popular discourses.

The media coverage of the Middle East since September 11, 2001, points to the necessity of a cultural critique that can attend to the discourses of representation through which those tragic events were made transparent. My work is located at the interstices of postcolonialism and feminism with a view to investigating the complex discourses of cultural representations in order to provide an interventionary and counterdiscourse. At a time when Western, and particularly (North) American, relations with the Middle East are in a state of crisis, this text attempts to provide historical perspectives and current insights into a nation branded by U.S. president George W. Bush as part of an "axis of evil," and examines the ways in which liberal feminist discourse has been and continues to be complicit with dominant discursive representations of "Other" nations and women.

A note on transliteration: I have used a modified version of the Library of Congress transliteration system throughout this book. In cases where names and places have circulated widely in English, I have kept the familiar spelling. All diacritical marks have been omitted. In citations, I have adhered to the transliteration system used by the authors.

Introduction

"AN IMAGINATIVE AUNT who, for my ninth birthday, sent a copy of *The Arabian Nights* was, I suppose, the original cause of trouble." Thus begins Freya Stark's 1934 narrative of her travels in Persia, *The Valley of the Assassins*. This Orientalist evocation of *The Arabian Nights* is a common feature in the many texts written by British and American women who traveled to Persia in the late nineteenth and early twentieth centuries.[1] Behind this evocation lies a consistent representation of Persia as exotic, accessible, and passive, and at the heart of this structure of representation one finds—almost inevitably—the figure of the exoticized, veiled, and silent Persian woman. This structure of representation, I believe, enabled British and American women writers to counterpose a figural category—the subjugated female Other—against a more recognizably domestic image of female subjectivity, and thus to occupy a subject position of power in relation to Persian women.

This book explores the ways in which "first world" feminist empowerment, as represented in these narratives, depends upon a figural subjugation of Persian women. At the same time, it examines the ways in which Western women's representation of Persian women as abject is contested by Persian women's participation at significant junctures in

Iranian political history. This study also traces the ways in which Western women's structure of self-empowerment continues into contemporary Western and prerevolutionary, state-sponsored Iranian feminist narratives about Persia and Iran, and examines what happens to this structure of representation when it is contested by postrevolutionary, indigenous Iranian feminists in their own narratives of self-representation. I would like to clarify at the outset that this is not a study about "inside" and "outside"; this is not an argument formulated within a binary structure about the dominating West and the beleaguered East. Rather, it explores (Western *and* Iranian) feminism's responsibility for its imperialist gestures in Iran and its possibilities for social and political intervention at a particularly vexed, indeed critical, moment in East/West relations.

A word about terminology: In "'Under Western Eyes' Revisited," Chandra Mohanty reflects on the terms "Western" and "third world," both of which she uses throughout her oft-cited critique of Western feminist imperialist scholarship about "third world" women. She considers that terms such as "One-Third World" and "Two-Thirds World" that "incorporat[e] an analysis of power and agency that is crucial" might, in some instances, work more effectively in discussions that aim to "move away from misleading geographical and ideological binarisms" (Mohanty 1991, 506). I would be tempted to borrow these terms throughout my own work, since my argument is not predicated on the view that all Western feminists were oppressors and all Iranian women were victims. However, I agree with Mohanty's observation that the terms "Western" and "third world" have an explanatory power and referentiality to the history of colonialization and imperialism that the terms "One-Third World" and "Two-Thirds World" elide. I have thus chosen to use the terms "West" and, at times, "East" or "third world," with all their inadequacies, to hang on to the critical colonial/imperial investments that the terms evoke.

This study examines the ways in which the history of feminism in Iran is intertwined with the history of imperial expansion and class oppression, which at times limited its potential as an oppositional theory for social and political change. This book explores the confluence of the discourses of modernity, global sisterhood, and subjugated Persian womanhood in the works of Western feminists and what I call "Pahlavi feminists" (by whom I am referring to prerevolutionary, state-sponsored feminists).

The focus of this study is on the long and largely neglected history of Western women's involvement in Persia from the mid-nineteenth century to the present time. European and American women traveled to the country variously as Christian evangelicals eager to spread the good word of the Bible, as "intrepid adventuresses" bravely exploring the exotic and alien land of Persia, and as feminists who went to Iran in the name of global sisterhood. The language of global, or universal, sisterhood was developed with particular vigor during the nineteenth century and was articulated within a discursive framework of modernization and progress. It was through the discourse of sisterhood that elite Persian women of the late nineteenth century and the Pahlavi feminists of the twentieth century expressed solidarity with their Western counterparts.

The problem with the discourse of sisterhood remains, however, the inherent inequality between "sisters." Often using the veil as a marker of Persian women's backwardness, Western and (unveiled) elite Iranian women represented themselves as enlightened and advanced, while the veiled Persian woman was made to embody subservient womanhood. By mobilizing the language of sisterhood, Western and Iranian women from the privileged classes positioned themselves as fully formed subjects against whom less privileged Persian women were constructed as abject figures.

Although there are significant differences between the self-sacrificing missionary who claims to bring the light of Christ to a land of darkness, the intrepid, independent, and spirited adventuress who travels simply because she has the privileged circumstances to indulge her wanderlust, and the feminist who seeks to close ranks with her less fortunate sisters, this book attempts to explore the discursive similarities between the ways in which all these subjects position themselves against (often traditional, working class) Persian women. In other words, although these women may have occupied very different social and political positions in Britain or America, and certainly not all of them were sympathetic to the principles of what may generally be understood as feminism, they drew on similar discursive representations of Persian women in their writings. In representing Persian women, they drew on what Foucault has called the "already-said," or rather, the repressed "never-said" of manifest discourse (1972, 25). The truth of Iranian women's representation as abject, veiled subjects is thus further entrenched by the self-referentiality of the "already-said" of colonial discourse.

The Western woman, modeled on an Enlightenment figure of autonomous subjecthood, contrasts herself in each instance to the Persian woman, represented as the devalued Other against which Western woman consolidates herself. Privileged Iranian women in the nineteenth and twentieth centuries also participated in the discursive subjugation of their working-class Persian counterparts. By positioning the Persian woman as the embodiment of oppressed womanhood, Western and elite Iranian women represented themselves as epitomical of modernity and progress.

Despite the large body of Western women's writing on Persia and the Persian woman, there has been very little critical attention paid to these works. In 1991, Sara Mills argued that women's travel writings have been largely ignored in the field of colonial discourse analysis. Those who have studied women's travel texts are, she claims in *Discourses of Difference*, women critics. These critics, she says, tend to romanticize and idealize women travelers as intrepid and indomitable "globetrotteresses" who bravely challenged Victorian gender roles by daring to travel on their own in spaces previously accessible only to men. Since Mills's influential work, however, there has been a growing body of feminist work in the field of colonial discourse analysis (which has traditionally overlooked women's travel writings) and feminist criticism (which has traditionally celebrated "adventurous" women) committed to viewing women's travel writings through a rigorous critical lens.[2]

Although Mills questions the absence of rigorous feminist critiques of women's travel writing, she appears occasionally to succumb to the temptation to exonerate the Western woman traveler, simply by virtue of her gender, from her participation in the reproduction of the colonial order:

> Because of the way that discourses of femininity circulated within the late nineteenth and early twentieth centuries, women travel writers were unable to adopt the imperialist voice with the ease with which male writers did. The writing they produced tended to be more tentative than male writing, less able to assert the "truths" of British rule without qualification. Because of their oppressive socialisation and marginal

position in relation to imperialism, despite their generally privileged class position, women writers tended to concentrate on descriptions of people as individuals, rather than on statements about the race as a whole. (Mills 1991, 3)

Despite Mills's claim that Western women writers avoided making "statements about the race as a whole," I would suggest, along with such feminists as Antoinette Burton, Inderpal Grewal, Kumari Jayawardena, Cheryl McEwan, and Meyda Yeğenoğlu, that Western women, in their capacity as missionaries, as "eccentric" or "intrepid" travelers, or as feminists, used their gender as a vehicle for unique emplacement within the colonial project. McEwan has observed that

many Victorians viewed lone women travelers as oddities, eccentric "globetrotteresses" with little to contribute to scientific and geographical knowledge. . . . Accounts of [women's] "vagaries" add spice to already colourful biographies, but at the same time underestimate the contribution of women to British imperial culture and overlook the part they played in the production of imperial knowledges. (2000, 4–5)

As women, they had a mobility denied Western men; they could transgress the gendered boundaries of the public and the private so carefully observed in the East. Armed with a privileged access to the women's quarters, to the mothers of the Oriental races and nations, and thus to the "heart of empire," Western women in Persia very much gave themselves the authority to make sweeping statements about the "race" as a whole.[3]

In 1894, Gertrude Bell published *Persian Pictures,* an account of her travels in Persia. At the end of a chapter describing her visit with three (veiled) women of the nobility, she writes, "We left them gazing after us from behind their canvas walls. Their prisoned existence seemed to us a poor mockery of life as we cantered homewards up the damp valley, the mountain air sending a cheerful warmth through our veins" (Bell 1894, 67). In February 1999, more than one hundred years after Bell's *Persian Pictures,* Elaine Sciolino published a feature article in the *New York Times* travel section on her experiences touring Iran with a group of "intrepid, well-traveled and well-prepared" Americans (1999, 9). The trip offended the feminist sensibilities of the women in the group, one of whom she quotes as saying, "Before I came here, I believed in women's liberation. Now I believe in women's domination" (Sciolino 1999, 8). In each instance, from Bell's 1894 observations to Sciolino's 1999 adventures, Western women position themselves against Persian women, contrasting their own independence and liberation with the miserable, "prisoned existence" of their Persian counterparts.

Mills admits that women travel writers "cannot be said to speak outside of colonial discourse," but she believes that their relationship to "the dominant discourse is problematic because of its conflict with the discourses of 'femininity'" (1991, 63). Simon Gikandi describes Western women's discourses as ambivalent because of their ambiguous relationship to the colonial enterprise, resulting in a "complicity/resistance" dialectic, which he explains as "a schema whose primary goal is to show how women saw empire as an opportunity for freedom and advancement but found it impossible, given their own subordinate positions in the domestic economy, to unconditionally valorize the imperial voice" (1996, 123). I would like to suggest that, despite their unequal relationship to men and, initially, to the colonial project, Western women argued successfully for their full and important participation in the colonies not despite, but indeed in substantial part *because of,* their gender. They argued that, as women, they had unique access to the "harems" or women's quarters in the Orient. Since a country's level of progress was for them measured by the status of its women, Western women located themselves within a particular position of authority initially by declaring the backwardness of their Eastern sisters and then by setting themselves the task of civilizing their inferiors. In this way, Western women defined their own unique burden, which they chose to bear in the civilizing project.[4] Western women could alter the masculinist tenor of colonial discourse by occupying a central position within the colonial project because of the mobility awarded them due to their gender and their class.

In Helen Barrett Montgomery's 1910 study of women's missionary work in the Orient, she forecasts dire predictions for Oriental women should Western women be prevented from ministering to their medical needs:[5]

> We cannot pursue the story of this chapter in the expanding life of women further than to note its bearing on foreign missions. These lion-hearted pioneers in the field of medicine were blazing a trail whose importance they little dreamed. If the contracted ideas of propriety held by the vast majority of men and women in the civilized

world of that time had triumphed, one of the most powerful agencies in the Christian conquest of the world would have been wanting. Whether there were to be women physicians was a question of interest in America: but in Asia it was a question of life and death. The women of half the world were shut out from medical assistance unless they could receive it at the hands of women. So with God and nature leading them, the women pioneers pressed out into the untried path; hundreds of more timid souls followed them, and the protesting old world settled back grumbling to get used to the new situation. (119)

Montgomery's contrast of "old world" propriety with "new" world models of male and female roles emerges from a particular historical moment. Theories of social evolution, which became increasingly popular in the nineteenth century, supported the argument that women were biologically inferior to men. In this climate of increasing conservatism and rigid gender differences, "woman became a symbol of . . . nonmodern identity" (Felski 1995, 18).

Rita Felski has traced the history of the "modern" and the contradictory significations of the term. Felski argues that the idea of the "modern" as expressed during the French Revolution enabled a subversive and revolutionary challenge to established social and political hierarchies (1995, 13). At the same time, she states, the concept of modernity is inextricably woven with the colonial enterprise. By denying what Johannes Fabian has termed in the context of anthropological writing "temporal coevalness" to the Oriental Other, the West can justify its presence in the East by claiming to bring educational, medical, and technological progress to a less modern nation. The concept of the modern also excluded women, but women of the middle class appropriated the idea of newness to posit the "New Woman" as the vanguard of modernity. According to Felski, in "the early twentieth century the figure of the New Woman was to become a resonant symbol of emancipation, whose modernity signalled not an endorsement of an existing present but rather a bold imagining of an alternative future" (1995, 14).

Montgomery's appeal to the "new situation" when describing the valiance of missionary women doctors evokes the figure of the "New Woman." She describes medical missionary women as "lion-hearted pioneers" on the threshold of a new enterprise: that of converting Oriental women. Montgomery writes:

> The women of the Orient, shut in, illiterate, superstitious, are naturally
> the hardest to win. They do not want to learn, they resist the pain of
> new ideas. To one argument they are open. The woman who ministers
> to them in their suffering, who redeems the lives of their little ones,
> who fights for them the pestilence that walks in darkness, may say
> anything she pleases to them about her religion, and they will listen.
> (1910, 131–32)

Not only does Montgomery make a space for women in the traditionally patriarchal discourse of modernity, but she also forwards a strong
argument in favor of including Western women as an integral part of the
traditionally male colonial project.

Contrary to the conventional perception that the discourse of Victorian femininity was disenabling for Western women, Vron Ware has
argued that the colonies offered a number of opportunities to British
women in the nineteenth century:

> At a time when evolutionary theories defining women's physical and
> mental capabilities were beginning to pass into the realms of "common
> sense," the Empire provided both a physical and an ideological space
> in which the different meanings of femininity could be explored or
> contested. Corresponding ideas about racial or cultural difference
> provided a context for these conflicts to be played out in their full
> complexity, so that, for example, the Englishwoman abroad could be
> at once a many-faceted heroic figure: from an intrepid adventuress
> defying racial and sexual boundaries to heroic mother responsible for
> the preservation of the white "race"; from the devoted missionary
> overseeing black souls to the guardian of white morals; from
> determined pioneer and companion to the white man to a vulnerable,
> defenceless piece of his property. (1992, 120)

Indeed, if the discourse of femininity hampered the mobility of Western women, as Mills and Gikandi suggest, then the discourses of feminism and of modernity enabled them to move outside their scripted and
restrictive lives in England and the United States.[6]

Certainly not all the women who went to Persia self-identified as
feminists or supported feminist causes, such as women's suffrage. But
they all shared a willingness to take advantage of the gains of feminism
to move outside their restricted domestic spheres in England and America. Leila Ahmed has argued that the *language* of feminism (if not actual
feminist principles) became an important rhetorical tool deployed by

men and women in the nineteenth century in the service of the colonial project (1992, 151). In *Western Women in Eastern Lands,* Montgomery uses Lord Cromer's denunciations of Muslim women's lives to bolster her own argument for the presence of women missionaries in the colonies:

> It cannot be doubted that the seclusion of women exercises a baneful influence on Eastern society. The arguments on this subject are, indeed, so commonplace that it is needless to dwell upon them. It will be sufficient to say that seclusion, by confining the sphere of woman's interest to a very limited horizon, cramps the intellect and withers the mental development of one-half of the population of Moslem countries. An Englishwoman asked an Egyptian lady how she passed her time. "I sit on this sofa," she answered, "and when I am tired I cross over and sit on that." (qtd. Montgomery 1910, 80–81)

Cromer's indignation at Muslim women's seclusion and oppression—as he represents them—did not arouse his sympathies for English women's feminist activities at home. In fact, as Ahmed points out, although Cromer was an outspoken critic of the practice of veiling in Egypt, he was a "founding member and sometime president of the Men's League for Opposing Women's Suffrage" in England (1992, 153). British patriarchs focused on certain practices in other cultures that they identified as oppressive, such as the practice of suttee in India, veiling in the Middle East, and foot binding in China, and used the rhetoric of feminism to justify their colonial presence in the offending country:

> Even as the Victorian Male establishment devised theories to contest the claims of feminism, and derided and rejected the ideas of feminism and the notion of men's oppressing women with respect to itself, it captured the language of feminism and redirected it, in the service of colonialism, toward Other men and the cultures of Other men. (Ahmed 1992, 151)

Gayatri Spivak has, now famously, described the patriarchal colonial impulse to protect women from their native cultures as "white men saving brown women from brown men" (1988, 297). Western women also used the language of feminism, and of women's rights, to highlight the differences between their independent, capable selves and their subjugated colonial counterparts. Ahmed writes:

Whether in the hands of patriarchal men or feminists, the ideas of
Western feminism essentially functioned to morally justify the attack
on native societies and to support the notion of the comprehensive
superiority of Europe. Evidently, then, whatever the disagreements of
feminism with white male domination within Western societies, outside
their borders feminism turned from being the critic of the system of
white male dominance to being its docile servant. Anthropology, it has
often been said, served as a handmaid to colonialism. Perhaps it must
also be said that feminism, or the ideas of feminism, served as its
other handmaid. (1992, 154–55)

Ware has acknowledged the dearth of Western feminist scholarship
that attempts to engage with the historical, political, and social conditions that enabled the growth of first-wave feminism by asserting that
"feminist ideology and practice were shaped by the social, economic
and political forces of imperialism to a far greater extent than has been
acknowledged" (1992, 119). Although the missionary woman and the
"intrepid adventuress" did not necessarily see themselves as feminists,
they believed, like the early feminists, that it was the moral duty of Western women to introduce the idea of women's rights to the Orient, and
their argument hinged on the concept of a shared sisterhood. Western
women missionaries, travelers, and feminists thus identified Eastern
women as their "sisters," and did so by drawing on the Enlightenment
idea of universal rights and equality.

Although universal or global sisterhood is commonly associated with
the second wave of feminism, which reached its peak during the 1970s,
the concept of global sisterhood can, in fact, be traced back to nineteenth-
century missionary women's discourse. As Susan Thorne has argued,
the "missionary connection between British feminists and the empire
helped to establish the imperial coordinates of Western feminism's conception of global sisterhood. Missionary tracts appealed explicitly to
women's solidarity across 'racial' divides by condemning the patriarchal
abuse of heathen women in the colonies" (1999, 52).

One significant difference between the rhetoric of 1970s global sisterhood and that of the late nineteenth and early twentieth centuries
centers on the notion of oppression. In the 1970s, the official rhetoric
of global sisterhood was one of the common oppression of women. Although nineteenth-century British and American women also deployed

the language of sisterhood to acknowledge women's universal oppression, they invariably used the Eastern woman as a symbol of women's "collective past" (Nair 1990, 16). Middle-class Victorian women were represented as the highest caliber of womanhood on the socio-evolutionary scale. According to Felski, middle-class women used evolutionary theories to their advantage by "frequently present[ing] themselves as an intellectual and political vanguard at the forefront of history. Within this scenario, women of other races and classes were often depicted as primitive and backward" (Felski 1995, 149). The image of the backward Eastern woman, who belongs to a more primitive era, served as a contrast to the more highly evolved figure of womanhood in the West and enabled Western women to place themselves in a leadership position vis-à-vis their Eastern sisters.[7] This hierarchical model of sisterhood was also embraced by privileged women in the Orient who, in turn, used class differences to place themselves at the forefront of the women's movements in their respective countries.

In *Our Moslem Sisters: A Cry of Need from Lands of Darkness* (1907), a collection of papers on Christian missions in Muslim countries presented at a 1906 conference in Cairo, Annie Van Sommer appealed to Presbyterian missionary women to bring salvation to women in "Moslem lands":

> We ask you to enter into a covenant of prayer with us, that we may not cease to intercede for our broken-hearted sisters, that they may be comforted, and for the captives of Satan, that they may be set free, that the prison gates may be opened for them so that the oil of joy may be given them for mourning, the garment of praise for the spirit of heaviness.
>
> "Life! life! eternal life!
> Jesus alone is the giver.
> Life! life! abundant life!
> Glory to Jesus for ever."
>
> When this Life becomes theirs, Our Moslem Sisters *will be our own sisters in a new sense of the word,* and we shall see the evangelization of the Mohammedan home and of all Moslem lands. (Van Sommer 1907, 298; emphasis mine)

The idea of sisterhood, as represented here, is predicated upon a hierarchical, pedagogical relationship between those sisters who know and those who passively await enlightenment. Van Sommer's claim that, after conversion to Christianity, the women will become their sisters "in a new sense of the word" betrays a recognition that the sisterhood she is currently advocating is predicated on an assumption of inequality.

The language of women's rights, and the idea of the universality of those rights, was developed with particular vigor during the nineteenth century and was articulated within a discursive framework of modern progress and global sisterhood. The problem with the discourse of sisterhood, however, remains the inherent inequality between "sisters." This hierarchical relationship between women who know and those who require instruction continues to haunt contemporary Western and diasporic Iranian feminist discourses that celebrate the universal experience of all women. Bruce Robbins has argued convincingly that "defenses of universalism, like attacks on it, are increasingly a trivial pursuit" (1995, 166). He believes that there is no such thing as what he calls a "clean universalism" and that critiques of universalism that aim to include the particular only reproduce a new universalism in the place of an old one. Although I agree with Robbins's point about the futility of arguing about universal inclusiveness, I believe that Meyda Yeğenoğlu's argument in *Colonial Fantasies* is an important one to consider here. She states that the universal sisterhood proclaimed by Western feminists since the nineteenth century is "a particular that masquerades as universal. But it should be emphasized that not any particular has the power to enforce itself as universal" (Yeğenoğlu 1998, 102).

Joan Scott has traced the history of feminism and that of universalism back to two conflicting notions of the individual in Enlightenment discourse. In "Universalism and the History of Feminism," Scott describes the first definition of the individual as an "abstract prototype for the human" (1995, 2). This definition, according to Scott, was used to prove that there were certain universal and natural rights to which citizens of a nation were entitled. However, those who for reason of gender, race, or class did not fit the definition of the abstract human prototype were excluded from this system of supposed universal inclusion.

The second Enlightenment definition of the individual was that of a unique being, a distinct person who was defined (necessarily) in relation to an Other. Western women were excluded from the political rights of the citizen since they did not fit the definition of the human prototype and because they were the Other to the male individual. The universal definition of the individual—the "abstract prototype for the human"—was necessarily male, and the definition of the individual as unique required, in Spivak's words, a "self-consolidating other." By virtue of their Otherness to men, Western women were excluded from the political rights of the citizen.

Scott argues that the power of feminism lies in its subversive nature. By revealing the contradictions of Enlightenment definitions of the individual as both universal and unique, feminism challenged the ostensibly democratic foundation of French Republicanism. For this reason, Scott believes that feminism proved itself to be a dangerous and subversive political force. However, the subversiveness of Western feminism appears less convincing in light of its own attempts to insert women into the discourse of universalism. If European men used the idea of sexual difference to exclude women from the universal rights of man, then Western women used the idea of cultural difference to insert themselves into universalist discourse—and they did so by turning to the colonies. Yeğenoğlu writes:

> It is in the East that Western woman was able to become a full individual, which was the goal desired and promoted by the emerging modernist ideology. . . . It is not far-fetched to argue that Western woman's recognition of herself as a subject was possible only outside national boundaries, in the encounter of a *sexually same yet culturally different other.* (1998, 107; emphasis hers)

In fact, early twentieth-century Western feminists were so successful at adopting the originally masculine Enlightenment discourse of individualism to achieve their political goals that it continues to permeate the language of global sisterhood.[8] It is the confluence of the discourses of modernity and of global sisterhood, as well as the mobilization of the figure of the subjugated Persian woman in the works of Western and Pahlavi feminists, that I would like to explore in this book. I will also examine contemporary representations of Iranian women by feminist filmmakers active in the Islamic Republic. One of the predominant forms of cultural expression in Iran has become contemporary cinema, which reaches an international audience and whose metaphoric and coded images have subversive implications for postrevolutionary feminist articulations.

This book is divided into four chapters, and is structured contra-puntally so that the last chapter (which focuses exclusively on contemporary Iranian feminist filmmakers) gestures back to the first chapter (which focuses exclusively on Western women's discursive representations of Persian women). Chapter 1 investigates Western women's construction of the Persian woman as the degraded other. Chapters 2 and 3 examine the intersection of Western and Pahlavi feminist voices through the discourse of global sisterhood, and explore the ways in which both Western and Pahlavi feminists participate in occluding the dissenting voices of other Iranian feminists. The final chapter considers the expression of an indigenous postrevolutionary Iranian feminism through the popular medium of Iranian cinema.

Chapter 1, "Enlightening the Other: Christian Sisters and Intrepid Adventuresses," examines the writings of Presbyterian and Anglican women missionaries who published accounts of their work in Persia (1899–1911), as well as Gertrude Bell's *Persian Pictures* (1894) and Ella Sykes's *Through Persia on a Side-Saddle* (1901) and *Persia and Its People* (1910). This chapter provides a historical background to the Western construction of the Persian woman as abject and the troubling of that construction by Persian women themselves. The argument will be structured around what historians have identified as the first "modern" period in Iran: that of the 1905–1911 Constitutional Revolution. I will be examining Western women's writings of that period to explore the ways in which the languages of modernity and sisterhood were mobilized to position the Persian woman in an unequal pedagogical relationship to Western women.

Chapter 2, "Scopophilic Desires: Unveiling Iranian Women," traces the intersection of Western and Iranian feminist discourses surrounding the familiar trope of the veil as oppressive. One of the most obvious sites upon which the dominant discourses of Western feminism and Pahlavi feminism intersect is the subject of veiling. The veil as the ultimate symbol of the degradation of Muslim, and in this case Persian, women, continues to circulate in both popular and academic feminist narratives in the West. After traveling to Persia in the early decades of the twentieth century, Clara Colliver Rice described the pitiable lives of Persian women thus: "Behind the veil out of doors, behind the curtain indoors, left out of every social function, public or private, in which men play any part, they are seldom educated, trusted, valued or respected. How can a country progress with its womanhood handicapped to this extent?" (1923, 38). Debates about veiling have often generated unequivocal positions on the oppressive or, alternatively, liberating aspects of this article of clothing. While a significant number of Western women from the late nineteenth century to the present have configured the veiled Persian woman as submerged beneath the suffocating folds of the chador, this chapter examines the complicity of many state-sponsored Iranian feminists and nationalists in the association of the veil with backwardness. Taj al-Saltanah, generally celebrated in Iranian academic circles as one of the early "modern" Iranian feminists, declared, "The veiling of women in this country has spawned and spread thousands upon thousands of corrupt and immoral tendencies" (1993, 292). This chapter attempts to move outside binary representations of the veil by gesturing to the complexities of the practice of veiling within an Iranian context, by grounding the argument in the historical moments of state-enforced unveiling (1936) and veiling (1983) and the participation of Western and Iranian women in these debates.

Chapter 3, "Global Sisters in Revolutionary Iran," offers a closer look at the discourse of global sisterhood as it manifested itself during the second wave of American and European feminism. It explores the ways in which 1970s global sisterhood was adapted to an Iranian context by considering the connections between the work of prerevolutionary Iranian feminists (or Pahlavi feminists) within the state-sponsored Women's Organization of Iran and the involvement of prominent second-wave feminists such as Betty Friedan, Germaine Greer, Kate Millett, Robin Morgan, Gloria Steinem, and others in the Iranian feminist movement before and during the 1979 revolution. The active participation of Western feminists in the volatile Iranian feminist arena during the revolutionary period needs to be understood in light of the history of global sisterhood, since, as Burton points out, "the concept of international feminist solidarity was an ideal which Western European feminists were able to imagine partly through representations of non-Western women as compliant in their own salvation by their feminist 'sisters'" (1991, 70–71).

Chapter 4, "Female Homosocial Communities in Iranian Feminist Film," grows out of the figure of the politically vigilant *hijabi* (veiled woman) discussed at the end of chapter 2. By turning to contemporary Iranian cinema, with a particular focus on Tahmineh Milani's *Two Women* (1999) and *The Fifth Reaction* (2003), Ziba Mir-Hosseini's and Kim Longinotto's *Divorce Iranian-Style* (1998) and *Runaway* (2001), and Mahnaz Afzali's *The Ladies' Room* (2003), I argue that these movies provide a forum for the articulation of an indigenous Iranian feminism that has taken shape in the postrevolutionary era. The figure of the articulate and agential *hijabi* expresses herself and her desires through female bonding. This concept of "female bonding," I suggest, presents a viable and important challenge to the dated and imperialist model of hierarchical "global sisterhood" by refusing to offer false promises of equality. The figure of the postrevolutionary Iranian feminist, I claim, dissociates herself from her earlier predecessors who were marked by the imperialism of global feminism. This chapter thus sees fit to focus, through the medium of cinema, on the agency of the feminist subject in contemporary Iran as she redefines her own subjectivity in the face of an oppressive liberal feminist discourse and an antifeminist state invested in her abjection.

CHAPTER I
Enlightening the Other: Christian Sisters and Intrepid Adventuresses

THIS CHAPTER EXAMINES ONE ASPECT of Western women's investment in Persia in the late nineteenth and early twentieth centuries: the involvement of American and British women during the 1905–1911 Constitutional Revolution and the period before it. Historians interested in locating a "modern" moment in Iran have argued that Iranian modernity was born out of the ideas leading to the Constitutional Revolution. Parvin Paidar has remarked that the discourse of Iranian modernity was mutable and that it went through four distinct phases in Iran; the Constitutional Revolution, she suggests, is the first of these four phases (1995, 27).[1] The idea of the modern emerged in the late nineteenth century and was influenced by Western models of modernity; in fact, the 1831 Belgian Constitution was used as a blueprint for the proposed Iranian Constitution in 1906 (Afary 1996, 65; Paidar 1995, 506). By the late 1970s, however, Iranian modernity had developed into "an anti-Western political discourse" (Paidar 1995, 29).

I would like to explore here the ways in which the discourses of modernity and of sisterhood intersect to position the Persian woman as the subjugated and passive Other to the modern (Western) female subject. I will attempt to trace the shared desire, in the writings of Presbyterian

1

and Anglican missionaries and of such independent travelers as Gertrude Bell and Ella Constance Sykes, for a particular figuration of the Persian woman as passive through the displacement of a more agential image. Although there were understandably some Western women in Persia who did not participate in the discursive subjugation of Iranian women, the women on whom I focus in this chapter illustrate quite clearly, I believe, the power/knowledge nexus. I have chosen this particular group-ing of very different women because they belong to established and rec-ognized missionary groups or to a privileged social and economic milieu with colonial/imperial affiliations. Thus, they participate in the pro-duction of colonial discourse through their affiliations with authorized and recognized institutions or their social and economic ties to a rul-ing, colonial class.

This glimpse of the historical roots of the politics of sisterhood is important to understanding the ramifications of its later manifestations in second-wave and Pahlavi feminist discourses.[2] By tracing the anxi-eties that surface in these texts in response to the (active) presence of the Persian woman, I hope to demonstrate the ways in which the figu-ration of the passive Persian woman is disrupted in Western women's discourses. Before elaborating upon the similar discursive strategies deployed by Western women in their texts about their Persian coun-terparts, a contextualization of their varied positions and a brief sum-mary of this period in Iranian history are in order.

Although Persia was never a formal colony of a European power, it was subjected to indirect political and economic rule for centuries.[3] Because of its strategic geographical location, neighboring countries such as Afghanistan, India, and Russia, and because of its oil-rich terri-tories, Iran figured as an object of desire for England and Russia, and later for the United States. Beginning in the 1850s, Iran became a bat-tleground for European powers, mainly Russia and England, competing against each other for economic concessions. The corrupt practices of the Qajar regime ensured the economic colonization of the country, and profits from European concessions often went directly into the royal purse while the rest of the country suffered the erosion of the country's resources.[4]

In August 1907, the British and Russian governments signed the infamous Anglo-Russian treaty that proposed to divide Iran into three sections: northern and central Iran would fall under Russian influence, southeastern Iran would fall under British influence, and the area in between was declared the neutral zone.[5] This agreement was drawn up between the two countries without the consent of the Iranian government; indeed, "the Iranians were neither consulted on the agreement nor informed of the terms when it was signed" (Keddie 1991, 75).

It was during this volatile period of predominantly British and Russian competition for economic control of Iran that British and American missionaries established themselves in the country. Two prominent missionary groups in Persia were the British Anglicans of the Church Missionary Society, or CMS, and the American Presbyterians from the Board of Foreign Missions. The CMS became increasingly active in the country through the work of Robert Bruce, who settled in Persia in 1869, and later through the work of Reverend E. F. Hoernle, who went to Persia in 1879 and was also "a medical man" (Vander Werff 1977, 165).[6] It was in 1875, six years after Bruce's arrival, that the Church Missionary Society established itself in Persia, and by the late nineteenth century the CMS had a significant number of missionaries working in the country. According to James Addison, "Before 1900 the C.M.S. had six clergy on its staff and had opened stations with either hospitals or dispensaries at Kerman, Yezd, and Shiraz" (1942, 181).

The American Presbyterians became actively involved in Persia in the 1870s. In 1871, the Presbyterian Board of Foreign Missions (PBFM) assumed responsibility for the Persian mission from the American Board of Commissioners for Foreign Missions (Zirinsky 1994, 187). Shortly thereafter, the PBFM started foreign missions in Tehran (1872), Tabriz (1873), Hamadan (1880), Rasht (1906), Qazvin (1906), Kermanshah (1910), and Mashad (1911) (Zirinsky 1994, 187).

Enlightening the Other: Christian Sisters in Persia

In the nineteenth and early twentieth centuries, "Christianity had a dual role—conversion and modernization" (Jayawardena 1995, 22). While evangelical Christians encouraged and promoted individual conversion, they also believed in creating the domestic conditions that would enable a life of continuing faith (Davidoff and Hall 1987, 183). In *Persian Women and Their Creed,* CMS missionary Mary Bird writes, "There is no word for home in the Persian language, because it has not been required; the Moslems have none of the associations and tender memories which that word awakens in us" (1899, 22). The dismissal of the idea of a Persian home life positions Bird within a wider discourse: the dissemination of a Christian domestic ideology. The rise of evangelicalism in England at the end of the eighteenth century was, according to Leonore Davidoff and Catherine Hall, a response to the French Revolution and to what the middle classes perceived to be a crisis in English society (1987, 73): "The nation, they believed, was suffering from moral degeneracy. Events in France were a warning of what was to come if individuals did not inspire a revolution in the 'manners and morals' of the nation, a transformation which must begin with individual salvation" (82). Evangelicals placed a high value on the conversion experience, and the family became an important site of individual spiritual growth. By the nineteenth century, the evangelical drive was displaced by a greater focus on the family as the locus of spiritual and moral development. Indeed, Christian domestic ideology, which promoted the feminine realm of the family as crucial to the moral and spiritual development of individuals, played a leading role in nineteenth-century evangelical missionary projects.

In this period of active missionary work, Christianity was seen as embodying superior cultural and religious values, and the "backwardness" or "primitiveness" of Muslim cultures—and of Muslim men's treatment of women—was attributed to the false beliefs propagated by the unenlightened religion of Islam. Through the light of Christianity, it was believed, Muslims would recognize their degraded status and reject Islam, "which rises as a stone wall to resist every real true ideal" (qtd. Van Sommer 1911, 37). Bird, who worked in Persia from 1891 to 1904, paints a picture of the dismal life that Persian women led under the "false prophet Mohammad" (1899, 2). Before she begins a point-by-point refutation of "the five points of the Moslem faith, which every true believer must accept," Bird writes:

> You know Mohammedans have as the symbol of their faith the crescent moon. A truer one could not have been found, for, like the crescent, the Moslem religion has but a little light and much shadow, and its light, like that of its symbol, is a reflected one borrowed from the Jewish and Christian religions. (5)

Bird's representation of Islam as a religion of darkness repositions her argument within Enlightenment discourse and "the scopic regime of modernity," which valorizes the visual and "refuses to tolerate areas of darkness" (Yeğenoğlu 1998, 12, 40). The association of Christianity with the Enlightenment, with reason, and with progress is set against Islam as its antithetical Other, steeped, in the language of nineteenth-century missionaries in Persia, in darkness and ignorance.

Jayawardena has argued that it is difficult to read the presence—and, I would add, the language—of the Christian missionary in the Orient outside of the project of colonial expansion (1995, 24–25). Given the political history of Persia in the nineteenth century, it is no accident that in 1890, Reverend James Bassett refers to "the *occupation* of Eastern Persia by resident American missionaries" when describing the establishment of the first Presbyterian mission in Tehran (74; emphasis mine). Michael Zirinsky has suggested that twentieth-century Iranian suspicions of the United States as a successor to British imperialism can be traced back to the early presence of the missionaries (1994, 187). Indeed, the 1895 Anglo-American agreement to partition the mission field resembles, rather disconcertingly, the territorial division in the Anglo-Russian Treaty of 1907, as it was agreed that "the Presbyterians confin[e] their work to northern Iran, leaving the south to the Anglican Church Missionary Society" (187).

Foreign missions were initially a predominantly male enterprise, but as Jane Haggis writes, by the late nineteenth century, female missionaries significantly outnumbered their male counterparts:

> Though missionary work was originally conceived of as purely a male endeavour, by 1899 it was estimated that women missionaries outnumbered men in the "foreign field" by over a thousand. This numerical ascendancy reflected the recruitment of single women as missionaries by the major missionary societies during the last three decades of the century. (1998, 51)

The mission fields in Persia were no exception to this rule. In his work on Presbyterians in Persia, Zirinsky writes that most of the missionaries were women:

> As in other mission fields, some two-thirds of the Presbyterian missionaries in Iran were women. . . . Over half of the mission women

went to Iran unmarried. A few wed while on the field, but the mission establishment discouraged this practice. . . . Missionary service was one of the few careers open to unmarried women, and in some respects it offered more freedom and opportunity than did those few choices open to them in America. (1992, 175)

British and American women missionaries who went to work in Persia claimed that their goal was to work with Persian women, and their reasons for this, according to Zirinsky, were twofold:

In the first place, the missionaries believed that all women were sisters, and they acted on the principle that sisters should help sisters. In the second place, male missionaries could work only with Iranian men outside of their homes. Although Iranian women and their families' private quarters were forbidden to unrelated men, women could gain access to them. Hence, women's work for women theoretically opened more than half of the population to the mission. (1994, 191)

These two reasons, universal sisterhood and Western women's unique access to what they called the "harems" of the East, resonate throughout the writings of missionary women and women travelers. It is this rhetoric of universality that permeates 1970s Western and Pahlavi feminist discourses, enabling them to place themselves in a hierarchical relationship, similar to that assumed by early missionaries, in relation to the unenlightened Persian woman.

Although women missionaries appeared to be genuinely dedicated to issues of social justice, it cannot be denied that this commitment was articulated through a problematic conception of the West as the model of progress and enlightenment. Indeed, the concepts of women's rights and social justice and the evangelical mission were inextricable from the imperializing mission:

[During the nineteenth century], in the United States and Europe, a network of Christian women emerged proclaiming "global sisterhood" and venturing out of their homes into the male world of work, travel and adventure in the name of the "noble cause" to serve God and improve the condition of women. The main concern of the women missionaries was the amelioration of the lives of colonized women. But in the "Age of Empire," Christianity was linked with imperialist conquest and capitalist expansion, and the main current of missionary activity became identified with colonial rule. (Jayawardena 1995, 24–25)

The women's quarters in Persia provided American and British women with a legitimate reason for traveling to the country and educating Persian women in matters of religion, health, and schooling. The fact that women's living quarters were located in the *andarun,* the inner space of the home, and thus forbidden to men, enabled Western women to formulate a convincing argument in favor of their active participation in the traditionally male colonial enterprise. Western women could travel to the East not just as companions to male colonizers, but as colonizers in their own right. The foreign missions provided British and American women with one means of achieving this goal.

Undoubtedly, many women missionaries performed important roles in the "Orient"; they played instrumental roles in forming women's groups and establishing girls' schools and orphanages;[7] some practiced medicine and educated local women in matters of health and hygiene. The Presbyterian missionaries, for instance, established hospitals and schools in northern Iran and introduced modern medicine and a formal system of education to the country (Zirinsky 1992, 174). Mary Bird, who was not a trained medical doctor, "opened a clinic in Isphahan to dispense medicine, Gospel, prayer and hymn in equal measure" (Vander Werff 1977, 166). Yet, as Mary Taylor Huber and Nancy C. Lutkehaus have argued,

> religious causes enabled many Western women to go overseas, and
> women missionaries helped provide many subject women with access
> to education and opportunities they would not otherwise have
> enjoyed. Yet neither of these liberating, enlightening moves was
> without deep shadows, and their intersection, especially, created
> problems whose implications are just now being explored (1999, 7–8).

Missionary women in Persia articulate their concerns for the lives of Persian women through their belief that the practice of Islam and the concept of social justice are incommensurate. According to one Presbyterian missionary, "The one fact of educating and emancipating woman, it would seem, must be a great blow to the whole doctrine of Islam" (Van Sommer 1911, 37). They claimed that through religious conversion, they would educate and enlighten the mothers of the nation, the women who were responsible for the future of the race.

In 1906, the American Presbyterian Society sponsored a conference in Cairo on Christian missions. The papers on Muslim women were published separately under a volume titled *Our Moslem Sisters: A Cry of Need from Lands of Darkness Interpreted by Those Who Heard It* (1907). In the first chapter, "Our Moslem Sisters," one of the editors of the volume, Annie Van Sommer, writes:

> "We must concentrate attention upon the mothers, for what the mothers are, the children will be." These words, spoken recently by a British statesman, are but the thoughts of many who have tried to save the children. And in looking at the millions of Moslems in the world to-day, and wondering why they are still as they were a thousand years ago, rather drifting backward than advancing, we turn to their women and find the cause. Mohammedan law, custom, and the example of their founder place woman on a level with beasts of burden and no nation rises above the level of its women. (1907, 15)

By identifying women as the singular reason for the backwardness of "the Moslem world," Van Sommer rhetorically accomplishes several things: first, she participates in the denial of temporal coevalness to the Other typical of colonial discourse. This gesture of denial is "a persistent and systematic tendency to place the referent(s) of anthropology in a Time other than the present of the producer of anthropological discourse" (Fabian 1983, 31). Second, by denying temporal coevalness to the Oriental woman/Other, Van Sommer positions Western woman as a more highly evolved model of womanhood to which women of other races and classes must aspire. Third, by locating the "problem" of the Muslim world with the backwardness of Muslim women, she advances Western women's argument for the importance of their presence in the East.

Identifying a feminized domestic space as the locus of the problem enables Western women to remain in a traditionally female space—that of the home, albeit in the Orient—thus appeasing members of the patriarchal colonial order. Inderpal Grewal has argued that "'home' is a crucial category within European travel because it is the space of return and of consolidation of the Self enabled by the encounter with the 'Other'" (1996, 6). The home functions in similar ways in the Orient as the Western woman's encounter with the Persian woman in the *andarun*, or women's quarters, serves as a means of self-consolidation; the life of the Persian woman is represented as all that a Western woman's (thankfully) is not.

The coeditors of *Our Moslem Sisters*, Reverend Samuel Marinus Zwemer and Annie Van Sommer, decry the sad state of the Muslim world, but in particular of Muslim women. In the introduction, Zwemer writes: "This book with its sad, reiterated story of wrong and oppression is an indictment and an appeal. It is an indictment of the system which produces results so pitiful. It is an appeal to Christian womanhood to right these wrongs and enlighten this darkness by sacrifice and service" (1907, 5). He then reproduces in his introduction the "Women's Appeal," written and presented at Cairo by a group of missionary women:

> We, the women missionaries, assembled at the Cairo Conference, would send this appeal on behalf of the women of Moslem lands to all the women's missionary boards and committees of Great Britain, America, Canada, France, Germany, Switzerland, Denmark, Norway, Sweden, Holland, Australia, and New Zealand. . . . The number of Moslem *women* is so vast—not less than one hundred million—that any adequate effort to meet the need must be on a scale far wider than has ever yet been attempted. (8–9; emphasis his)

In her chapter, "Our Moslem Sisters," Van Sommer urges Christian women in the West to heed the call of Christ in the Orient and to help their less fortunate sisters who are suffering under the weight of ignorance:

> You cannot know how great the need unless you are told; you will never go and find them until you hear their cry. And they will never cry for themselves, for they are down under the yoke of centuries of oppression, and their hearts have no hope or knowledge of anything better. And so to-day, we want to make our voices heard for them. We want to tell you, our sisters at home, in words so plain that you can never again say: "Behold, we knew it not." (16)

Muslim women are presumably so much submerged in darkness that they cannot recognize their own wretchedness, and it is incumbent upon their Western sisters to come to their aid. Even male missionaries urged the presence of the Western woman in the Orient by stressing the dire situation of Muslim women. In *Persian Women: A Sketch of Woman's Life from the Cradle to the Grave, and Missionary Work among Them, with Illustrations*, Reverend Isaac Malek Yonan declares:

> The Christian apologetes need no longer spend their valuable time and fertile brains in vindicating Christianity. The treatment of women is in itself, sufficient proof of its superiority over any other system. The uncontrovertible facts of history and the strong testimony of experience show clearly that one of the distinguishing features of the so-called moral and philosophic religions of the world is the slavery and degradation of the female sex. (1898, 129)

This quote establishes the abjectness of Muslim women while simultaneously confirming Christianity's rightful place as a colonizing religion by virtue of its superior treatment of women. Further, Van Sommer makes clear, the entire Muslim world is submerged in darkness and in need of the edifying light of Christ: "Although the voices in *[Our Moslem Sisters]* sound from many lands: Egypt, Tunis, Algiers, Morocco, Hausa Land, East Africa, Arabia, Palestine, Syria, Turkey, Bulgaria, Persia, India, one story is told and one cry heard everywhere" (1907, 17).

As women missionaries increased in number, the concept of universal sisterhood became further linked with the feminization of missionary work. It is important to recognize, however, that missionary work was not an entirely philanthropic endeavor, since the colonies presented professional opportunities otherwise not available to British and American women. Huber and Lutkehaus write:

> The movement of missionary and other professional women into the colonies cannot be separated from the entry of middle-class women into philanthropy and the professions that took place at the same time. Women needed the colonies, which provided opportunities for professional service rarely available at home, and the colonies needed professional women to make good the humanitarian commitments by which imperial expansion in the late nineteenth century was increasingly justified. By attributing to women virtues crucial to social improvement, Victorian ideology enabled them to be cast in a special role as civilizers. In turn, women's movements for access to education and the professions at home were increasingly justified in imperial terms. (1999, 9)

In a romanticized imagining of Mary Bird's life titled *She Went Alone: Mary Bird of Persia,* C. Savery describes Bird patiently awaiting her "Master's" "summons overseas" (5):

It came in 1891 when she was asked to go to Persia as a pioneer of women's work. The Land of the Lion and the Sun was stirring in the dead sleep of centuries. Age-old barriers were breaking down; even in the stronghold of Mohammedanism it was becoming possible for a woman to work among women. Would Mary go? Most certainly Mary would. (1942, 6)

On the one hand, what we have here is the familiar invocation of the concept of sisterhood: the idea that women separated by cultural, racial, geographical, and economic barriers would come together and that the more fortunate women would enlighten their sisters shrouded in darkness. But one of the interesting slippages in the passage cited above is the recognition that Mary Bird is indeed a pioneer, not only in the "stronghold of Mohammedanism," but perhaps even in the more advanced nation of Britain. The recognition that "age-old barriers were breaking down" allows for an interestingly ambivalent reading; it is unclear whether the referent here is Britain or Persia, thus opening a space for recognition of gender inequality among the "more progressive races." As well, the "stronghold of Mohammedanism" offers exciting job prospects for British women otherwise confined to the domestic realm; in other words, the perceived wretchedness of Muslim women becomes an employment opportunity for British women.

Although "global sisterhood" was certainly a concept and a term used by missionaries, they were not the only women to brandish a universal sisterhood as a way of inserting themselves in the (traditionally male) colonial and imperial project. In *Burdens of History,* Burton writes, "Sisterhood was the watchword of women's suffrage in Britain in much the same way it was in other discourses about female social reform" (1994, 172). Organizations such as the International Woman Suffrage Alliance (IWSA), created in 1904, held biennial conferences to discuss women's suffrage worldwide.[8] At the 1926 conference in Paris, the organization decided to broaden its scope and renamed itself the International Alliance of Women for Suffrage and Equal Citizenship (Schreiber 1955, 37). Despite its claim to "internationalism," the IWSA conferences were usually held in European capitals and the organization was made up primarily of Western, particularly European, members: "Having typed the Eastern woman as silent and impassive, suffragists were willing to speak for her in the name of universal womanhood" (Burton 1994, 195).

Secular European feminists used the degraded status of their "Oriental" sisters as a yardstick with which to measure their own social and political advancement. The time consciousness of fin de siècle culture, argues Rita Felski, inspired the sense of an ending coupled with an exhilarating sense of a new beginning (1995, 146). Western feminists' embrace of a "modern time awareness . . . affirmed a sense of history as chronological development and as embodying a linear, irreversible flow of time" (147). The middle-class members of the feminist movement thus located themselves at a more advanced stage along the axis of time in relation to women of the working classes and to women of other races and nations. As such, British middle-class feminists worked from within the modern discourse of evolution and progress, molding it to their own advantage. They argued that women were more highly evolved than men and that their roles as progenitors of the new white race placed them in an exalted position as the mothers of progress and of evolution. This feminist narrative of evolution could only be secured by holding up "other" women as examples of a "retarded development" (155).[9]

Burton traces the mobilization of the discourse of motherhood with discourses of evolution and progress to Victorian feminists, whom she describes as follows:

> a strong sense of female superiority combined readily with other
> assumptions of imperial supremacy to make British feminists conceive
> of "the Anglo-Saxon woman" as the savior of her race, not to mention
> as the highest female type. (1992, 138)

In her oft-cited work *Women's Orients: English Women and the Middle East,* Melman takes the position that the "women's vision of the Middle East undoubtedly reflects their prejudices, as well as hegemonic notions on the exotic and 'oriental.' However, the vision was shaped primarily by gender and class" (1992, 307). While gender and class were certainly important factors in how women missionaries and travelers saw and related to the Orient, their active participation in the "discursive colonization" of Persian woman cannot be denied. It seems to me that Melman's detailed and impressive study of British women in the Middle East tends to offer a more generous reading of their representations of Middle Eastern women than is at times warranted. Indeed, one of the trends she identifies in Western women's writings is "the emergence of an empathy with the other and a solidarity of gender which undercuts the differences of religion or race. Solidarity arises from the sheer fact of a co-existence as women in a shared world" (Melman 1992, 310). To make this claim, I believe one has to make a concerted effort to over-look the connections between religious missions and the discourse of sisterhood, both of which are predicated on a notion of inequality: one group of women is seen as more advanced than another, and thus one group determines the (social, cultural, economic, political) "development" of "the Other." One has to ignore pointedly the ways in which "sister-hood" has been historically abused as a term with which to deny (some) women's agency rather than a term with which to create women's com-munity or solidarity.

Many middle-class women, Christian missionaries, and secular fem-inists in Britain used the discourses of sisterhood, and of progress and evolution, to enable their mobility outside the bounds of their pre-scribed lives and to justify a more exciting life of travel and adventure for themselves. Of course, not all middle-class British women with inter-ests in Persia aligned themselves with the feminist project or with the Christian missions, but they generally were closely affiliated with the imperializing mission.

Gertrude Bell and Ella Constance Sykes: Intrepid Adventuresses

Gertrude Bell and Ella Constance Sykes reaped the advantages of trav-eling in the colonies without specifically positioning themselves within the feminist or religious discourses of the period. Both were members of the privileged classes (Bell was a member of the aristocracy, and Sykes was comfortably middle class); both were single women with the means and the opportunity to travel. Although Sykes does mention the "plight" of Persian women in her writings, and contrasts the situation of Per-sian women to that of their British counterparts, she avoids an explicit alignment with the suffragists. Instead, she embraces the role of the "determined . . . companion to the white man" whose affiliation with the British colonial administration takes him to Persia (Ware 1992, 120). Gertrude Bell, on the other hand, was an outspoken and active member of the Women's Anti-Suffrage League; indeed, she was made honorary secretary of the organization (Wallach 1996, 82). Janet Wallach, author of the encomiastic biography *Desert Queen: The Extraordinary Life of Gertrude Bell: Adventurer, Adviser to Kings, Ally of Lawrence of Arabia,* explains Bell's antisuffrage position thus:

> Gertrude saw herself as the equal of any man, but most women, she was firmly convinced, were not. Their votes would certainly be questionable; they could even prove to be dangerous. Like her mother Florence, or her father Hugh, or their friends Lord Curzon, Lord Cromer and Lord Robert Cecil, Gertrude argued that the female role was fundamentally different from that of the male: women were meant to rear children; men were meant to run the country. Furthermore, they all believed, only men had the sound judgment to rule the colonies, to determine foreign policy and to decide matters of the constitution; therefore, only men should have the right to cast a ballot. Rare was the woman knowledgeable enough to make a contribution to the affairs of state. Yet even as she promoted the agenda of the Anti-Suffrage League, Gertrude worked on her book about Byzantine Anatolia and yearned to penetrate the mysterious regions of the Arabian desert. (1996, 83)

Throughout the book, Wallach paints a portrait of Bell as an intrepid, independent, and contradictory figure who, despite her antifeminist activism, remains a model of feminist strength and spiritedness. Bell undertook a number of voyages to and through the Orient on her own and eventually won much fame and admiration for her diplomatic work in Iraq. But Bell's first trip to the Orient was chaperoned. In May 1892, Bell accompanied her aunt, Mary Lascelles, to visit her uncle, Frank Lascelles, who was British minister in Persia at that time. She stayed in Persia until October of that year and upon her return to England wrote *Persian Pictures,* published in 1894.

Almost two years after Bell's trip, Ella Sykes made the first of two visits to Persia as a companion to her brother, Sir Percy Molesworth Sykes, a British colonial administrator. Although she accompanied her brother on both trips to Persia, Sykes did travel on her own in the presumably "safer" colony of Canada.[10] Sykes's first book, *Through Persia on a Side-Saddle* (1901), describes her and her brother's travels through Persia from October 1894 to March 1897. *Persia and Its People,* published in 1910 after their second trip to Persia, discloses a more authoritative tone and serious agenda that, I believe, makes a case for a British colonial presence in the East.[11]

Although there are notable similarities between Bell's and Sykes's travel narratives, one of the significant differences between them is that Sykes offers a very gendered account of travel in *Through Persia on a Side-Saddle*. Indeed, Sykes foregrounds her gender in the book's title and throughout her narrative; in the preface, she writes:

> This book has no pretensions to be either historical, scientific or political, being merely the record of a very happy period of my existence which I have, in a way, re-lived by writing about it. My information, however, may claim to be correct as far as it goes, my brother, Major Sykes, who has travelled for several years in Persia on Government service, having revised my manuscript. As I believe that I am the first European woman who has visited Kerman and Persian Baluchistan, my experiences may perhaps interest other women who feel the "Wanderlust" but are unable to gratify their longing for adventure. (1901, vii)

While she disavows any claim to political or historical expertise, Sykes establishes the authenticity of her narrative by invoking a figure of male colonial authority, her brother Sir Percy Sykes, who "knows" Persia as a British colonial officer. Percy Sykes is most famous for organizing, in 1916, the South Persia Rifles to fight encroaching Turkish and German armies in southern Persia during World War I (Keddie 1981, 80).[12] By gesturing to her brother's colonial position, Sykes substantiates her travel narrative through her kinship with a respected figure of colonial officialdom. Having in this manner established her credibility, she joins the clamor of voices competing for recognition as the original traveler to the Orient: she purports to be the first European woman to visit Kerman and Baluchistan. Sykes directs her narrative to (women) armchair travelers, presumably more timid than she, who are unable to gratify their wanderlust.

Sykes's gender does not exclude her from her participation in the colonial enterprise. In fact, her narrative belongs to a body of work by Western women travelers who contrasted themselves with Oriental women, a strategy that enabled them to assert their own independence and mobility as Englishwomen. The position of the "intrepid adventuress" was in this way unambiguously complicitous with the colonial project. While Sir Percy Sykes conducted his duties in an official capacity as a representative of the British Empire in Persia, his sister occupied herself with the domestic aspect of colonialism. In a chapter titled "Housekeeping at Kerman," Ella Sykes details the exhausting task of setting up an English home in a primitive land among uncivilized people. Her main complaint is with the servants:

> We found our Persian servants, from highest to lowest, afflicted with an incurable laziness, and although we had over a dozen men to minister to our various wants, yet three or four good English servants would have done all the work they did and a great deal more besides. (1901, 81)

While her brother is busy managing the affairs of the country and civilizing the Persian population, she manages the affairs of the home and attempts to civilize her Persian servants. This is by no means an easy task, she complains:

> It is no exaggeration to say that to keep things up to even a very low European standard is an exceedingly exhausting task. And every lady in Persia with whom I discussed the "servant question," confessed to an intense irritation of the nerves, engendered by struggling with these lazy Orientals. (83)

Despite the taxing work of domestic colonization, she seems to derive some pleasure from the overwhelming challenge presented to her, and she catalogs, for the benefit of her female readership in England, the numerous tasks and responsibilities to which she must attend daily.

In the next chapter, "Four Visitors and a Maid," Sykes faces the hardship of finding a new maid in Persia as her Swiss help "proved entirely unsuited to a life of travel" (123). As a result, she hires "one of the despised *Gabres,* or Fire-worshippers" to wait on her (123). The reader might well imagine the arduous task of training an Oriental maid, Sykes confides, but eventually she familiarizes "Baji" with European ways, thus making her more agreeable, honest, and efficient. After praising her maid's newly developed virtues, Sykes writes:

> In common with many Orientals she considered her skin to be of lily whiteness, and was much upset when I presented her with a photo of her brown little self, saying that I had made her black, and that her mother had wept over the insult to her daughter when shown it. For answer I placed one of my hands beside her dark one, but, not to be

outdone, she said promptly, "Yes, *Khanum,* you are white because you use that beautiful Feringhee *sabūn,*" and henceforth she always begged for scraps of my soap, which she took when she went to her bath. I used to wonder if she imagined that she became whiter in consequence, but of course never dared to make inquiries on a subject that was evidently a tender one with her! (125)

Sykes plays her role in the project of domestic colonization by instructing her maid to behave in a fashion appropriate to a European maid, while at the same time attempting to put Baji, who aspires to whiteness, in her place as a colonial native. Sykes positions herself as an instructor to the indigenous woman, but also to her counterparts in England who are reading her travel narrative. Not only does she unveil Persia and Persian women to the female armchair traveler, but she also unveils Persian women to Persian women themselves. She insists on proving Baji's Otherness to her by asserting that she is not white, that she is brown, and therefore Sykes's inferior.

At the same time, Baji's persistent belief that Sykes owes her whiteness to her possession of the "Feringhee sabūn," or foreign soap, and regularly demands the use of Sykes's soap when she bathes, opens a space for what Michel de Certeau recognizes as the political potential of "everyday practices."[13] The telling exchange between Baji and Sykes enables a reading of what de Certeau calls the "tactics of consumption"— the ways in which the subaltern subject works from within the system and through "everyday practices" to work against the system (1984, xvii).

By the late nineteenth century, soap had highly overdetermined imperial connotations, epitomized by racist Pears soap advertising linking contemporary concerns about empire, domesticity, and the enlightenment of colonial savages.[14] Baji's rejection here of the inherent "whiteness," "cleanliness," and consequently moral superiority of Europeans is a radical rejection of imperial ideology. Baji's repeated demands to use Sykes's soap implies that she too can have access to the privilege of whiteness. Even in her consumption of the imperial significations of European soap, Baji rejects the inherent superiority of the culture that ties the concept of the "white man's burden" to the circulation of British consumer goods in the colonies (McClintock 1995, 32). This way of consuming dominant ideology by "manipulat[ing] the mechanisms of discipline and conform[ing] to them only in order to evade them" is

what interests de Certeau (1984, xiv). He writes: "[Consumption] is devi-
ous, it is dispersed, but it insinuates itself everywhere, silently and almost
invisibly, because it does not manifest itself through its own products,
but rather through its *ways of using* the products imposed by a dominant
economic order" (xii–xiii; emphasis his). In Baji's rejection of Sykes's
representation of her as brown and inferior, and in her steadfast belief
that the only difference between them is the quality of European soap,
there is a leveling of the ground between *khanum* and maid, between the
European self and the colonial Other. At the same time, Sykes's insistence on her own inherent (and unquestioned) whiteness betrays an
underlying anxiety about the civilizing British presence in Persia.

For her European readers, Sykes's self-representation further underscores two images she is keen to convey: first, that she is a respectable
European lady who, despite her travels through the Orient, abides by the
social codes and mores of England (as evidenced by the numerous times
she mentions having to ride her horse sidesaddle); second, that she is a
loyal servant of the Empire. Upon their departure from Kerman, Sykes
claims to feel sad at leaving behind their new home, but then launches
into an exuberant celebration of the adventurous colonial spirit:

> And perhaps what distracted my thoughts more than anything else
> was the fact that I was riding a new horse for the first time—a horse
> that had never had a lady on its back before, or a side-saddle and
> English bridle; and to me there are few things more interesting than
> to get mastery over a spirited animal, and to establish that delightful
> sympathy which makes the rider and his steed as one. So hurrah for
> the road again! hurrah for nomadic existence! and hurrah for the
> *Wanderlust* that lurks in each man's blood, and drives our English race
> so far from home and kindred over the face of the globe! (1901, 191)

Sykes's self-positioning within the rhetoric of Empire as she celebrates
the "wanderlust" that drives her and her kindred to other nations in the
quest to civilize their inhabitants manifests itself in her panegyric language. Her description of breaking in a horse and the pleasure that the
sense of control provides her can be extrapolated to the exhilaration
she feels upon arriving in Persia and conducting the business of Empire
in her home at Kerman.

Nevertheless, the sense of freedom that Sykes extols as she travels
through the country with her brother is compromised by her gender:

I used to vary my position by taking my cramped knees from the
pommels and letting my feet hang down; but the more I rode the
more I saw the disadvantages of the saddle to which I was condemned.
The side-saddle is by no means an ideal invention in my eyes. It is
difficult to mount into it from the ground; it is dangerous in riding
among hills to be unable to spring off on either side in case of accident;
the habit is very apt to be caught on the pommels if the rider falls, and
the position in which she sits cramps her much if persisted in for
many hours at a slow walk, which is the usual thing in hilly and stony
countries. (1901, 248)

Of the local reaction to her presence in Persia, she writes: "I heard after-
wards that I was the great attraction, as it passed their comprehension
how I could sit on a horse sideways and not come off when I cantered!"
(69). Her observations—and complaints—about riding sidesaddle under-
score her position as a gendered traveler and serve as a contrast between the European woman's femininity and the absence of feminine
charm in the Persian woman. Her celebrity status due to her sidesaddle
highlights the fact that Persian women do not have the freedom to
travel through their own country on horseback, and even if they did,
they would most likely not do so in as dignified a fashion as Ella Sykes.
In this way, she, like other women travelers to the Orient,

> prov[es] . . . the power of an Englishness that could be supposedly
> inviolate while living and being in the "East," which was depicted as
> the antithesis of the "West," even while their narratives were gendered
> to show the extra effort required to do so and the difficulties faced by
> women attempting to live in these lands. (Grewal 1996, 65)

On the other hand, the freedom Sykes purports to feel when traveling
seems elusive since she is clearly frustrated by the Victorian class, gender, and cultural restrictions that hamper her mobility and comfort during travel. The pity with which she regards her unfortunate Persian sisters
becomes ironized by the restrictions placed upon British women, including herself, in the Victorian and Edwardian periods.[15]

The question of the sidesaddle never arises in Bell's *Persian Pictures*.
This is not surprising, since Gertrude Bell does not foreground her
gender in her writings. According to her biographer, Bell—like Sykes—
did travel through Persia on a sidesaddle; it was only on her second trip
to the Middle East, when she was in Palestine, that she was taught how

to ride like a man: "'No more feminine saddles for me on a long journey,' she announced to her parents. 'Never, never again will I travel on anything else; I have never known real ease in riding till now'" (Wallach 1996, 50). Yet, in *Persian Pictures,* there is no mention of any of the discomforts she may have suffered while traveling; indeed, there is little to distinguish it as a text written by or for a woman. Bell spent much of her life in a man's world and was not interested in drawing attention to her gender. In fact, according to Grewal, Bell expressed a significant amount of disdain for Englishwomen in the colonies and dissociated herself and her work from her female counterparts:

> Gertrude Bell, the famous traveler who lived many years among the Bedouins, blamed the Englishwomen in the colonial settlements in Egypt for creating an exclusive society and taking no interest in Arab life. She claimed that such attitudes had brought about the downfall of the British government in India. Bell saw herself as different and superior to the Englishwomen who had accompanied the colonists. (1996, 80)

Although there are differences between *Persian Pictures* and *Through Persia on a Side-Saddle,* there are also a number of similarities between the two accounts. Both books conform to the genre of travel writing, a genre that is, in the words of Ali Behdad, "an (af)filiated discourse: it maintains both an institutional affiliation with colonial power and a kind of 'filial' relation with other orientalist representations" (1994, 111); both writers engage with the Orientalist trope of desire and disappointment as the reality of Persia does not conform to the exoticized Persia of their imagination; both writers represent Persian women as simultaneously exotic and oppressed beings.

In the opening lines to her book, Sykes declares that her passion for the Orient began with a book: "The 'gorgeous East' has always possessed a strong fascination for me, and after reading [Kinglake's] *Eöthen,* that most delightful book of travels, the indescribable attraction of the Orient became, if possible, stronger than before" (1901, 2). According to Behdad, the late nineteenth-century European traveler arriving in the East on the heels of earlier European travelers always experiences a sense of disappointment upon her arrival. The disappointment of the belated traveler stems from the disjunction between the romance of the Orientalist text and the reality of the Orient. Sykes, however, claims to be wholly enamored of Persia:

> The glamour of the East penetrated me from the first moment of landing on its enchanted shores, and although many a time I encountered hard facts, quite sufficient to destroy the romantic illusions of most folk, yet they struck against mine powerlessly. . . . I was, in a way, prepared for much that might come by the perusal of Lord Curzon's comprehensive work on the country. . . . For we were bound to see the real East, where we should have none but Orientals for our daily society, and our home would be in a city by contrast with which Tehran would seem almost Western. (3–4)

Sykes's self-representation appears to work in contradiction to Behdad's argument, as she claims to have read travel narratives on Persia in which the "romance is stripped away remorselessly, and Persia, bare and barren as she is in reality, exposed, to the view" (3). She claims that, despite the fact that the reality of Persia would have discouraged other travelers, she remains as enchanted as always by the country. Equipped with Lord Curzon's definitive study of Persia, she claims to be prepared to face the difficult conditions of Kerman, where they planned "to see the *real* East" (4; emphasis mine).

Nevertheless, despite Sykes's protestations that her favorable impressions of Persia remained unchanged by the reality of its conditions, her access to the "real East" is mediated through what Behdad has termed the "Orientalist intertext" (1994, 26). Indeed, despite her claims to the contrary, Sykes succumbs to the disappointment of the belated traveler who yearns for the primitive, untouched land of a mythical past:

> When the traveller looks back on the past history of Persia and remembers what a mighty kingdom it was, and how many powerful rulers it counted among its tributaries, he is surprised not to come across more frequent relics of its departed grandeur. Tehran, the capital, is, to all intents and purposes, quite modern; there is but little to admire in Kasvin, one of the old royal cities, while I am told that even in Isfahan it is difficult to conjure up from the buildings that remain a clear picture of its magnificence and splendour in the days when Shah Abbas held his court there. (1901, 90)

Determined as she is to represent herself as an experienced, well-prepared, and intrepid traveler who has consulted a number of books on Persia before embarking upon her journey, Sykes refuses to concede her disappointment with the ugliness of modern Iran; she merely remarks that Persia would not be the ideal place for "the ordinary globe-trotter," a category in which she clearly does not place herself.

Gertrude Bell was a well-educated and intelligent woman who studied Farsi before she went to Persia and pursued her study of the language while there. Upon her return to England, she completed and published *Persian Pictures* and began translating the poems of Hafiz. In 1897, she published *Poems from the Divan of Hafiz,* which A. J. Arberry describes as "a remarkable monument to her scholarship and literary gifts; though some twenty hands have put Hafiz into English, her renderings remain the best" (1947, 6). Bell, in some ways, is a more interesting figure than Sykes, as she appears to have a greater understanding of the country to which she is traveling and a more sophisticated understanding of the politics of travel. Indeed, Bell appears to have some fun at the expense of the figure of the British traveler to the Orient when she writes:

> Many, many years have passed since the ingenious Shahrzad beguiled the sleepless hours of the Sultan Shahriyar with her deftly-woven stories, and still for us they are as entrancing, as delightful, as they were for him when they first flowed from her lips. Still those exciting volumes keep generations of English children on wakeful pillows, still they throw the first glamour of mystery and wonder over the unknown East. . . . The supply of bottled magicians seems, indeed, to be exhausted, and the carpets have, for the most part, lost their migratory qualities — travellers must look nowadays to more commonplace modes of progression, but they will be hard put to it from time to time if they do not consent to resign themselves so far to the traditions of their childhood as to seek refuge under a palace roof. (1894, 104–5)

Throughout her narrative, Bell conjures up images of *A Thousand and One Nights* or the *Arabian Nights,* and laments — albeit in tongue-in-cheek fashion — that the stories are part of Persia's past. Bell's (playful) wistfulness that the reality of Persia does not conform to the Orient of her childhood imagination suggests a self-ironizing moment during which she recognizes the fantasies produced by the Orientalist intertext:

> On our way home we stopped before a confectioner's shop and invited him to let us taste of his preserves. He did not, like the confectioner in the Arabian Nights, prepare for us a delicious dish of pomegranate-seeds,

but he gave us Rahat Lakoum, and slices of sugared oranges, and a jelly
of rose-leaves (for which cold cream is a good European substitute),
and many other delicacies, ending with some round white objects,
which I take to have been sugared onions, floating in syrup—after we
had tasted them we had small desire to continue our experimental
repast. (1894, 137)

Bell devotes a number of passages to her putative disappointment that
the tastes, sights, and sounds of Persia do not conform to those described
in the *Arabian Nights*.[16]

Despite their differences, Bell's *Persian Pictures* and Sykes's *Through
Persia on a Side-Saddle* offer portraits of Persia as a quaint, if primitive,
and fascinating country. Although Bell was a staunch imperialist throughout her life, Sykes's narrative—perhaps due to the fact that she was
traveling with her brother—is more explicit in its support of Empire.
For example, Sykes writes:

Not far from the British Legation are the headquarters of the Indo-
European Telegraph line, which deserves mention, as it is one way by
which India is connected with Europe. The line runs from Karachi
along the Persian Gulf to Bushire and then traverses the whole of
Persia, being a wonderful achievement of English energy over Oriental
obstructiveness. As in many places, the wire crosses high passes, it
naturally often gets broken down during the winter snows, and the
telegraph clerks, whose duty it is to test it so many times daily, are
frequently forced to sally forth to repair it, however inclement the
weather may be. (1901, 15–16)

In her second book on Persia, which will be discussed at greater length
in the final section of this chapter, Sykes becomes more aggressive in
her pro-colonialist rhetoric. As her representations of oppressed Persian
women are challenged by their political activism during the Constitutional Revolution, Sykes makes a more emphatic and unambiguous argument for the presence of British men—and women—in Persia.

Reading the Constitutional Revolution
from the Postcolonial Time Lag

I propose to read Western women's representations of Persian women
during the 1905–1911 Constitutional Revolution by drawing on Homi

Bhabha's notion of the "time-lag" and opening a space for what he calls a "postcolonial contramodernity" (1994, 244). Postcolonial contra-modernity, or the "postcolonial translation of modernity," he argues, is enabled by "introduc[ing] the question of subaltern agency into the question of modernity" (244). There is, according to Bhabha, a caesura, a time lag "effected in the continuist, progressivist myth of man," and it is this temporal break that enables the postcolonial or diasporic subject to emerge into full presence (236). It is through the time lag, or caesura, in the discourse of modernity that the belated body of the raced subject can be read, and it is the presence, the "readability," the enunciative site of the racialized, the colonized body, that disorders and disrupts the narrative of modern progress. The final section of this chapter will examine Western women's evolutionary narratives about Persia and Persian women from the time lag of postcolonial contramodernity, thus attempting to effect a disruption of the figure of the passive, abject Persian woman and to facilitate the emergence of an agential counterfigure in Western women's discourses about early twentieth-century Persia.

Despite the many differences between the narratives of American Presbyterian women, British Anglican women, and the travel writings of Gertrude Bell and Ella Sykes, all of whom are writing approximately in the same historical period, there exists a shared desire in their texts for an inscription of the passive body of the Persian woman. In *Persia and Its People,* Sykes offers a detailed and rather alarming trajectory of the dejected and degenerate life of the Persian woman since "from the cradle to the grave — nay, even in the life beyond the grave — the balance weighs heavily in favour of the Persian man as compared with the Persian woman" (1910a, 63). In her talk to the National Geographic Society in October 1910, the same year *Persia and Its People* was published, Sykes describes Iranian gender relations by turning to a "kind of 'projective' past" (Bhabha 1994, 238):

> In order to understand Persian domestic life at the present day, we
> must carry ourselves back to patriarchal times. The Persian is lord and
> master of his house much as was Abraham or Jacob. . . . When a
> woman is handed over to her husband with her dowry, he regards her
> far more as a chattel than as a wife. (Sykes 1910b, 851)

Bhabha argues that representations of a culture as timeless or as part of a distant past are "a mode of 'negativity' that mak[e] the enunciatory

present of modernity disjunctive" (1994, 238). The concept of timeless-
ness, he claims, opens a time lag within the myth of modern progress
and "displays the *problem of the ambivalent temporality of modernity*" (239;
emphasis his).

The most intriguing passages in *Persia and Its People* are those that
create a temporal disjunction between Sykes's colonialist, progressivist
narrative and the emergence of counternarratives that challenge the
time scheme she uses to describe the lives of Persian women. In a chapter dedicated to "The Persian Woman," Sykes begins thus:

> Europeans travelling in Asia sometimes assert cheerfully that all is well
> with the Eastern woman, and that she would not change lots with her
> Western sister if she could, as she is thoroughly contented with things
> as they are. When, however, we come to look at the facts of the case,
> we shall find that the picture they compose is by no means one of
> roseate hue. (1910a, 196)

The anxiety here emerges in reaction to contradictory representations:
if the Persian woman emerges as independent and as contemporaneous
with her British counterpart, then the presence of the British woman,
and indeed, that of the British man, in Persia becomes superfluous. If
Persia—and Persian women—cannot be represented as part of a collective past from which European nations and European women have
evolved, then the project of British imperialism, and consequently, the
mobility of the British woman, becomes threatened. To counteract what
she perceives to be misleading representations of Persian women as
"thoroughly contented," Sykes catalogs the appalling facets of a Persian
woman's life. She concludes the chapter by reiterating the pronounce-
ment that a Persian woman leads a life of unadulterated misery:

> The life of a Persian woman, taken as a whole, cannot be considered
> a happy one, and the victims of Islam recognise that their fate is hard
> when they are brought into contact with European women. . . .
> Certainly the yoke of Mohammedanism presses heavily on the Persian
> woman, and, through her, on the entire race, for how can a nation
> make real progress if the mothers of its men are kept in bondage and
> ignorance? (1910a, 208)

Sykes claims that upon becoming acquainted with a few Persian women,
she "found that a latent discontent with their restricted surroundings

was fanned into life by the tremendous contrast between the unfettered existence of an Englishwoman and their own" (1910a, 208–9). By ensuring that her reader has a vivid picture of the horror that is the life of the Persian woman, she makes a case for the importance of the presence of the British woman in Persia. For, according to Sykes, it is only when Persian women come into contact with European women that a "latent discontent" with their lot is realized and articulated. Indeed, Persian peoples in general could only benefit from their contact with British travelers and colonial officers; in this manner, Sykes inscribes her support for British colonialist policies and betrays her complicity with British imperial interests in Persia.

Sykes's *Through Persia on a Side-Saddle* is a travel narrative meant for the female armchair traveler, depicting the rigors of living and traveling through the Orient. *Persia and Its People,* published nine years later, claims to be an "objective" analysis of the political and social climate in Persia. It is most notable for its validation of the British colonial presence in Persia at the time and for Sykes's misrepresentation of Persian and British diplomatic relations. She begins by describing the country's primitive infrastructure and preindustrial state. After painting a picture of Persia as technologically backward and desperately in need of the assistance of more advanced European nations, she suggests that British statesmen could come to its aid:

> Persia has merely single-wire telegraph lines, the rickety poplar poles of which are often seen lying on the ground, in which case the Persian official at the nearest station will calmly remark that the line "does not speak to-day." In great contrast to this is the British three-wire line, supported on iron posts, which runs from the Persian frontier on the north-West down to Bushire on the Persian Gulf. . . . Sterile as Iran appears to be, yet an able ruler might do great things for his country, and the Englishman cannot but long for a man of the type of Lord Cromer to be allowed a free hand in remodelling the administration of the kingdom. (1910a, 9–10)

The distinctions Sykes makes between the primitive Persian telegraph lines on "rickety poplar poles" and the sophisticated "British three-wire line, supported on iron posts" conjure up the image of the primitive colony in contrast to the modern seat of Empire. By revealing the backwardness of Persian society and infrastructure, Sykes adds her voice to those clamoring for British "assistance" to Persia. Indeed, her concern that some of the country's natural resources are controlled by the Russians emerges from the continuing competition between Russia and England for economic and political control of Persia. Sykes's anxiety over Russia's involvement in Persia comes from a sense of colonial entitlement, and she "long[s] for a man of the type of Lord Cromer" to be allowed the freedom to mine and control the number of resources that she lists as being available for exploitation.

In light of the history of British and Russian competition over ownership of Persia and its resources, and Sykes's obvious investment in British presence in the country, her ostensible support for the Constitutional Revolution appears suspect:

> It is too soon to judge how the change from an autocratic rule to that of a Constitutional Government will work; but owing to the agreement of 1907 between England and Russia, Persia has every chance of working out her own salvation. . . . That Persia may succeed in her arduous task of regeneration is the earnest wish of all Englishmen who take any interest in the country. (1910a, 38)

It is particularly audacious of Sykes to suggest that the 1907 Anglo-Russian treaty, which effectively colonized the country by awarding territorial control to the Russians in the north and to the British in the south, and was drawn up without the knowledge of the Iranians, secured the potential for a constitutional democracy. In *Persia and Its People,* the subject of her narrative is the male colonial traveler; she extols the virtues of the British Empire and praises the spirit of "wanderlust" that she celebrates in *Through Persia.* Sykes invokes the language of racial progression as she glorifies the involvement of British colonial officers in the country. But the evolutionary model upon which she draws to justify the intervention of British men in Persia also enables her to make a case for the presence of British women in the country.

The argument in favor of European women's work in the colonies is a central theme at the second conference sponsored by the American Presbyterian Society held in Lucknow, India, in 1911. In their papers, Christian missionary women lament the unenviable social status of their Muslim "sisters" in much the same vein as they did at the Cairo Conference. These papers, edited once again by Annie Van Sommer and

Reverend Samuel Zwemer, were published separately as a "Women's Volume" under the title *Daylight in the Harem: A New Era for Moslem Women*. This volume, like its 1907 predecessor, *Our Moslem Sisters*, targets a Christian female audience, and the editors "send it forth, with a prayer that God may use it to stir into flame the embers of devotion to the cause of Moslem Women which are as yet only smouldering in the hearts of Christian Women" (Van Sommer and Zwemer 1911, 5). In a speech summarizing the work of missionaries in Oriental countries, Van Sommer reads from a letter sent to her by a missionary woman in Persia. The letter details the efforts made by Christian missionaries to prevent child marriage in Persia and to encourage the pursuit of education for Persian girls:

> As for twenty years at least, we have always had some Moslem girls in our school, and have continually striven to impress upon the women the inexpediency and wrong of sending little girls into homes, where they are strangers, just when they need their mother's careful guidance; the time in school has in many cases gradually lengthened, and this term we have many older girls in the Boarding Department of our school. In all, this year, we have had about twenty-seven Moslem Boarders; some of them would in the old time have been given years ago to husbands. I have had special opportunities for telling Moslem women of Christ, and they listen as well, if not better, than they have before. As in all religions the women are much more tenacious in their hold on Islam than the men are. (41)

The unnamed letter writer emphasizes the importance of missionary work in Persia and of the various accomplishments of missionary women in their interactions with Persian women. But the letter also reveals an anxiety that the missionaries' efforts to convert their Muslim sisters have not been entirely successful because "the women are much more tenacious in their hold on Islam than the men are." The implication here is that the missionaries are not quite as welcome as they had imagined and that Persian women might not be necessarily awaiting "liberation" through the intervention of Christian missionaries. This discordant note in the narrative of progress and of emancipation for Muslim women introduces an anxiety that repeatedly resurfaces in the missionary texts. The anxiety that emerges in Sykes's writings about the misrepresentation of Persian women as contented, and in the British missionary's letter read at the Lucknow Conference regarding the unwillingness of Muslim women to convert to Christianity, has a particular resonance in the context of the historical moment: the 1905–1911 Constitutional Revolution.

During this period, there was widespread demand among secular nationalists and religious clerics in Persia for "public welfare, public education, a House of Justice (Edalat Khaneh), equality, protection of life and property and liberty through secular law, and the establishment of parliamentary democracy" (Paidar 1995, 52). To mitigate further economic devastation and colonization of the country's resources, Persian reformists demanded a constitutional democracy whereby the shah would be held accountable to the people. According to Paidar, "Women's political activities in this period ranged from circulating information, spreading news, acting as informers and messengers, participating in demonstrations and taking up arms in protest" (1995, 52).

In December 1905, a large group of clerics, merchants, and women occupied the shrine of Shahzadeh Abdolazim, demanding that Muzaffar al-Din Shah convene a House of Justice (Paidar 1995, 53). Large groups of women outside the shrine used their bodies as barriers to protect the demonstrators from armed government forces; these women also surrounded the shah's carriage and demanded that he respect the peoples' wishes for a constitutional democracy. Iranian feminist historians have remarked that one of the first threats against the life of the shah was uttered by a woman:

> As Muzaffar al-Din Shah descended from his carriage, [Mrs. Jahangir] cut through the circle of guards and handed him a letter. This was a warning from the Revolutionary Committee of Tehran that if he did not set up a "Majlis of the representatives of the nation to spread justice as in all civilized nations of the world" he would be killed. Mrs. Jahangir's house was a meeting place and an arms cache for the radical constitutionalists during the years of the revolution. She lost both her son and her nephew during the June 1908 coup. (Afary 1996, 371, n 8)

The occupation of the shrine ended in January 1906, when the shah conceded to convening a House of Justice.

In July 1906, several consecutive days of public demonstrations broke out when it became clear that the shah was reneging on his promise. The demonstrations resulted in a three-week occupation of the British

Legation, and the protesters were vociferous in their demands for a constituent assembly and for a constitution (Paidar 1995, 54). Despite efforts by Persian and British men to prevent the active participation of Persian women at this time, large numbers of Persian women held demonstrations outside the Legation and the royal palace while other women chose to support the protests financially (54).

The first Majlis, or parliament, opened in October 1906 and drafted a Fundamental Law, "which was basically a translation of the Belgian Constitution" and severely curtailed the shah's power while granting "extensive powers to the Majles" (Paidar 1995, 55). One of the decisions made by the Majlis was to reject the government plan to request loans from Britain and Russia to pay its debts. Iranian male constitutionalists donated their own money, and women their jewels, to the national coffers to set up a national bank. Women were strong nationalists, but they also demanded the right to vote, which alienated some members of the clergy, who subsequently abandoned their "nationalist" position and joined the royalist forces opposed to the Constitution.[17]

In June 1908, the government bombed the Majlis and thus sparked a civil war between the constitutionalists and the royalists. The shah surrounded the city of Tabriz, which had strong constitutional support, and launched a ten-month siege of the city. During this time, Persian women—disguised as men—fought alongside Persian men in defense of the city and in defense of an ideal of democracy and equal rights for all citizens. Janet Afary writes:

> *Anjuman* [newspaper] published reports that bodies of armed women dressed in men's clothing had been found in the battlefields of Amirkhiz and Khiaban alongside those of the men. Peasant women in the small villages of Azerbaijan "bundled their new-born babies on their backs, picked up guns," and fought alongside the men. *Habl al-Matin* [newspaper] reported that in one of the battles of Tabriz twenty women, disguised in men's clothing, were found among the dead. (1996, 194)

In July 1909, after ten months of fighting, Persian men and women nationalists regained control of the city and a constitutional government was established.

In 1911, the Majlis employed an American, Morgan Shuster, to help organize the country's finances. The Russians—to whom the Persian government was heavily in debt—issued an ultimatum to the Majlis: dismiss Shuster immediately or the Russians would invade. This sparked an outrage in the country and another series of mass protests in which women were once again actively involved. Persian women stormed the Majlis, carrying pistols under their veils, and threatened to kill their husbands and sons and themselves if the Majlis succumbed to the threats of the Russian government (Paidar 1995, 58; Afary 1996, 204–5). Despite the waves of protest across the country, the Majlis dismissed Shuster within three weeks of the Russian ultimatum and the Qajar monarch succeeded in closing the Majlis and sending its members into exile. However, the disintegration of the parliament and its goals for a constitutional monarchy did not hinder the massive proliferation of women's political organizations and women's schools during that period.

Persian women, veiled, unveiled, or disguised in male garb, emerged into the public sphere demanding national and international recognition of their rights as women and as nationalists. The visibility of the Persian woman, to borrow Bhabha's words, "displays the ambivalent temporality of modernity" by threatening the self-representation of Christian missionaries in Persia as benevolent instructors to their servile Persian sisters, of intrepid adventuresses such as Ella Sykes and Gertrude Bell as liberated and modern in contrast to imprisoned and backward Persian women, and of suffragist women as leaders of the international women's movement.

On December 5, 1911, the *Times* (London) published, under the caption "Appeal from the Women," a telegraph from the Persian Women's Society addressed to women suffragists in Britain: "To Women's Suffragist Committee, London.—The Russian Government by an ultimatum demands us to surrender to her our independence; the ears of the men of Europe are deaf to our cries; could you women not come to our help?" In reply, the Women's Social and Political Union wrote this message:

> Badrod Doja, Persian Women's Society, Tehran.
> Your touching appeal received. Unhappily we cannot move British Government to give political freedom even to us, their own countrywomen. We are equally powerless to influence their action towards Persia. Our hearts deeply moved by sympathy with Persian sisters and admiration for their militant patriotic deeds. (*Times* 1911, 5)

The telegram is signed by Emmeline Pankhurst and Emmeline Pethick Lawrence, leading members of the Women's Social and Political Union, which was seen as the more "militant" branch of the suffragist movement (Holton 1996, 110; Rupp 1997, 137). The most significant part of this exchange is, for me, an admission on the part of the suffragists that they are equally disadvantaged and powerless in their own country. The concept of sisterhood and a shared oppression is expressed here, as well as a recognition on the part of British women of Persian women's political activism. The fact that these moments of recognition tend not to surface in dominant discursive representations of Iranian women underscores the importance of attending to how discourse works: how do certain representations (in this case, the subjugated Persian woman) become fixed as "truth" despite all evidence to the contrary?

The missionary women at the Lucknow Conference also appear aware that they cannot ignore the prominent role played by Persian women in the demonstrations, particularly since the *Times* published extended coverage of the political events and of the feminist movements in Persia. Nevertheless, the missionary texts attempt to contain the tremendous implications of these events in two ways: first, they claim that the reforms do not address the fundamental problem of Islam as a degenerate religion. In a letter read by Van Sommer at the conference, the (unnamed) writer observes:

> There is very much to be desired in the so-called reforms. It is all apparently outward and not inward, *i.e.* expressing no change of heart or contrition for sin. Not all that they have adopted is good; with the commendable change in bad customs and the efforts to obtain education have come many of the vices of Europe. Wickedness is much increased, while the decline of faith and observance of Islam only leaves the people with no restraining motive. The problem of the Missionary is the same old difficult one, how to bring the Gospel to impenitent hearts. (Van Sommer 1911, 34)

The Christian missionaries thus attempt to contain the threat of the enunciative presence of the Persian woman by lamenting the religious ignorance of the Persians and by justifying the continuance of their own work in Persia so as "*individuals* [Persians may] be *regenerated* while as a nation they are seeking reform" (36). "Miss G. Y. Holliday" ends her talk on "Awakening Womanhood" in Persia by referring to the feminist anti-veiling protests in Persia as follows:

> As to discarding the veil, I should be very sorry to see them going with uncovered faces till they have a religion which requires purity of heart instead of outward restraint, and which knows neither polygamy nor divorce. There are no more beautiful, capable, or clever women in the world, than many of our Persian sisters. It rests largely with us to say how much longer they shall be deprived of the privileges we have so long enjoyed that we have ceased to appreciate them. (Van Sommer 1911, 129)

The uncompromising presence of the agential Persian woman is anxiety-producing for the Christian missionaries, and they attempt to contain its implications by proffering an image of the ignorant (and passive) Persian woman swept up in the reform movements out of "false consciousness" and without "purity of heart."

The second way in which the missionaries attempt to defuse the significance of the Persian nationalist and feminist movements is to claim responsibility for igniting the desire for reform among students at the missionary schools. Holliday claims that "one of our school boys, in a public meeting, boldly advocated the removal of the veil, and the equal education of men and women. He is a young man of some importance, having a government position. The veil will not soon pass, but there is a noticeable carelessness in its use" (Van Sommer 1911, 126). Furthermore, the missionaries attempt to reinscribe the image of the passive Persian woman who needs the Christian missionary—or the product of missionary schools, such as the Persian "school boy"—to advocate for their rights on their behalf. In this way, the missionaries reaffirm their necessary presence in Persia.

Sykes, on the other hand, categorically refuses to acknowledge the presence of the Persian woman in the nationalist struggle. She reinscribes a particular vision of the Persian woman as subservient by refusing to acknowledge her active participation in the public protests during the revolutionary period. The manifestation of the agential Persian woman presents a threat to Sykes, who represents British involvement in Persia as paradigmatic of the Empire's benevolence and of its commitment to guiding primitive races along the path to democracy and enlightenment.

Although the Christian missionaries and Sykes deploy different strate-gies in recuperating the figure of the passive Persian woman, they share the need to re-veil the threatening "present and presence" of the Persian woman by claiming that she is always already shrouded in the shadow and darkness of Islam (Bhabha 1994, 251).

The active participation of the Persian woman in the political future of Persia disturbs the temporality of British women's narratives. The constitutional revolution and Persian women's revolutionary activities represent a caesura, a temporal break in the teleological narrative of European imperial progress. If the Persian woman's body could be seen as "civilized" and "modern," then the body of the British woman in Per-sia would become superfluous.

The anxiety about Persian women echoes in all the papers on Persia at the Lucknow Conference because the constitutional reforms and the women's movements in Persia at the time were perceived to be indica-tive of a growing, indigenous, "modern" period in the country—and nothing could be more disturbing to the concept of imperial time and progress than a concomitant move toward "social progress" and eman-cipation in a backward and primitive country. The time lag of post-colonial contramodernity thus moves in contradiction to the myth of progress. It is a movement that is "neither teleological nor is it an end-less slippage. It is a function of the lag to slow down the linear, progres-sive time of modernity to reveal its 'gesture,' the pauses and stresses of the whole performance" (Bhabha 1994, 253). Reading the enunciative present or presence of the Persian woman's body in the caesura of modernity enables a reading of national and cultural histories as dialec-tical and atemporal and as moving outside the binarisms of past/pres-ent, primitive/modern. Reading history from this time lag presents a fundamental challenge to imperial discourse and, as a consequence, to the contingent subject position of Western women within the linear narrative of progress and evolution. More important, however, it en-ables a rereading of the "value-coding" of imperial texts and creates a space for the presence of the agential Persian woman (Spivak 1990, 228).

CHAPTER 2

Scopophilic Desires: Unveiling Iranian Women

OR THE PAST TWO HUNDRED YEARS, the practice of veiling is the site upon which discursive representations of enlightened feminists and their subjugated sisters intersect perhaps most markedly. Since the eighteenth century, the figure of the veiled Muslim woman has occupied a privileged place in the Western literary and cultural imagination, leading to overdetermined representations of the veil as a symbol simultaneously of abstention and debauchery. Accounts of erotic, mysterious, threatening, and enslaved harem women figure in the works of such writers as Richard Burton, Gustave Flaubert, Pierre Loti, Charles-Louis de Secondat Montesquieu, Alexander Kinglake, Thomas Moore, James Morier, and Gérard de Nerval.[1]

Mohja Kahf's informative study of Western representations of the Muslim woman traces the trajectory of representations of Muslim women from that of "termagant" in Medieval and Renaissance texts to "odalisque" in Enlightenment and Romantic texts, thus demonstrating that Western representations of Muslim women are historically not static (1999, 5, 6). Although the Muslim woman emerges as a powerful figure in early Western narratives, she metamorphoses into a symbol of oppressed, enslaved womanhood in the age of Enlightenment:

> In the eighteenth century, the Muslim woman becomes [the harem's] inmate definitively—and the seraglio inmate's lack of liberty turns into an issue in a century veering toward revolution. . . . The sexuality of the Muslim woman is increasingly organized as a scopophilic experience, both voyeuristic and fetishistic. . . . Now she emphatically becomes the erotic object of male visual pleasure. Such a transformation follows inherently from the cementing of the seraglio in the dominant (i.e., male elite) Western discourse as a structure which operates on the basis of teasingly concealing and revealing the woman, both delaying and heightening the male gaze through narrative technique. Subtly, the veil begins to slip into the place of a defining metaphor. (Kahf 1999, 113)

In contrast to the representation of the dissipated Eastern harem woman, the image of the ideal woman in eighteenth-century England buttressed the language of thrift, labor, and morality endemic to the middle class; these middle-class values would become part of the dominant discourse by the end of the eighteenth and the beginning of the nineteenth centuries. The late eighteenth century saw a shift toward a middle-class domestic ideology that posited the mother as the center of the home and the moral fulcrum of the family. By the nineteenth century, the indolent, upper-class socialite was replaced by the "angel of the hearth" as the ideal model of femininity and maternity.[2] By comparing the upper-class Englishwoman to a harem inmate, eighteenth-century Western feminists such as Mary Wollstonecraft criticized the indolence of the aristocracy and lauded the middle-class woman as a worthy example of motherhood and feminine domesticity.

Excluded since the seventeenth and eighteenth century from the definition of the fully articulated individual in masculine Enlightenment discourse, Western women, especially in the nineteenth century, sought to include themselves in the grand narrative of progress and evolution by celebrating their roles as progenitors of their race, placing themselves in the exalted position of mothers of progress and social evolution. They used the language of the Enlightenment to insert themselves in the discourse of individual liberty, and they did so by contrasting their own position in European societies against that of their Eastern sisters in the Orient.

By the twentieth century, this form of representation was commonplace in Western women's narratives about the Orient. The most visible marker of difference between European and Oriental women was the veil, which came to symbolize the epitome of Eastern backwardness and oppressive patriarchal traditions. In *Moslem Women Enter a New World,* an American woman, Ruth Frances Woodsmall, writes:

> Undoubtedly the barometer of social change in the Moslem world is the veil. Where the veil persists without variation, the life of the Moslem woman is like the blank walled streets of Bhopal, India, which afford no outlook from within and no contact from without. But the Bhopal streets within the last few years have been pierced by a few small windows, very high up to be sure, but breaking the dead monotony, and one can imagine some purdah woman unseen looking out on the street life below. (1936, 40)

Western women mobilized to their advantage the popular significations of the veil as evidence of women's subjugation and claimed the unveiling, hence liberation, of Muslim women as their prerogative. In Western discourses, the practice of veiling was represented as tantamount to imprisoning women; it was enforced by the male patriarchy and symbolized a dogmatic faith that enlightened Europeans had discarded in favor of a democratic and secular system of government. By the nineteenth century, Western models of modernity garnered increasing attention in the Orient, and the emancipation of women was adopted as a viable political cause by nationalist men and women who believed that progress entailed the emulation of Western cultural, economic, and political models.

To discuss the ways in which representations of the veil as an unequivocal symbol of either female oppression by patriarchy or of female emancipation from Western imperialism have been mobilized in Western and indigenous discourses, my argument here is structured around two historical moments in twentieth-century Iran. The first moment is in 1936, when the ruling monarch Reza Shah Pahlavi legislated the Unveiling Act, which prohibited women from appearing veiled in public. The second is in 1983, when revolutionary leader Ayatollah Ruhollah Khomeini implemented the Veiling Act, which prohibited women from appearing unveiled in public. My focus on these specific moments in Iran's history enables a detailed exploration of the general hypothesis of this chapter, and indeed of the larger study: that when discussions of the veil are undertaken at the microlevel with a view to examining the material conditions of veiling, the inadequacies of definitive postulations on the veil in patriarchal nationalist and contemporary feminist discourses are foregrounded. By examining the dominant discourses around these two historical moments, I hope to demonstrate how these two pieces of legislation, which claimed to initiate revolutionary nationalist positions by two very different leaders, had remarkably similar effects on the body of the Iranian woman. In both instances, legal and feminist discourses proffered the Iranian woman as a visible marker of the nation as either secular, modern, and Westernized, or alternatively, as Islamic, modern, and anti-imperialist. Beneath these two polarized representations lies a desire to possess and to control the figure behind the veil by unveiling or re-veiling her.

Following Gayatri Chakravorty Spivak, my aim is to "revers[e], displac[e], and seiz[e] the apparatus of value-coding" in relation to the veiled woman (1990, 228). Spivak defines Karl Marx's discussion of value as "something 'contentless and simple' . . . that is not pure form, cannot appear by itself and is immediately coded" (1989, 272). She argues that this coding operation should not be understood as taking place solely in the realm of the economic, but also "in the fields of gendering and colonialism" (1989, 272). According to Spivak, the anticolonial nation secures its independence from imperial powers by reversing the interests of the four great codes of imperialist culture: nationalism, internationalism, secularism, and culturalism (1989, 269–70). However, as she indicates, "there is always a space in the new nation that cannot share in the energy of this reversal" (1993, 78). This is the space of the subaltern woman, who is represented in dominant discourse as the "*object* of protection from her own kind" (Spivak 1988, 299; emphasis hers).

It is my argument that it is through the language of protection the discourses of feminism and of patriarchal nationalism converge to perform a coding operation whereby the veiled Iranian woman circulates as a signifier of oppression.[3] The complicity of Western and dominant Iranian feminist discourse with that of imperialism has worked in tandem with patriarchal nationalist discourse to occlude the agential subject position of the Iranian woman. The intersection of these discourses elides the increasingly urgent category of the *bad-hijabi* (inappropriately/badly veiled) woman, whose manipulation of state-sanctioned dress codes suggests that the *hijab,* rather than a mere signifier of oppression or emancipation, remains the site of a continuous contestation of categories of gender and of class in contemporary Iran.

To discuss the moments of legislated unveiling and veiling, a brief historical overview of the veil in twentieth-century Iran is in order. In the early part of the century, *hijab*—which means "modest clothing"—was worn by women across classes, but the ways in which it was worn were markers of a woman's social and economic status.[4] Upper- and middle-class urban women wore the chador, a floor-length cloth from head to toe, usually accompanied by a separate facial veil, a *pichih.* The *hijab* of peasant or tribal women who worked mostly in the fields consisted of a colorful *rusari* (headscarf) and baggy clothing, which provided them with more freedom of movement than the floor-length chador. At this time, the widespread use of *hijab* reflected cultural standards of gender roles and class distinctions rather than practices enforced through legal discourse. In her groundbreaking work on Iranian women's autobiographies and the concept of veiling, Farzaneh Milani has argued that the veil is a physical reflection of the gendered concept of *sharm,* a combination of charm and shame (1992, 6). *Sharm,* which connotes modesty, timidity, and soft-spoken charm, remains one of the most valued qualities in a traditional Iranian woman. At the turn of the century, the more a woman concealed with her dress, and the more *sharm* in her demeanor, the more she indicated her privileged social status.

As Milani and Shahla Haeri have noted, the *hijab* was also a reflection of architectural space in the affluent Iranian home, divided between the *andarun* (inner) and the *biruni* (outer) (Haeri 1980, 215; Milani 1992, 5). The *andarun* was a realm occupied exclusively by women. The only men who had access to the women's quarters were close members of the family and servants. The *biruni,* in contrast, was reserved only for the men of the household, their male guests, and servants. Contrary to the beliefs of nineteenth-century missionaries, some American and British feminists, and women such as Gertrude Bell and Ella Sykes, who traveled to Iran in the late nineteenth and early twentieth centuries, these separate spheres did not automatically suggest that the *andarun* constituted a place of women's imprisonment or oppression. The *andarun* has been recognized in contemporary historical and political writings as the site of political intrigue and activism. An oft-cited example by Iranian historians of the *andarun*'s political role tends to be the tobacco protests of 1890. In response to a total monopoly awarded Major G. F. Talbot, a British entrepreneur, to cultivate and sell Iranian tobacco, there were large-scale protests and boycotts, but it was the uncompromising boycott of tobacco by the women in the *andarun* of the shah's palace that finally forced the shah to cancel the concession (Bayat-Philipp 1978, 297–98).[5]

The voices of privileged Iranian women, who would traditionally have belonged in the realm of the *andarun*, intersected with those of Western women to promote the language of women's rights and suffrage in Iran. Elite Iranian women and Western women mobilized the discourses of modernity and of sisterhood to argue for the unveiling of women and for their rights as citizens of the new nation during the Constitutional Revolution of 1905–1911. Often represented as one of the early proponents of progress and women's rights, Taj al-Saltanah, the daughter of Nasir al-Din Shah, and her memoirs deserve some attention here.

The structure of Taj al-Saltanah's autobiographical text is epistolary. She chooses to address her thoughts in the form of a letter addressed to her male mentor and cousin, whom she says reminds her of members of "Prince de Condé's family, whose noses were always compared to eagles' beaks" (1993, 109). She sets up her narrative by drawing on European frames of reference and makes frequent comparisons between her own writing style and that of French intellectuals, between the status of Iranian women and that of their European counterparts. She writes: "I wish I were a competent writer like Victor Hugo or Monsieur Rousseau and could write this history in sweet and delightful language. Alas, I can write but simply and poorly" (134). In her memoirs, Taj al-Saltanah argues that the postconstitutional nation of Iran can achieve its Enlightenment goals of sovereignty, individual rights, and technological progress only by discarding the traditional, oppressive practice of veiling and by promoting women's education:

> It disheartens and grieves me to think that my fellows—that is, the
> women of Persia—are ignorant of their rights and make no effort
> to fulfill their obligations as human beings. Completely deficient in
> character and unsuited for any task, they crawl into the corners of
> their homes and spend every hour of their lives indulging wicked
> habits. Excluded from the community of civilization, they roam the
> valley of confusion and ignorance. (118)

The representation of traditional Iranian women as ignorant and backward remained prevalent in Iranian feminist discourses well into the twentieth century. In the 1960s, Badr ol-Moluk Bamdad, another celebrated Iranian feminist, echoed Taj al-Saltanah's sentiments regarding the lives of Iranian women before the 1905 Constitutional Revolution:

> In the days when Iranian mothers were imprisoned in a corner of the house and knew nothing about rights or freedom, the Iranian children and youngsters growing up beside them had to spend their formative years in idleness and mental stress. (1977, 17)

Like their Western sisters, Bamdad and Taj al-Saltanah emphasize the importance of women's roles as mothers for the future of the nation; "[e]very mother's first responsibility is the edification of her children," Taj al-Saltanah opines (1993, 116).

The concept of motherhood as integral to the project of national progress and development is articulated as early as the eighteenth century by Wollstonecraft in *A Vindication of the Rights of Woman:* "If children are to be educated to understand the true principle of patriotism, their mother must be a patriot" (1792, 102). Iranian modernists in the late nineteenth and early twentieth centuries looked to the West as they constructed a model of social and political change for the nation and embraced the role of mothers as vital to the modern nation. Afsaneh Najmabadi has argued that Mirza Aqa Khan Kermani, one of the leading Iranian intellectuals of the nineteenth century, concerned with the creation of the perfect nationalist Iranian man, envisaged the womb as a school. According to Najmabadi, during this time in Iran, motherhood "became a mediating term between two concepts central to modernity: progress and women's rights" (1998, 94).

It is, however, the practice of veiling and segregation that emerges initially in Western women's discourses, and later in Iranian women's discourses, as the root of all the nation's problems. Taj al-Saltanah laments the lives and education of Iranian women, and bemoans their fate thus:

> Alas! Persian women have been set aside from humankind and placed together with cattle and beasts. They live their entire lives of desperation in prison, crushed under the weight of bitter ordeals. At the same time, they see and hear from afar and read in the newspapers about the way in which suffragettes in Europe arise with determination to demand

their rights: universal franchise, the right to vote in parliament, the right
to be included in the affairs of government. They are winning successes.
In America their rights are fully established and they are striving with
serious determination. The same is true in London and Paris. (1993, 285)

The portrayal of Iranian women as comparable to "beasts of burden" is
a familiar image in the writings of nineteenth-century missionaries and
feminists (Van Sommer 1907, 15). In fact, Reverend Samuel Zwemer goes
one step further by expressing his outrage at the barbarous practice that
ensures "a way by which *all* females could be buried alive and yet live
on—namely, the veil" (6; emphasis his). In her memoirs, Taj al-Saltanah
includes a questionnaire from a Caucasian Armenian, "a militant and a
freedom fighter for Persia," during the Constitutional Revolution (1993,
288). In response to his questions regarding the political future of the
nation and the role of women in that future, she writes:

> The duties of Persian women consist of: insisting on their rights, like
> their European counterparts; educating their children; helping the
> men, as do women in Europe; remaining chaste and unblemished;
> being patriotic; serving their kind; eradicating laziness and a sedentary
> lifestyle; removing the veil. (1993, 288)

The European woman is posited as a model to be emulated here; this is
a theme that runs throughout the history of the (elite) Iranian women's
movement and that enabled anti-imperialist patriarchal nationalists in
1979 to dismiss feminist concerns by configuring feminism as a quintessentially Western movement. When Taj al-Saltanah's Armenian correspondent requests clarification on the connection between the nation's
progress and the unveiling of women, she makes a case for women's education and employment, which she claims would be beneficial to the
household and, by extension, to the national economy. She ends by declaring that "[t]he source of the ruination of the country, *the cause of its moral
laxity,* the obstacle to its advancement in all areas, *is the veiling of women*"
(1993, 290; emphasis mine).[6]

Despite the lip service she pays to feminism, Taj al-Saltanah cannot
be exculpated from contributing to the reductive and constrictive model
that positions women as embodying the state of the nation. Veiled and
segregated from male public life, they represented the backwardness
and traditionalism of an outdated and corrupt feudal system in Iran. From

Taj al-Saltanah's perspective, veiling, as a religious practice, represents the incursion of religion into what the West, dating back to the Enlightenment, cherishes as secular space. Unveiled, however, women would represent a modern and independent nation moving along the path of moral, economic, and social progress.

Taj al-Saltanah's lack of faith in the vigilance of backward Iranian women inspires her to launch an appeal to Western women:

> How I wish I could travel to Europe and meet these freedom-seeking ladies! I would say to them, "As you fight for your rights happily and honorably, and emerge victorious in your aims, do cast a look at the continent of Asia. . . . These are women, too; these are human, too. These are also worthy of due respect and merit. See how life treats them." (1993, 285)

Her appeal to a universal sisterhood and her desire to be saved by her Western sisters is indicative of the complicated colonial history of feminism in Iran. Early twentieth century Persian and later Pahlavi feminists made repeated appeals to Western feminists to come to the aid of their Persian "sisters"; Iranian feminists from the privileged classes in this way participated in their own subjection to Western models of feminist "emancipation." The telegraph sent by the Persian Women's Society on December 5, 1911, to the Women's Social and Political Union (discussed in chapter 1), asking for their assistance in pressuring the British government to support Persia in the face of growing Russian threats to the country's independence, is one example of Iranian feminists looking to the West for help. The suffragists' response that they were unable to help because they were powerless at the level of the state in their own country further ironizes the assumption on the part of elite British and Persian feminists that their relationship is predicated on a hierarchical teacher/student model.

Nevertheless, this assumption continued into the period of 1919 to 1932, which Eliz Sanasarian has identified as the rise of the Iranian women's movement. During this time, there was a proliferation of feminist organizations, feminist periodicals, and schools for girls. Sanasarian notes that twentieth-century feminists, whom she identifies as belonging primarily to the upper classes, continued to look to the West for models to emulate:

> An interesting feature of feminist periodicals in Iran were translations
> and articles about the status of women in other countries, especially in
> England and the United States. Some of these articles would elaborate
> on the superior status of Western women as compared with Iranian
> women. Women's rights—to divorce, to marry by choice, to vote, and
> to work outside the household—were constantly praised. In fact, one
> article asserted that Western women were two centuries ahead of
> Iranian women. (1982, 38–39)

Belief in the superiority of Western feminist models continued to influence the state-sponsored Iranian feminist movement throughout
the twentieth century and contributed to the alienation of more traditional and especially rural women from mainstream Iranian feminist
discourse.

The history of cross-cultural feminism in the Iranian context is not
only one of unequal power relations between Western women and Iranian women, but also between Iranian women of the privileged classes
and those of the lower classes.[7] Contemporary Iranian feminists continue to celebrate Taj al-Saltanah as one of the great early feminists in
Iranian history without acknowledging her participation in reproducing the reductive binary of the traditional, veiled woman as backward
and the so-called modern, unveiled woman as progressive.[8] In the early
twentieth century, the discourses of nationalism, modernity, and sisterhood were mobilized by both Western women and their elite Iranian
counterparts to argue for the figure of the emancipated Iranian woman
who was necessarily unveiled, both physically and metaphorically, from
the constraints of Iranian patriarchal society and who would thereby
assist in the development of the country's nationalist goals.

The manipulation of veiling practices to reflect the aspirations of the
nation remained a powerful political tool, first used by the monarchical
state and later by the Islamic Republic. Upon his return from a trip to
Turkey in 1934, where he was impressed by Kemal Ataturk's modernization policies, including advocating the unveiling of women, Reza Shah
Pahlavi began introducing measures to unveil Iranian women. In 1936,
he legislated the Unveiling Act and ordered his soldiers to arrest veiled
women or to tear the veil off their heads should they appear in public
with any form of *hijab*. Despite the violence of these actions, the dominant feminist response to the new law was one of celebration.

The Iranian feminist language of gratitude and celebration surrounding the Unveiling Act can be attributed to what Eliz Sanasarian calls the period of "coercion and decline" of the women's movement during the Pahlavi period.[9] Among the factors contributing to this decline—and later co-optation—of the feminist movement was the brute force to which Reza Shah, sometimes personally, resorted to mute political opposition (Sanasarian 1982, 69). An example of Iranian feminists' complicity with the Pahlavi regime was their, albeit forced, celebration of January 7 (or the seventeenth of the month of *Day* in the Iranian calendar), the anniversary of the Unveiling Act, as Women's Day instead of International Women's Day on March 8.[10]

Iranian feminists from the social elite feted Reza Shah as an enlightened ruler who was "modernizing" the country by destroying the boundaries of *andarun* (inner, private space) and *biruni* (outer, public space) through his enforcement of the public appearance of women. The architecture of Iranian homes altered so as to reflect this new change in Iranian social life; the structure of *andarun* and *biruni* was discarded in favor of a more democratized space where men and women could travel freely. Similarly, the new Unveiling Act was represented as an effort to democratize gender roles by unveiling women and by encouraging mixed social gatherings at official state functions. While many women in Iran had protested the discarding of the veil, the fiction of democracy and of equal access to public space was nevertheless underscored by the violent enforcement of this law that ostensibly liberated women while denying them the freedom to choose how to present themselves in public.

In her work on the subaltern woman, Spivak has argued that "it is in terms of this profound ideology of the displaced place of the female subject that the paradox of free choice comes into play" (1988, 300). In the 1930s, the Iranian woman occupied the unenviable position of "choosing" to accept the enforcement of legal discourse, and thus acquiescing to the rhetoric of emancipation, or of being cast as an archaic figure responsible for retarding the modernizing impulses of the nation. The dominant patriarchal nationalist discourse and feminist discourses thus converged at this time in pursuit of the same goal: the strategic manipulation and control of women's social identities and appearances to reflect the interests of the nation and of the imperial feminist project.

In *From Darkness into Light: Women's Emancipation in Iran*, Bamdad describes the day that Reza Shah publicly pronounced the unveiling of all women. In a section titled, "A Momentous Decree," Bamdad describes in glowing terms the effects of the 1936 ruling:

> After that day, women wearing veils were forbidden to circulate in the main streets of Tehran and the provincial cities. They were guided by the police into side streets. . . . The women themselves at first found their new situation strange and startling. Thanks to the unshakable strength of will of the *nation's liberator,* the difficulties were overcome. (1968, 96; emphasis mine)

The "liberation" of women in 1936 is unintentionally ironized by Bamdad's admission that veiled women were barred from the main streets and were forced to walk along side streets.[11] Thus, rather than dissolving the boundaries of *andarun* and *biruni,* Reza Shah in fact extended those boundaries to city streets. More significantly, Bamdad neglects to mention the verbal and physical harassment to which veiled women were subjected as the shah's soldiers forcibly unveiled them. Indeed, the Unveiling Act ultimately ensured that women who had spent their entire lives wearing the veil would remain in the private space of their homes since, for them, walking the streets unveiled was tantamount to walking the streets naked.

In general, Pahlavi and Western feminists applauded state-imposed unveiling as a symbol of social progress; meanwhile, lower middle-class urban women felt the acute impact of this law as a violation of their bodies and their sense of self. By becoming forcibly unveiled, they felt coerced into a state of *bisharmi* (a state without charm/shame). Homa Hoodfar's notable article on veiling provides a nuanced argument on the social and political complexities of veiling in Iran. Describing the repercussions of the Unveiling Act for the class of women who identified strongly with the veil, Hoodfar writes:

> For many women it was such an embarrassing situation that they just stayed home. Many independent women became dependent on men, while those who did not have a male present in the household suffered most because they had to beg favors from their neighbours. . . . Women became even more dependent on men since they now had to ask for men's collaboration in order to perform activities they had previously performed independently. This gave men a degree of control over

women they had never before possessed. It also reinforced the idea
that households without adult men were odd and abnormal. (1993,
261–63)

Furthermore, Hoodfar writes, devout families prevented their daughters
from attending school because of the assumptions of immorality and
wantonness traditionally associated with being unveiled (263). State-
sponsored feminists, insensitive to the sufferings of lower-class women,
consolidated their feminism and nationalism along class lines with Western feminists and with patriarchal nationalists. Moreover, the discursive
practices of these groups positioned women as the yardstick by which
the progress of the nation was measured.

An enthusiastic description similar to that of Bamdad's of the progress of the nation and of women under Reza Shah is offered by Woodsmall, present in Iran on what she calls "the eventful day of emancipation"
on January 7, 1936:

> A number of definite regulations against the *chaddur* and the *pecheh*
> have been passed since this event, which will probably make unveiling
> inevitable. For example, no veiled woman can now receive treatment
> in Iran at a public clinic, or ride in a public conveyance. These two
> regulations will doubtless for a time work genuine hardship on
> conservative Moslem women but eventually their conservatism will
> doubtless be overcome. (44)

Bamdad's and Woodsmall's reflections on the Unveiling Act are remarkably similar in their unquestioning support of a patriarchal law that
imposed its nationalist vision on the bodies of women. The penalties
exacted by the act are quickly written off and the reluctance on the part
of some women to unveil for cultural or religious reasons is dismissed
as false consciousness. Bamdad writes:

> The majority of the nation's women had been trammelled by their
> upbringing with outworn ideas and notions; they had been trained, as
> the saying goes, "to enter the husband's house in a veil and leave it in a
> winding sheet." Feelings of inadequacy and servility had thereby been
> thoroughly inculcated into them. Now it was necessary to inform
> them of the rights which they had acquired and of the duties which
> would henceforth fall on them, and generally to prepare them for
> enjoyment of freedom and recognition of its limits. (1977, 121)

Bamdad and Woodsmall alike appear confident that once working-class women are exposed to the enlightened ways of their upper-class and/or Western counterparts, they will happily discard the shackles of the veil. The shared perspective of Bamdad and Woodsmall highlights a persistent problem with the history of the (Iranian and Western) feminist movement: the silence on issues of class inequities and colonial violence.[12] The imbrication of Western and Pahlavi women's discourses and their strategic alliance on the subject of veiled Iranian women were thus enabled through class solidarity.

Western and Pahlavi feminist discourses on unveiling women, and their representation of Iranian women's "liberation," were, in the words of Yeğenoğlu,

> linked not only to the discourse of Enlightenment but also to the scopic regime of modernity which is characterized by a desire to master, control, and reshape the body of the subjects by making them visible. Since the veil prevents the colonial gaze from attaining such a visibility and hence mastery, its lifting becomes essential. (1998, 12)

The emphasis on the visual in Enlightenment discourse and in the discourse of modernity leads to "a new form of institutional power which is based on visibility and transparency and which refuses to tolerate areas of darkness" (Yeğenoğlu 1998, 40). In her analysis of Western representations of the Islamic veil, Yeğenoğlu draws on Foucault's discussion of Bentham's model prison, the Panopticon, an architectural structure composed of a central tower surrounded by a circular building. Each room in the building is visible to the supervisor in the tower; however, the inmates are unable to see each other or the authority figure in the tower, thus, according to Foucault, "induc[ing] in the inmate a state of conscious and permanent visibility that assures the automatic functioning of power" (1979, 201). Bentham's institutional structure ensures a self-regulating system whereby the inmates discipline themselves for fear of the possibility of being watched.

Najmabadi has argued that the discourse of Iranian modernity, which advocated women's physical unveiling as a symbol of the nation's evolution, necessitated the development of "a veiled language and a disciplined de-eroticized body" (1993, 510). The desexualization of women's bodies was necessary to facilitate the shift from traditional "homosocial" spaces to a "heterosocial" space in which men and women were encouraged to socialize (489). In her article, Najmabadi cites a satirical poem by Iraj Mirza, published in the 1920s, in which he presents opposing images of two women: one veiled and the other unveiled. The poem describes in vivid detail a poet's sexual encounter with a veiled woman who "is described as a fully lustful participant, although she continues to hold tightly on to her veil, lest her face be seen by a male stranger" (510). According to Mirza, the educated and unveiled woman does not require the veil because, in his words, "when you see chastity and modesty in her / you will only look at her with modest eyes" (qtd. Najmabadi 1993, 511).

Mirza's conception of veiled women gestures to the complex representations of *hijab* in indigenous and Western discourses. The idea of the veiled woman as licentious was popular among male Orientalist writers who projected their own sexual fantasies on the East. The discourse of modernity, which originated in the West and influenced nineteenth-century Iranian nationalists and feminists, maintained the representation of the simultaneously dissolute and abject veiled woman. American and British missionaries in Iran also drew on the popular depiction of the veiled woman as oppressed and sexually permissive. Presbyterian missionaries Van Sommer and Zwemer comment on the moral laxity of veiled Muslim women:

> Not the least feature of the moral ruin into which they have fallen,
> is the impurity which seems to permeate every thought; so that they
> delight in obscene songs, vile allusions, and impure narratives. A
> missionary lady visiting at the home of a high-born Moslem woman,
> very religious and devout according to their standards, was so shocked
> by the character of the conversation with which her hostess was trying
> to entertain her, as to be forced to say, "If you talk to me like this, I
> shall be obliged to excuse myself and leave your house." (1907, 239)

While Western discourse portrays veiled Muslim women as licentious and crude, this representation translates into differences of class in Iranian discourses. Privileged Iranian women represent their (veiled) working-class counterparts as lewd and immoral, with the compulsory physical barrier of the veil to keep them in check, while they position their unveiled selves as models of sexual restraint and morality.

In her efforts to emphasize the benefits of unveiling, Bamdad relays an anecdote about "one of the worst consequences of veiling":

Not infrequently women of bad character played vile tricks on other women in pursuit of advancement for themselves. For example, with the help of marriage brokeresses who had access to particular houses, they would make their way into the presence of wealthy men and get lavish gifts from them by pretending that they were the reputedly beautiful and charming female members of well-known families. Naturally, such dishonesty and perfidy often gave rise to nasty incidents. (1977, 69)

If, in Iranian modernist discourses, the veiled woman conjures up scenes of wantonness and debauchery, the unveiled woman represents chastity and self-restraint. The veiled woman requires the barrier of the veil to control her sexual impulses. The unveiled woman, on the other hand, regulates her own behavior by imposing a form of self-disciplinary control. Because the unveiled subject is no longer concealed beneath the *hijab,* she becomes fully exposed and subject to the mechanisms of disciplinary power; she also emerges within the field of vision, knowledge, and control of the seeing subject.

However, the veiled woman also challenges the Enlightenment concept of visibility and power because she

seems to provide the Western subject with a condition which is the inverse of Bentham's omnipotent gaze. The loss of control does not imply a mere loss of sight, but a complete reversal of positions: her body completely invisible to the European observer except for her eyes, *the veiled woman can see without being seen.* (Yeğenoğlu 1998, 43; emphasis hers)

The threat posed by veiled women as they obstruct and frustrate the gaze of the colonizer has been addressed most famously by Frantz Fanon in "Algeria Unveiled." He argues that the French in Algeria focused on veiled women as a metaphorical symbol of the nation's resistance to colonial rule: "This woman who sees without being seen frustrates the colonizer. There is no reciprocity. She does not yield herself, does not give herself, does not offer herself" (1959, 44). While Western men and women fixated on the veil as a barrier, and its rending as a passage to the heart of the Orient, Oriental men constructed the veil as a symbol of national and cultural honor. This honor was necessarily gendered, and although the (veiled) body in question was female, its veiling or unveiling was a reflection of male honor and respectability.

In 1941, Reza Shah was forced to abdicate by the Allied powers because of his Nazi sympathies, and his son, Mohammad Reza Pahlavi, was enthroned as the new monarch. At this time, the Unveiling Act was rescinded and women were ostensibly free to wear or to discard the veil as they chose. Whereas earlier in the century, upper-class women were among the most heavily veiled, the situation was reversed by the 1940s. Upper- and middle-class urban women, who now embodied the modern secular state, remained unveiled while traditional working-class women returned to wearing the *hijab.* The ways in which the *hijab* was worn also changed at this time: the *pichih,* or face veil, was for the most part discarded, but some women returned to wearing the floor-length chador while others chose to wear the *rusari* (headscarf). Despite the illusion of free choice, there remained a marked prejudice against veiled, and thus working-class, women in professional and social circles. Hoodfar remarks:

> The government, through its discriminatory policies, effectively denied veiled women access to employment in the government sector, which is the single most important national employer, particularly of women. The practice of excluding veiled women hit them particularly hard as they had few other options for employment. Historically, the traditional bazaar sector rarely employed female workers, and while the modern private sector employed some blue-collar workers who wore the traditional chador, rarely did they extend this policy to white-collar jobs. A blunt indication of this discrimination was clear in the policies covering the use of social facilities such as clubs for civil servants provided by most government agencies or even private hotels and some restaurants, which denied service to women who observed the *hejab.* (1993, 263)

In what appears to be a direct inversion of, or response to, the discriminatory anti-veil policies under the Pahlavi regime, there are numerous signs in the Islamic Republic stipulating the virtuosity of *hijabi* women, as well as notices in restaurants and shops denying service to *bad-hijabi* (improperly veiled) women.

In the 1960s and 1970s, prominent Iranian feminists and Western feminists continued to forge strong relationships, mostly through the efforts of the Women's Organization of Iran (WOI). In the 1970s, the organization came under attack by Iranian women who felt that their needs were not addressed by the top-down policies of an organization closely affiliated with the monarchy. In an important essay, Zohreh T. Sullivan launches a forceful critique of the project of modernity during the Pahlavi period and of the regime's specious commitment to feminism. One of the examples she offers to illustrate the repressive nature of Mohammad Reza Shah's modernizing program is an event described to her by one of the "agents of development." Pari, a pseudonym used by her interviewee, visited Iranian villages to promote women's rights and to "modernize" rural women; the pedagogical agenda of this development program included forcing women—who were unfamiliar with sleeping on beds—to sleep on bunk beds:

> Pari tells of how, when they persisted in falling off their bunk beds in the middle of the night, the administrators found a bizarre solution. They tied the woman on the top to her bed with her chador. The image of the woman bound to her bed with the veil in the larger cause of progressive rights and freedoms, a paradox of modernity, captures the simultaneity of modernity and its underside, of the forces of reason and their bondage. . . . The image recalls the monumental hegemonic vision of Pahlavi Iran, and of the Enlightenment project of modernity that enforced selected citizen rights through repression and violence. (Sullivan 1998, 224)

Another consequence of the forays of urban-based "agents of development" into villages was the resultant physical abuse of rural women at the hands of their fathers and husbands who felt their honor was besmirched by the intrusiveness of urban women whose concerns appeared so far removed from those of their rural counterparts (225).

As was the case with members of the WOI, the leaders of the second-wave feminist movement in the West, with whom the WOI established a close relationship, have been criticized for their elitist vision of women's role in society and for their inattention to the needs of women who do not belong to the white, heterosexual, bourgeois nuclear family.[13] In her 1975 article for the *Ladies' Home Journal,* Betty Friedan extrapolates from her brief visit to Iran that there is very little difference between the concerns of women in the United States and those of women in Iran, despite the fact that she associated mostly with women of the elite class.[14] Friedan describes how she playfully wears the veil at the WOI while her Iranian sisters coach her in chador etiquette:

> They put the *chodor* on me, showing me how they tie it around the
> neck or waist to get work done—and how to peer around it to flirt. . . .
> I looked at myself, draped in the *chodor,* in the Women's Center in
> Iran, and realized that that piece of cloth is easier to throw aside than
> those invisible veils trapping our spirits in the West. My sisters in Iran
> laughed at me in their *chodor,* and I realized how far we all have come
> out of the veil. (104)

The call for a universal sisterhood is strongly advocated here, and Friedan
advances the standard second-wave feminist claim that all women are
united under the same banner of oppression. In this instance, the veil
becomes a universal signifier of the unequal positions of men and
women in society, a symbol that translates cross-culturally.

Billie Melman has argued that the period from the eighteenth century to post–World War II marked the emergence and development of
an alternative discourse regarding the veil. Unlike Mohja Kahf, Melman
believes that Western women's writings about veiled women in this period
emphasize the similarities between Western and Eastern women and
"humaniz[e] the colonial subject" (1992, 439). The veil, in eighteenth-
century discourses, she claims, is configured as a cross-cultural symbol:

> Here the veil is perceived not as a divide between veiled and unveiled
> women but as a moving contact zone between spaces: interior and
> exterior, personal and political, Eastern and Western. It may not be
> identified as "oriental" because it is also prevalent in the West. The
> veil is transcultural in the sense of this prevalence in most cultures
> but also because it mediates across cultures. Furthermore, Western
> women's responsiveness to this transcultural aspect makes it difficult
> for them to construct their identity as colonists by simply pitting it
> against the identity of a nonwhite female colonial subject. . . . The
> literature on veils reveals that the very notion of the other, or fixation
> on alterity as the basis for the construction of a discrete Western
> identity, is unworkable and probably unhistorical. (465)

In *Sexual Anarchy,* Elaine Showalter also draws on the idea of the "tran-
scultural" nature of the veil. Although she concedes that "the Oriental
woman behind the veil of purdah stood as a figure of sexual secrecy and
inaccessibility for Victorian men in the 1880s and 1890s," Showalter
suggests that the veil is "associated with female sexuality and with the
veil of the hymen" (1990, 145). It is, in fact, the "unhistorical" work of

both Melman and Showalter that elides the social, religious, and political context out of which representations of the veil emerge. Celebratory feminist work of this nature commits the error of absolving Western women from their active participation in the figuration of the Oriental woman as abject, thus sustaining the colonial creed that "the protection of woman (today the 'third-world woman') becomes a signifier for the establishment of a good society" (Spivak 1999, 288).

Representations of the veil as a cross-cultural symbol of female sexuality overlook the ways in which it emerged in feminist discourses, mobilized by both Western and elite Iranian feminists, as the epitome of Iranian women's degradation. The abject position of veiled Oriental women served as a justification for the Western civilizing project, which advocated women's unveiling as a step toward the progress and evolution of the nation. This configuration of the veil as quintessentially backward and primitive inspired the politicization of the veil, in various national and cultural contexts, and gave rise to its use as a form of anti-imperial resistance. Leila Ahmed has observed that

> the veil came to symbolize in the resistance narrative, not the inferiority
> of the culture and the need to cast aside its customs in favor of those
> of the West, but, on the contrary, the dignity and validity of all native
> customs, and in particular those customs coming under fiercest colonial
> attack—the customs relating to women—and the need to tenaciously
> affirm them as a means of resistance to Western domination. (1992, 164)

In Iran, the veil as a symbol of anti-imperial resistance was gaining popularity in the years preceding the 1979 revolution. During the period of Friedan's visit to Iran, in the 1960s and 1970s, there was growing dissatisfaction with the Shah's aggressive modernization policies and with his close political and economic ties to the West, particularly to the United States.

In a powerful speech in October 1964, which became the immediate cause for his forced exile to Iraq in November of that year, Ayatollah Khomeini publicly condemned a bill passed in parliament affording legal immunity to all American citizens in Iran. In exchange, the Iranian government would receive a two hundred million dollar loan from the United States. Khomeini decried the bill as yet another manifestation of Western imperialism in Iran:

[The government has] reduced the Iranian people to a level lower than that of an American dog. . . . If the Shah himself were to run over a dog belonging to an American, he would be prosecuted. But if an American cook runs over the Shah, the head of the state, no one will have the right to interfere with him. . . . The government has sold our independence, reduced us to the level of a colony, and made the Muslim nation of Iran appear more backward than savages in the eyes of the world. . . . If the religious leaders have influence, they will not permit this nation to be the slaves of Britain one day, and America the next. (1981, 182–83)

Khomeini went on to condemn the notorious "White Revolution," which the shah heralded as a new era of economic, cultural, and political modernity in Iran. The shah's vision of Iran, as exemplified in his six-point reform program, was one of an industrialized economy coupled with the increasing "Westernization" of Iranian culture. The reforms of the "White Revolution," however, were perceived by critics of the regime as benefiting only the Iranian elite who had close ties to the royal court and to American investors in Iran.

In *Gharbzadegi,* loosely translated as *Westoxification,* Jalal Al-e Ahmad launches a powerful critique of Iran's colonial relationship to the West, but he makes Iranian women the target of his criticism, as the embodiments of a Westernized and corrupt state. Although his point about the disingenousness of the 1936 Unveiling Act's claim to redress gender inequities is well taken, Al-e Ahmad's nostalgic harking back to a time when women knew their place as mothers and daughters is deeply disturbing:

In reality then what have we done? We have only allowed women to appear in public. Just hypocrisy. Pretense. That is, we have forced women who were in the past guardians of our customs, the family, the new generation, and our bloodlines to become frivolous. We have brought them outside of the home into the streets. We have compelled them to be shallow and flighty, to paint their faces, to wear a new outfit everyday, and to run around with nothing to do. Work, duty, responsibility in society, esteem? Never—very few women can achieve these. (1962, 47)

The responsibility that Al-e Ahmad places on Iranian women as the personification of the nation's status as independent, dignified, and resistant evokes Fanon's contention that "unveiling [the Algerian] woman is revealing her beauty; it is baring her secret, breaking her resistance, making her available for adventure" (1959, 43). In 1943, shortly after the abdication of Reza Shah, Khomeini condemned those who "regard the civilization and advancement of the country as dependent upon women's going naked in the streets, or to quote their own idiotic words, turning half the population into workers by unveiling them (we know only too well what kind of work is involved here)" (1981, 171–72).[15] Unveiled women, Khomeini implies, are immoral, "loose" women who invite (sexual and imperial) penetration and epitomize the depraved and degenerate nature of the "Westoxified" soul. The incursion of Western values, culture, or knowledge into the Oriental nation is configured in sexual terms and thus undermines the honor of the indigenous patriarchy.

One of Khomeini's followers (unnamed here) from the early days explains his allegiance to Khomeini by evoking the idea of cultural *hijab*, and by extension, the *ghiyrat*—the concept of male honor, which has deep cultural roots—of the Iranian man:

> Before Ayatollah Khomeini raised his voice, we had lost our identity. We had to bow our heads down to American dogs that had as much right in Iranian courts as Iranians. . . . You see, we had lost our cultural *hejab* . . . inside and outside. We had also lost social justice. Ayatollah Khomeini had the bravery to fight for our Islamic culture and to stand up for justice. (qtd. Mackey 1996, 249)

At issue in anti-Pahlavi, anti-imperialist discourses, then, especially in the 1960s and 1970s, was the question of *hijab* in its physical as well as its cultural manifestations.

Patriarchal nationalist discourses carry within them the anxiety of emasculation; colonial domination or imperial influences are perceived as a direct challenge to male potency and control. Thus, the threat of colonial powers or the infiltration of imperialist influences in a "third world" country is seen as a personal affront to the masculinity and the *ghiyrat* of the "third world" man. The sexualization of the colonized "third-worlder" feeds into the powerful and oppressive metaphor of the nation as woman who is always vulnerable to penetration and rape. The more powerful the imperialist presence, the weaker the position of the third-world subject, and the more this subject position becomes associated with effeminate and weak female identities. Al-e Ahmad asserts that the "West-stricken man is a gigolo. He is effeminate. He is always primping; always making sure of his appearance. He has even been known to pluck his eyebrows!" (1962, 70). To be colonized or to be susceptible to imperialist cultures, then, is to be weak and female; women's actions and women's bodies, therefore, must be controlled by indigenous (male) cultures to protect the nation from colonization and emasculation and to prove the *ghiyrat* of the Iranian man.

The positioning of (unveiled or veiled) women as embodying the state of the nation is a typical feature of anticolonial writings. In the Iranian context, Al-e Ahmad's desire to dispense with the image of what was generally referred to as the (unveiled) "painted doll of the Pahlavi regime" was motivated by his desire to return to the feminine concept of *sharm*. The quality of feminine charm and shame, embodied by the veiled woman, would restore the *ghiyrat* of the Iranian man whose honor has been besmirched by the presence of the Westoxified woman. Ali Shariati, an influential Shiite modernist of the 1970s, built upon Al-e Ahmad's Westoxification argument by criticizing the new Iranian woman in her support of capitalism. The Westoxified woman enabled the capitalist agenda in two ways: first, as a sexualized object under the Pahlavi regime, she distracted the working man from class revolt; second, her dependency on cosmetics and fashion transformed her into the quintessential capitalist consumer (Paidar 1995, 180). Shariati thus offered the figure of Fatimih, the Prophet Mohammad's daughter, as an alternative and superior (veiled) role model for Iranian women (Paidar 1995, 181). Fatimih signified all that was desirable in an Iranian woman: she was shy, modest, and chaste; in other words, she was a woman with *sharm*. More important, her *sharm* was now politicized as an anticapitalist, anti-Pahlavi, anti-Western quality.

As a symbolic manifestation of growing discontent with the shah's regime, many secular, middle-class women who had never before worn the veil, but were attracted by Shariati's charismatic speeches, chose to adopt some form of *hijab* (modest clothing) and to emulate Shariati's Fatimih as a visible sign of their dissatisfaction with social, political, and economic affairs in Iran. This move did not go unnoticed by prominent Iranian feminists. In a *New York Times* article of July 30, 1977, the minister of state for women's affairs and the secretary general of the WOI, Mahnaz Afkhami, offers the idea of a "spiritual revivalism" in response to journalist Marvine Howe's observation that "more and more women are seen on the streets of this Middle Eastern capital [Tehran] wearing the chaddour, a long enveloping veil, in what looks like a women's backlash" (20). Aware of the implications of a growing opposition to the feminist rhetoric of the WOI, Afkhami is quick to promote herself as an example of an Iranian woman who manages to balance her feminist ideas with her Islamic faith:

> "I found it in myself," the 36-year-old Minister said, speaking of her own experience with religion. She said that last spring she had visited the Islamic holy city of Mecca in Saudi Arabia and shrines in Iraq. "The experience would have been impossible for me five years ago," she said. "There seems to be a need for religion, as if we have moved too fast in a direction that is not native to us," Mrs. Afkhami said. She calls it a revival "against emptiness" and compares it with spiritual trends among young Americans, such as the interest in Zen Buddhism. (Howe 1977, 20)

The article is fascinating in the way that it exposes an underlying sense of panic that the WOI and, by extension, the Pahlavi regime felt with regard to their own vulnerability as members of the ruling class in a politically unstable time. It appeared just weeks after Iranian student demonstrations in New York City against what the protesters saw as the Empress Farah Pahlavi's fraudulent self-representation as a champion of women's rights. Afkhami recognizes that, to contain the discontent of the growing numbers of people, she must, as minister of state for women's affairs, distance herself and the WOI from the image of feminism as a wholly Western phenomenon divorced from Iranian cultural traditions. As Sandra Mackey writes, in 1978 the shah "tried to restore some of the royal family's Islamic credentials. Empress Farah went on pilgrimage to Mecca and the Shah touted the amount of money he had spent on the beautification of the shrine at Mashhad" (1996, 280). The shah and his coterie's reinvention of themselves as devout Muslims was a politically savvy move but one to which they resorted too late, since, by July 1977, the political winds were already blowing in another direction.

By the late 1970s, the anti-shah movement had gained in popularity and force across social classes in Iran. Contrary to general Western perceptions that the 1979 revolution was Islamic, it was supported and enabled by Iranians who held radically different political and national visions but who came together in their one shared desire: the overthrow of the shah. In the late 1970s, revolutionary women moved away from the model of the modest Fatimih and chose to adopt her daughter, Zaynab, as the new female role model. The popular narrative surrounding the figure of Zaynab was of an aggressive, militant warrior who reputedly divorced her husband so that she could devote her energies to the Shiite cause by fighting the Sunni forces (Paidar 1995, 218). That this figure was embraced as a symbol of women's agency rather than of Islamic piety is evident by women's prompt removal of *hijab,* which they had worn only as a symbol of anti-Pahlavi protest, after the shah's departure in January 1979.

However, one month after the revolution in March 1979, revolutionary leader Ayatollah Khomeini announced that "women should not be naked in these ministries. There is nothing wrong with women's employment. But they must be clothed according to religious standards" (qtd. Jaynes 1979a, A1). Once again, women took to the streets in five consecutive days of feminist demonstrations, only this time they were unveiled. Renowned second-wave feminist Kate Millett went to Iran at this point to lend support to her Iranian sisters. Once again, the veil was adopted as a universal feminist cause by Western women, but in contrast to Friedan's 1975 representation of the veil as a cross-cultural phenomenon, the *hijab* was now reconfigured as belonging to a space of incommensurable difference from the West. Upon her arrival in Tehran airport in March 1979, a horrified Millett proclaims:

> The first sight of them was terrible. Like black birds, like death, like fate, like everything alien. Foreign, dangerous, unfriendly. There were hundreds of them, specters crowding the barrier, waiting their own. A sea of chadori, the long terrible veil, the full length of it, like a dress descending to the floor, *ancient,* powerful, annihilating us. (1982, 49; emphasis mine)

Millett's aversion to the sight of veiled Iranian women situates the veil in a time and space of radical Otherness. By deploying temporal terms of progress and regression, she reinserts the discourse of modernity into the debate. In so doing, she is speaking out of a long, discursive tradition of Western women's representation of their Eastern sisters as existing in an earlier, more primitive temporal order. In 1936, Woodsmall declared that the principal difference between the cultures of the East and West centers on "the position of woman" (39). While Western cultures offer a "unified" culture in which men and women occupy the same realm, Eastern cultures enforce a distinction between the worlds of men and women by placing women behind the veil and in the home. Woodsmall then provides an explanation for these radical differences:

> This present unified basis of Western society is undoubtedly the result of evolution as the Western world of the twentieth century is very different from the Western world of the Middle Ages, especially in regard to the position of women. . . . The Islamic world with its integrated system of religion and society, has preserved with little if any variation, the social customs of the seventh century. *Between the social practices of the East and of the West, there has always been until recently the cleavage of centuries.* (1936; emphasis mine)

Thus Millett's denial of temporal coevalness to the veiled Iranian woman belongs to a discursive tradition in which, to paraphrase Edward Said, the Orient becomes Orientalized through its radical difference from the West (Said 1978, 3). If the veiled woman represents a primitive seventh-century Islamic tradition of female enslavement, then the image of the independent, emancipated, unveiled woman serves as the projected fantasy of Western and privileged Iranian women.

The language of Millett and the contingent of European feminists who arrived in Iran in 1979 to support their beleaguered Iranian sisters was framed within the rhetoric of oppression and emancipation and provided fodder for anti-imperialist patriarchal nationalists who saw the intervention of Western feminists in Iranian domestic affairs as an opportunity to advance their arguments about Western imperialism and the Westoxification of the nation.[16] In turn, they offered a vision of independence and emancipation through anti-Western nationalist discourse. The presence of Western feminists in Iran forced a larger wedge between feminist discourse and nationalist discourse, especially in the context of the WOI's historical association with Western feminism. Iranian women were forced to choose allegiances at that time, but again it was a spurious choice since to declare oneself a feminist was to declare oneself a member of the "counterrevolutionary" Westernized elite who were purportedly at the root of all the nation's problems. This moment of cross-cultural feminism was overdetermined by the colonial history of the international feminist project, and the figure of the anti-imperialist feminist subject was elided and displaced between dominant patriarchal nationalist discourse and dominant Western and Pahlavi feminist discourse.

In 1980, the Islamic Republic passed a regulation prohibiting unveiled women from working in offices. In 1983, the Veiling Act was ratified and the penalty for women appearing unveiled in any public space was seventy-four lashes with a whip. This law was presented in the language of women's emancipation once again: their emancipation from their status as sexualized objects under the Pahlavi regime. The Veiling Act claimed to facilitate a more professional work space, where women could work alongside men without fear of sexual harassment. This argument implicitly suggested the symbolic reconfiguration of Iranian architectural space: the literal boundaries of *andarun* and *biruni* were dissolved because women could venture anywhere as long as they remained veiled. As with the 1936 Unveiling Act, this was a fallacious argument because the requirement of veiling was applied to all public spaces and forced gender segregation on public transport, in government offices, on beaches, and even on the streets, as only men and women who were related could be seen together in public.[17]

The debates on the subject of *hijab* in Iran remain as divisive and oppositional now as those arising from the 1936 and 1983 legislations. It has been especially true of the post-1979 revolutionary period that Western women's, as well as some diasporic Iranian women's, representations of veiled Iranian women has been, for the most part, unequivocally associated with oppression.[18] In Susan Faludi's 1991 best seller, *Backlash: The Undeclared War against American Women,* she criticizes what she perceives to be a backlash against feminism in the popular media. She also suggests that outspoken second-wave feminists have tempered their arguments in the face of the antifeminist sentiment of the 1980s. Faludi offers Germaine Greer as one such example and accuses her of celebrating the ultimate symbol of female oppression—the chador:

> Formerly the media's favourite as a flamboyant advocate of sexual emancipation . . . Greer now championed arranged marriages, chastity, and the chador, and named as her new role model the old-fashioned peasant wife, happily confined to kitchen and nursery and happily concealed under her chador. (1991, 320)

In fact, Greer makes no such claims. She does, however, offer a perspective on the chador that recognizes the complexities of the issue, thus distancing herself from dominant Western and Pahlavi feminist discourses of the time. Greer writes:

> When the shah of Persia outlawed the veil in 1937, he did not so much liberate his people as announce their dependency upon the West. Older women, humiliated by the possibility that soldiers might tear off their veils in the street, made themselves prisoners in their own houses. Gradually a version of the veil re-established itself; peasant women marked the rise in their status when their husbands gained work in the cities by assuming a lighter and more coquettish version of the chador, nowadays replaced in revolutionary Iran by the old heavy chador or the unbecoming uniform of Islamic Marxism, which confers upon young women the aspect of military nuns. (1984, 123)

Rather than celebrating the Unveiling Act as a moment of women's liberation, Greer recognizes it for what it was: a state-enforced legislation that aimed to promote, through the use of brute force, a particular vision of national modernity on women's bodies. Thus, Greer seems to be aware that there needs to be a nuancing of (mainstream) Western feminism's tendency to unequivocally equate women's unveiling with women's liberation. Yeğenoğlu has argued convincingly in favor of contextualizing the practices of veiling and unveiling in their cultural and historical specificities:

> The presumption of the naturalness of not-to-be-veiled has come to secure the truth of bodies and is used as the universal norm to yield Muslim woman as a knowable and comprehensible entity for the West. In other words, it is the naturalness and truth of the unveiled body that legitimates and endorses colonial feminist sentiments and certitude in the necessity of interventionist action against Muslim women's veiling. Although the beliefs and values about not veiling are also incorporated in the existential and embodied being of Western women, the fact that this is a culturally specific inscription is effaced in colonial feminist representations. Such an effacement ensures that the beliefs and values that produce Western women's bodies stand in for the truth of women universally. (2002, 93)

There is a substantial body of work on the veil in the diasporic Iranian feminist community; while some diasporic Iranian feminists acknowledge

the complexities of the issue, a regrettable number tend to fall back on
the discourse of the veil as oppressive, thus endorsing a colonial feminist
position of the unquestioned naturalness of the unveiled body.[19] Haideh
Moghissi has queried, "In whose interests is it, except the present-day
champions of the reveiling of Iranian women, to present unveiling in
Iran as a concocted colonialist ploy, executed by the local, Westoxi-
cated modernizer, Reza Shah?" (1999b, 88). The question implies that
those who choose to critique some of the oppressive policies of the Pahlavi regime, and its problematic embrace of a particular Western feminist
discourse of women's liberation, can be unceremoniously dismissed as
dogmatic "Islamic fundamentalists." Moghissi's perhaps unwitting cen-
soring of dissenting voices serves to silence debate on the future of
Iranian feminism.[20]

The work of prominent diasporic Iranian feminist Azar Nafisi is
worth mentioning here, not least because of the extent to which her
work has been celebrated in the West. Her rise to fame in the West has
been primarily as a result of her book *Reading Lolita in Tehran: A Memoir in Books* (2003). Here, Nafisi offers an extremely conservative view of
what constitutes the "literary" as well as what constitutes "freedom." In
both instances, Nafisi turns to the West for validation: freedom comes
to her and her students, represented as suffocating in the stifling
atmosphere of repression in Iran, in the form of the "Great Works" of
European literature. In their weekly discussions of these Great Books,
they engage in a New Critical reading practice, long since abandoned in
most departments of literature in favor of more politicized reading strategies that demand readers contextualize and theorize the literary work
in its historical, social, and cultural moment. Furthermore, the turn away
from the "Great Works" approach has opened avenues of literary self-
expression to those people previously excluded from the Western canon:
postcolonial and women writers, for example, have greatly benefited
from this "opening" and this collapsing of hierarchical notions of "the
literary."[21]

Nafisi's adulation of the great European masters, and her attempts
to make them make sense in an Iranian context, has colonial echoes,
but more important, it perpetuates the highly problematic position that
Iranian self-identity comes through an embrace of Western cultural
forms and representations. Although Nafisi pays lip service to respecting

women's choice to veil, she nevertheless tends to reproduce in her book and elsewhere the stereotype of the veiled woman as effaced from public life, whose voice has been muted beneath the smothering folds of the veil.

Roksana Bahramitash has taken Nafisi to task for what she calls her "Orientalist feminism," which she defines as "a modern project and a type of feminism that advocates and supports particular foreign policies toward the Middle East" (2005, 221). Bahramitash argues that the commercial success of *Reading Lolita* and its enthusiastic endorsement by conservative supporters of the U.S. government needs to be understood in the context of the post–September 11 language of regime change:

> Azar Nafisi's book has remained on the bestseller's list for more than one year and during a time when the Bush administration has been preparing the American public to support its foreign policy against Iran. . . . For those who genuinely care about the status of women, this book has hijacked the issue of women's rights from them, and it helps to prepare broad acceptance for the neo-conservatives' Greater Middle East Initiative agenda—a Middle East dominated by the US economic and political interests. Simultaneously, the book's success hinders those who aspire to mobilize feminists against a possible military confrontation with Iran. Thus, the popularity of *Reading Lolita in Tehran* among North American feminists is extremely problematic, and the situation calls for a reconsideration of the reasons why gender rights advocacy, anti-war activism, and anti-racism have failed to come together in this case. (234)

Nafisi's endorsement of Western imperialist views on Iran, particularly Iranian women, is certainly not a new position for her. In a 1999 article titled "The Veiled Threat," published in the *New Republic,* Nafisi structures her argument around Edgar Degas's painting *Dancers Practicing at the Bar,* reproduced in an art book published in Iran. The dancers, according to Nafisi, are absent in this reproduction as they have been airbrushed out to satisfy the Islamic Republic's censors. She argues that this is indicative of the ways in which women have been rendered invisible due to the repercussions of state-enforced veiling. However, Nafisi suggests, by virtue of their absence from the public space, these women have become more fully present. The article plays off the tensions of modernity and tradition, progress and backwardness, as she waxes nostalgic about the disappearance of early Iranian feminists, who devoted their energies to emancipating women, in the collective national memory. Nafisi sets up a binary of state versus society as she grapples with the effects of the 1983 Veiling Act. While she acknowledges the various forms of women's resistance to *hijab*, she tends to universalize the stance of Iranian women with respect to the veil as one of unilateral resistance to a universally recognized oppressive legislation. I would like to suggest that, as long as we persist in the reproduction of a colonial feminist position that the *hijab* is in and of itself oppressive, we remain in a stalemate. In contemporary Iran, the *hijab* is the site upon which issues of class, gender, and nationalism are continuously contested, negotiated, and rethought. To illustrate this point, I would like to examine briefly the current effects of legislated *hijab* in Iran with regard to the traditional space of the *andarun* and the figure of the *bad-hijabi* woman.

The Veiling Act has ensured yet another reconfiguration of Iranian architectural space. Due to the strict enforcement of public segregation and veiling, the *andarun* has taken over the entire space of private homes. In memory of its past political role, such as in the 1890 Tobacco Protests, the Iranian middle-class home or *andarun* has become one of the sites of resistance to the regime by facilitating such illegal activities as drinking, dancing, and the viewing of smuggled Western videos. In 2002, Christiane Bird, the daughter of American missionaries, published a book about her return to Iran, where she lived as a child. Like many travel writers since the 1979 revolution, Bird was struck by the ways in which Iranian men and women managed to live their lives through myriad contradictions:

> Every Iranian lives in two worlds—the public and the private. The public is for wearing dark colors, obeying the laws of the Islamic society, and generally presenting a serious and pious face to the world. The private is for wearing bright colors, laughing and socializing with family and friends, and quiet contemplation and prayer. Among some Iranians, most notably the middle and upper classes of north Tehran and other large cities, the private is also for enjoying forbidden music and literature, watching banned videos and TV shows, wearing miniskirts and halter tops, drinking alcohol and doing drugs, and criticizing the Islamic government. (2001, 51)

Many others have commented on the schizophrenic nature of Iranian society developed as a result of excessive state-imposed codes of

behavior. Canadian travel writer Alison Wearing describes her burgeon-
ing friendship with a young man whose entrepreneurial spirit has led
him to a lucrative drug-dealing operation out of his trendy Tehran apartment (2000, 180). Wearing appears fascinated by his ability to navigate
his way through the elaborate cultural codes expected of him through
tradition, the stringent social codes imposed on him through state legislation, and the stealth required of him in his covert traffic in opium, a
profitable venture enabling him to maintain his fashionable lifestyle.
But as CNN reporter Christiane Amanpour's 1999 documentary on Iran
(discussed later in the chapter) indicates, the private spaces of Iranian
homes are the sites not only of drug deals, but of surreptitious sales of
bootleg Hollywood movies.

As was the case in 1936, the boundaries of *andarun* and *biruni* have
been displaced onto city streets but with different results, so that public
parks and ski slopes in northern Tehran are now renowned for accom-
modating surreptitious meetings between teenagers who defy the wrath
of the Islamic Republic by arranging social excursions in groups or as
couples. *New York Times* foreign correspondent Elaine Sciolino describes
the complexities of private and public spaces and the ways in which Iranians are continuously reconfiguring the two realms:

> Iranians . . . find refuge in the great outdoors, especially in the three
> small mountains north of Tehran. . . . All use the mountains as a place
> of release, beyond the watchful eye of the Islamic Republic. . . . A
> young Iranian woman I know goes camping with a coed group of
> friends in mountains where the police do not go. . . . For days, they
> sleep in tents and cook food over campfires. It is an act both of
> liberation and desperation. In reality, the mountains are not private at
> all, and if the campers were to be caught, they could be arrested, fined,
> and perhaps lashed. But the longing to feel free makes it worth the
> risk. (2000, 106)

Consequently, although the effects of legislated veiling were intended
to demarcate private and public domains, many Iranians are subverting
the rigidity of these categories by redefining and relocating these spaces.

An important factor that has been elided in scholarly discussions of
the *hijabi* (veiled) and *bi-hijabi* (unveiled) in Iran is the category of the
bad-hijabi. By draping a *rusari* (headscarf) around her head in creative
ways, teasing out a lock of dyed blond hair, wearing various shades of

lipstick, and sporting fashionably tailored *manteaus* (overcoats), the compelling figure of the middle-class *bad-hijabi* woman draws attention to her body. By manipulating state-sanctioned dress codes to flaunt the regime, she simultaneously displays her class privilege by the quality and style of *manteau* that she wears and the designer scarf she drapes over her semiconcealed hair. Ziba Mir-Hosseini has argued that the enforcement of *hijab* has paradoxically "empowered those whom it was meant to restrain: Westernised middle-class women" (1996, 157). I agree with Mir-Hosseini that this particular class of women effectively manipulates the terms of the legislation to display resistance to the regime. The *bad-hijabi*'s creative interpretation, indeed subversion, of state-enforced ideals of Islamic modesty exemplify what de Certeau identifies as the tactical nature of everyday practices. Following Foucault's analysis of the "microphysics of power," de Certeau reads the possibility of individual opposition from within an oppressive, disciplinary system:

> If it is true that the grid of "discipline" is everywhere becoming clearer and more extensive, it is all the more urgent to discover how an entire society resists being reduced to it, what popular procedures (also "miniscule" and quotidian) manipulate the mechanisms of discipline and conform to them only in order to evade them. (1984, xiv)

To explain how this form of internal opposition occurs, de Certeau focuses on the difference between a "strategy," which, he argues, is "organized by the postulation of power" since it emerges from an authorized, institutional, and recognized location, and a "tactic," which "is determined by the *absence of power*" (38; emphasis mine).

By mocking and parodying the form of modest dress that the state imposes on women, the *bad-hijabi* threaten one of the regime's most important political aims. The rhetoric of revolutionary days and of the revolutionary government championed the *mustaz'af*, the downtrodden poor. The government's aim was to redistribute the wealth of the country, and one of the ways they sought to do so was by forcing women to wear *hijab*, thereby concealing the inequalities of wealth and class in the country. The distinctive and tactical ways in which women are increasingly choosing to wear *hijab* presents a brazen challenge to the Islamic Republic's self-proclaimed efforts to redress social and economic inequalities.

Janet Afary suggests that the battle over the ways of wearing the *hijab* constitutes a form of resistance to the regime as well as to the previous generation of women:

> Young women, in contrast to their mother's generation—leftist radicals who abhorred bourgeois decadence—express their defiance toward the morality police by wearing makeup and streaking their hair in vibrant colours (the bit they can show from under their colorful scarves). Before the eyes of the clerics and police authorities on the streets, they claim the public arenas with elegant capes in creative designs that meet the minimum requirement of the morality police but are nowhere near the drab black veils that are recommended by them. (2004, 134)

The *bad-hijabi* thus pose simultaneously a challenge to the regime's self-described politics of economic and social equality and to the fashion politics of their mothers' generation, but they also defy the regime's enforcement of female chastity and morality by artfully testing the limits of *hijab*. It is the erotic aspect of veiling that the *bad-hijabi* exploit and manipulate to subvert the purpose of state-legislated *hijab*, which claims to equalize all women in terms of class and sexuality. By deploying a form of tactical resistance, or opposition, as de Certeau explains it, from within the limits of their precarious subject position, the *bad-hijabi* toy with the limits of the Islamic dress code. They push the boundaries between modesty and immodesty, testing the government's stance on these issues. The *bad-hijabi* have managed, through fashionable adaptations of the *hijab*, to challenge both the concepts of economic equality and of sexual neutrality. Not only do they tempt the scopophilic gaze by the provocative ways in which they wear *hijab* in public, but private homes have become the site of suggestive unveiling and sexual allusions.

Upon arriving at a party in affluent north Tehran, Bird is startled to find that

> all around [her] were gorgeous young women, dressed in revealing T-shirts or tube tops, and slinky blank pants, black miniskirts, or tight blue jeans. Some had long elaborately curled hair and most were wearing a light layer of makeup. All in all, they looked much like fashionable young women in the United States. (2001, 53)

While in Tehran, Sciolino visits an aerobics studio in the affluent north and is treated to an impromptu dance performed by the instructor for the viewing pleasure of the women in attendance:

> Ladan was dressed in a low-cut belly shirt, tight red and white paisley pedal pushers, big gold hoop earrings, and athletic shoes. But the dance she chose was pure Persian. She turned down the lights and put on the sinuous music. She thrust out her small breasts, revealing her slightly rounded belly and her navel, threw back her head, and put her arms over her head. She parted her wide lips in what I can only describe as an orgasmic smile. Then she moved, swaying and undulating her way around the room. She outlined the curves of her body with her hands and beckoned the audience to her. It was a moment of sheer sensuality like others I have been invited to see from time to time in Iran. Men can be wonderfully erotic when they show their skills in traditional dances that have survived, despite the Islamic Republic. But for women, there is an additional dimension of freedom. So much of a woman's body is covered in public, so much is forbidden and repressed, that when the veil falls, even for a moment, there is a heightened sense of excitement. (2000, 95)

Although this passage attempts to challenge contemporary stereotypes of the veiled woman as desexualized and abject, it does so by evoking the recognizable eighteenth- and nineteenth-century Orientalist fantasies about the Orient. Ironically, by attempting to subvert state legislation through a mockery of its emphasis on morality, the *bad-hijabi* invoke Orientalist representations of the East as a site of endless sexual possibilities and of veiled women as sensual and insatiable objects of desire.

In July 1999, the television program *National Geographic Explorer* aired an episode titled "Iran: Behind the Veil." The show follows photographer Alexandra Avakian through the country as she, according to the narrator, "capture[s] an Iran few Westerners know about or have ever seen." Avakian establishes her Middle Eastern pedigree by mentioning an Iranian grandfather, but takes pains to ensure that her audience will recognize her as American. In other words, she is just "Other" enough to represent her subject authoritatively, and at the same time familiar enough not to alienate her audience.

Central to the documentary is footage of women, black stripes over their eyes to conceal their identities, modeling clothes in a women's clothing store in Tehran, as well as still photographs, similarly doctored, of a wedding celebration in which we see unveiled women dancing with men. The narrator declares triumphantly: "Not only has Alex photographed Iranian women in traditional garb, but she's also managed *to get behind the veil,* photographing women in situations and circumstances that just a few years ago might have landed both photographer and subject in trouble" (emphasis mine). Not to be outdone, in February 2000, CNN *Perspectives* aired a personal documentary hosted by the network's foreign affairs correspondent, Christiane Amanpour. Amanpour's cultural credentials are even more authentic than those established by Avakian: she, too, is Iranian, but was born and raised in Iran and left the country as a teenager during the 1979 revolution. Not only does she have more cultural authority than Avakian, she also has more cultural capital because of her position as a respected CNN correspondent.

The CNN documentary, filmed in 1999, trumps the *National Geographic* episode as it provides an even more daring unveiling of the mysteries of postrevolutionary Iran and its women. In one scene, we are taken inside an affluent home in north Tehran to witness a party attended by a group of young adults. The CNN camera pans over scantily clad women (unprotected by the anonymity of black stripes); they are drinking alcohol, smoking cigarettes, and performing coquettishly for the camera. Amanpour exults in the fact that "no one has ever shown this side of Iranian life on television before. Single men and women are never allowed to mix like this. Especially when they're dressed like this."

Both documentaries participate in a long, discursive tradition. Western women have historically inserted themselves in the discourse of unveiling the Orient by using their gender as a strategy of unique emplacement. As women, they have argued, they have greater access to the women's quarters and are therefore in a better position to tear away the veil of the exotic East for the consumption of a Western audience. In this case, Avakian and Amanpour authenticate their narratives not only by their gender, but also by virtue of their cultural backgrounds. This scopophilic desire to get behind the veil to know and to contain the elusive Iranian woman has both a colonial and a feminist history. This history spans at least a century, from early missionary women's efforts to modernize Iranian women in the nineteenth century by unveiling them to Kate Millett's 1979 ventures into the Iranian feminist arena, and finally to more recent forays by Western feminists into debates about the oppressed status of their Iranian counterparts. Avakian's and Amanpour's photographs and documentary footage belong to a colonial tradition of prurient obsession with disclosing that which lies behind the veil. Indeed, they use their status as North Americanized Iranians to reveal the mystery of the Oriental woman to a Western audience long obsessed with peeking behind the veil.

Contemporary Iranian academics are also complicit in the revival of the veiled woman as exotic and sexually desirable. In his introduction to Taj al-Saltanah's memoirs, Abbas Amanat includes a reproduction of an Orientalist painting in which a semiclad yet veiled harem woman poses seductively for the painter. Amanat comments that "[e]ven though her appearance may have been embellished by the stereotypes of Orientalist paintings of the nineteenth century, Ziba Khanum as she is described by Madame Dieulafoy in 1881 was still a telling example of fashionable sensuality in the harem of the affluent" (1993, 31). Several pages later, Amanat issues this peculiar apology for the photographs of Nasir al-Din Shah's wives:

> The standards of female attractiveness in Naser al-Din's harem are puzzling to contemporary tastes. The pictures of the often badly dressed ladies, huddled together in front of their husband's camera, hardly support the stereotype of the harem beauty portrayed in Orientalist novels and paintings or idealized in the Persian lyrics. (39)

Thus, Amanat appears to insinuate, the projection of Western fantasies about the Orient as illustrated in the nineteenth-century Orientalist painting of the sensual veiled woman, *not* the photographs of the shah and his lamentably homely wives, is the authentic (or at least more desirable) image of Persian women.

On the one hand, the postrevolutionary figure of the *bad-hijabi* participates in reviving representations of eroticized (and amenable) harem women through her teasing performance of unveiling and reveiling, thus challenging the contemporary image of the scowling *chadori*. She sustains the axiom that "[b]eneath the shapeless black chador of Iran lie the sensuous curves of Persia" (Anderson 2001, 1). On the other hand, the *bad-hijabi* force the terms of the debate to move beyond the reductive veiling/unveiling binary, thus challenging Western stereotypes of

veiled Persian women. The *bad-hijab* woman is the site of Spivak's definition of catachresis, "a concept-metaphor without an adequate referent" (1990, 224). Arguably, one could equally postulate that the figure of
the *hijabi* circulates, in contemporary postcolonial feminist discourse,
as a referent without an adequate concept-metaphor.[22] If the veil is seen
unilaterally as a signifier of oppression or of emancipation, where is the
place of the *bad-hijab* woman who wears *hijab* while playing with the
categories of self-effacement and performance, modesty, and vanity? Is
the *bad-hijabi* disturbing categories of veiled women, or is her alluring
act of concealment and revealment merely an endorsement of Orientalist fantasies about the East?

Of equal interest, how do we read the figure of the politically vigilant *hijabi* who calls herself a feminist, and whose outspoken and visible
participation in Iranian political and national affairs undercuts the stereotype of the silent veiled woman? In the August 2001 issue of *Mother
Jones* magazine, Camelia Entekhabi Fard addresses the nuances and complexities of compulsory *hijab*, and the ways in which it is being contested,
in contemporary Iran:

> To feminists in the West, the veil epitomizes everything that is wrong
> with the Iranian revolution. But the hejab means different things to
> different people; it is simultaneously a symbol of domination and
> liberation, of piety and rebellion. For Iranian men, the hejab has
> traditionally been a means of defending women's honor and protecting
> their chastity. . . . But for Iranian women, the hejab has an entirely
> different meaning: It affords a convenient protection for their public
> lives. In a society where an unveiled female is seen as sexually available,
> most women would wear some kind of hejab outside their homes even
> without state coercion—and many who have entered the workforce
> and the academy would simply return to their traditional roles rather
> than remove their veils. (72)

In contemporary feminist discourse, the figure of the articulate, vigilant *hijabi* emerges as a chiasmus, the site of what Spivak has called "a
double contradiction" (1989, 274). To date, most feminist writings on
this topic suggest that to be veiled is to be silent and demure; to be
unveiled is to be an outspoken feminist. How can feminist discourse
come to terms with this seeming contradiction of the *hijabi* as feminist,
who does not celebrate or condemn the veil, and who in fact does not

appear to consider it a primary concern? How can secular diasporic Iranian and Western feminists grow to appreciate the position of women active within the Islamic Republic? These feminists are fighting for equal access to divorce and child custody, equal opportunities in the workplace, and equal representation in a legal system in which a woman's testimony is worth half that of her male counterpart. The challenge for cross-cultural feminist understanding and exchange between Iranian, Western, and diasporic Iranian feminists remains, particularly in light of the long and fractious colonial history of Western feminist intervention in Iran.

CHAPTER 3

Global Sisters
in Revolutionary Iran

IN THIS CHAPTER, I will examine the cross-cultural engagements of
1970s Western liberal feminists with Pahlavi feminists to explore
the tensions that arose between these two prominent feminist
groups and anti-imperialist Iranian feminists who participated actively
during the revolutionary period in Iran. The ultimate failure of cross-
cultural feminist collaboration during the anti-imperialist feminist demonstrations of March 1979 epitomize, I believe, the limitations of the
discourse of sisterhood.

I have been arguing that the subject-formation of the Western feminist is predicated upon the figural abjection of the Oriental (in this
case, Persian) woman, and that the prerevolutionary, state-sponsored
Iranian or Pahlavi feminist benefited equally from this figuration. In
the first two chapters, I have attempted to trace the development of an
essential feature to the discourse of sisterhood in its various incarnations:
the perceived superiority of Western women in relation to Oriental
women through the languages of religious salvation and international
suffrage. Although the language of gender oppression mobilized by missionary women and first-wave feminists recognized the mutual oppression
of women, "traditional" (often working-class) Persian women somehow

always emerged as requiring the guidance and enlightenment of their Western and "modern" (often privileged) Iranian sisters.

During the second wave of feminism, the discourse of international sisterhood stressed the notion of a shared and universal women's oppression. But the rhetoric of women's solidarity and collectivity was undermined by divisiveness among second-wave feminists from the movement's early days. Deborah Babcox and Madeline Belkin, editors of *Liberation Now! Writings from the Women's Liberation Movement* (1971), emphasize the differences between two dominant feminist positions in 1970s North America: the "reformers," led by the National Organization of Women's (NOW) Betty Friedan, and self-styled "revolutionaries" or "radicals" such as themselves.[1] The former founded NOW "as a direct result of the failure of America's Equal Employment Opportunity Commission (EEOC) to take seriously the issue of sex discrimination" (Thornham 1999, 30), and the latter claimed that they were inclusive of racial and class differences:

> Most of the women in NOW, like Betty Friedan, are white, middle class or upper middle class, and professional. From the outset the politics of NOW have been reformist, aiming to integrate women into the mainstream of American society. Radical women feel an analysis of our economic system shows that sex, race and class discrimination are necessary to maintain the control over wealth and resources by the ruling classes and that the role of women will not basically change until there is a radical reorganization of power in America. This view differs from NOW's reformism in that we believe that power will not voluntarily be relinquished by those who hold it and that only revolution will accomplish this end. (Babcox and Belkin 1971, 4)

Janet Jakobsen has observed that feminist movements have always been characterized by diversity and difference, but the reason for the repeated failure of alliance politics has been "a disarticulation of diversity from complexity" (1998, 5):[2]

> The predominantly white, middle-class, and heterosexual women's movement often described in the 1990s in the passive voice or as factual data about the 1970s, the movement which has existed "until recently" or which will soon change, is not a necessary fact of women's movement or even an unfortunate, but unavoidable, necessity of saying "women." It is instead produced in particular historical moments,

often out of a diversity of women activists and of their activisms and movements. (66)

Indeed, 1970s "Western feminism" was not a monolithic discourse; there were many women who were active feminists and who simultaneously voiced their displeasure about being relegated to the margins of a white, liberal, feminist agenda. Working-class women and women of color protested their lack of representation at conferences and rallies, and most significantly at the 1975 United Nations Conference on Women in Mexico City. By the early 1980s, there were publications such as *This Bridge Called My Back: Writings by Radical Women of Color* (1981), edited by Cherríe Moraga and Gloria Anzaldúa; Angela Davis's *Women, Race, and Class* (1981) and *Women, Culture, and Politics* (1989); *All the Women Are White, All the Blacks Are Men, But Some of Us Are Brave* (1982), edited by Gloria T. Hull, Patricia Bell Scott, and Barbara Smith; and *Frontiers: Selected Essays and Writings on Racism and Culture 1984–1992* (1992), edited by Marlene Nourbese Philip, in which women wrote about their exclusion from the mainstream feminist movement on the basis of race, class, and sexuality.[3]

Nevertheless, the myth of the "golden age of feminism," during which all women were purportedly united in a common goal, perpetuates itself in sentimentalized accounts by 1970s feminists, or in works that evoke the spirit of the second wave, such as *Sisterhood Is Powerful: An Anthology of Writings from the Women's Liberation Movement* (1970) and *Sisterhood Is Global: The International Women's Movement Anthology* (1984), edited by Robin Morgan; *The New Women: Motive Anthology on Women's Liberation* (1970), edited by Joanne Cooke, Charlotte Bunch-Weeks, and Robin Morgan; Marcia Cohen's *The Sisterhood* (1988); Susan Faludi's *Backlash* (1991); Marilyn French's *The War against Women* (1992); and the immensely popular stage production based on Eve Ensler's *The Vagina Monologues* (1998), and her more recent book, *The Good Body* (2004).

Some feminist critics of global sisterhood have argued that the crux of the problem with the language of 1960s and 1970s feminism was its call for solidarity among all women with the assumption that they were bound together in "common oppression" (hooks 1986, 127). bell hooks has remarked that global sisterhood failed in the 1970s because of the assumption of women's shared oppression, and because those who raised the banner of universal oppression were white bourgeois feminists who wanted to position themselves not merely as members of the feminist movement, but as its leaders (132). This kind of hierarchical structure within feminist organizations harks back to the origins of global sisterhood, when the missionaries of the nineteenth century claimed to bring the good news of the Bible, but also of women's rights and social justice, to their less fortunate sisters in the East. Global sisters in the 1970s, however, claimed that women the world over had one thing in common: regardless of race, culture, or class, all women suffered the indignity of patriarchal oppression. They also managed to recruit and showcase women representatives of the third world in more visible ways than did global sisters in the early part of the century. Global feminist relationships across class and cultural boundaries have been, and continue to be, played out in an educational arena where one group of "sisters" aims to enlighten and educate another, less informed group of "sisters."

The tensions that emerged out of what can be seen as a failed moment of a global feminist alliance have provoked divisions within the ranks of diasporic Iranian feminists, as well as between some diasporic Iranian feminists and indigenous Iranian feminists. These contentious relationships mirror the types of generational debates about the future of feminist criticism and activism occurring between Western feminists.[4] This chapter, which will examine the intersection of second-wave (Western) feminist voices with Iranian feminist voices in the 1970s, at a particularly vexed moment for Iranian women during the revolutionary period, attempts to move toward what Sherene Razack has called "a politics of accountability":

> [A politics of accountability] begins with anti-essentialism and the recognition that there is no stable core we can call women's experience. Equally important, it is a politics guided by a search for the ways in which we are complicitous in the subordination of others. A feminist politics of accountability cannot proceed on the assumption that as women we are uninvolved in the subordination of others. If we take as our point of departure that systems of domination interlock and sustain one another, we can begin to identify those moments when we are dominant and those when we are subordinate. Our implication in various systems of domination means that there are several ways in which we can perform ourselves as dominant at the same time that we understand ourselves to be engaging in liberatory politics. (1998, 159)

By studying this attempt at cross-cultural feminist collaboration in revolutionary Iran, I hope to demonstrate the political complexities hindering global feminist success in this instance. Although different types of feminisms existed (and continue to exist) in North America and Europe in the 1970s, a type of liberal feminism that embraced the notion of a unified, global sisterhood was the dominant feminist discourse. I will explore here the ways in which a particular (and exclusive) discourse of sisterhood inserted itself into the Iranian feminist arena during what Parvin Paidar has identified as the fourth and final phase of modernity in Iran, an era "characterized by the state's double strategy of political repression and aggressive modernization" (1995, 28).

By the late 1950s in Iran, the various independent women's organizations that had formed in the 1940s and early 1950s were now directly controlled by the newly formed High Council of Women's Organizations headed by the shah's twin sister, Ashraf Pahlavi (Najmabadi 1991, 60). In 1966, the shah, who was tightening his control over all aspects of public life, replaced the High Council with the state-sponsored Women's Organization of Iran (WOI). The women's organizations previously contained by the High Council were now dissolved and absorbed into one large state-controlled organization with a sizable budget controlled by the female royals, Ashraf Pahlavi and Faridih Diba, the queen's mother (Paidar 1995, 149).

The shah was certainly no champion of feminist goals, and the women of the WOI faced the challenging task of advancing women's rights in Iran from within a rigid and resistant system. Nevertheless, the fact remains that members of the WOI were, for the most part, royalists from privileged social and economic backgrounds, and the reforms for which they worked tended to overlook the particular needs of the urban poor or the peasant classes in rural Iran.[5] Regardless of significant disparities between the majority of Iranian women and their royal representatives, the figurehead of the organization, Ashraf Pahlavi, tirelessly represented herself as a progressive feminist and as someone who was leading Iranian women along the path to feminist enlightenment.

In a forceful article published in 1980, Azar Tabari draws attention to the "absent peasant woman" in Iranian feminist projects, contained and controlled by the shah under the guise of the WOI, in the 1960s and 1970s. Tabari contests official Pahlavi reports about the merits of the shah's "White Revolution"—his grandiose plans of taking Iran out of the category of a third-world country and placing it alongside the United States as a country with significant economic, political, and social power. As was the case during the Constitutional Revolution, Iranian women were used as indicators of the image of modernity the nation sought to project. The shah's dreams of modernization, claims Tabari, were carried out at the expense of the rural and urban working classes. Despite Ashraf Pahlavi and the WOI's claims about advancing the rights and the status of all Iranian women, Tabari contends that, in fact,

> many factors contributed to a sharp deterioration in the daily life of the peasant woman, intensifying her exploitation and reinforcing her traditionally degraded status. . . . As a direct result of land reform, the need for female and child labour on peasant family plots increased tremendously. (1980, 21)

She provides a list of the problems that emerged out of the Pahlavi project of modernization and nation-building, including the increased need for seasonal agricultural laborers and carpet weavers to satisfy a growing export market; this form of labor was supplied for the most part by peasant women and children (21). The link between feminism and modernity as articulated by the Pahlavi state, and sustained by the WOI, thus appeared to speak little, if at all, to the material needs and concerns of Iranian peasant women. Tabari suggests that the women who reaped most of the benefits from the work advanced by the state-controlled feminists in Iran were women of the privileged, educated classes who already had access to an "upwardly mobile" world (22). This led to an ever-widening gap between the working classes and the upper middle classes in the mid- to late 1970s in Iran, and the feminist agenda of the time appeared to address predominantly the concerns of a relatively privileged and educated class of women.

Claims about the elitism of the WOI have been strongly contested by Haleh Esfandiari, former deputy secretary general of the organization and presently the director of the Middle East program at the Woodrow Wilson International Center for Scholars. Esfandiari's position on women's rights needs to be contextualized, however, in light of her affiliation with state-sponsored Pahlavi feminism and, more recently, with the Wilson Center, whose mission statement proclaims as its aim "to unite the world of ideas to the world of policy by supporting pre-eminent scholarship and linking that scholarship to issues of concern to officials in Washington" (Woodrow Wilson Web site).[6] In a speech a year after 9/11 titled "Combating Terrorism and Protecting Our Homeland," the center's director, former congressman Lee H. Hamilton, states:

> A question that many Americans asked in the immediate aftermath of
> September 11 was: Why do they hate us? . . . Many militant radicals
> oppose or are jealous of the extent of American power in today's world,
> and reject our secular and open society. Fundamentalist Muslims are
> threatened by the spread of American culture—the respect for women's
> rights, materialism, and the tolerance of free expression. (2002, 2)

In these and other speeches, Hamilton serves to bolster the Bush administration's rhetoric of American innocence, perpetuating the myth that the United States was attacked because the Muslim world is "jealous" of its secular and free society. By so doing, he absolves the United States from any responsibility in the current state of world affairs. While it might not be entirely fair to equate the position of the director with that of all the scholars working at the Wilson Center, Hamilton's eagerness to support, indeed to reproduce, the inflammatory language of the Bush administration does raise the question of whether the Web site is accurate in its self-portrayal as a "nonpartisan" center for scholarship.

In 2003, the center published a collection of speeches titled *Middle Eastern Women on the Move: Openings for and Constraints on Women's Political Participation in the Middle East* (2003), which emerged out of a conference by the same name in October 2001. The conference was organized by Esfandiari and the participants included the usual diasporic Iranian feminist spokespersons such as Mahnaz Afkhami and Azar Nafisi, although there are other contributors and participants such as Roza Eftekhari, from a well-known feminist magazine in Iran, *Zanan;* Mansoureh Ettehadieh and Jaleh Shadi-Talab, from the University of Tehran; Golnar Mehran, from Al-Zahra University in Tehran; and Sussan Tahmassebi, from a nongovernmental organization in Tehran. This invitation to Iranian feminists is an important gesture from prerevolutionary Iranian feminists now in the diaspora, and can be fairly interpreted as a sign of increasing willingness to dialogue with their feminist counterparts in Iran.

In her introduction to this collection, Esfandiari takes a defensive tone against the criticisms leveled against the WOI and prerevolutionary Iranian feminists. She takes pains to emphasize the relevance of the organization:

In 1979 when the revolution occurred Iranian women had made considerable progress. I am not talking only about an elite class of women—absolutely not. The women's movement in Iran was not an elitist movement, nor was it run by a group of light-headed, flaky, westernized women cut off from their roots, as alleged by many in and outside Iran. Both the generation of Iranian women's activists in the sixties and seventies, and the generation that came before them, comprised groups of dedicated women who fought for women's rights in an inhospitable environment. The male-dominated establishment was not ready or willing to share power. Women activists gave up interesting careers to devote their time to the women's movement. . . . These women were able to change a dormant, cautious women's movement, that nevertheless deserves a lot of praise for its pioneering work, into an active Women's Organization. One has to give credit to Mahnaz Afkhami, who in 1970 became the Secretary General of the Iranian Women's Organization, for launching the women's movement in the seventies. (2003, 4–5)

Despite her efforts at demonstrating the inclusiveness of the organization and the agency of Iranian women, Esfandiari expresses herself from within the limits of an imperialist feminist discourse by portraying the Iranian women's movement as "dormant" and "cautious," evoking nineteenth-century missionary language about Iranian women's "awakening." Furthermore, her portrayal of Afkhami as the person single-handedly responsible for "launching the women's movement in the seventies" again has echoes of a hierarchical and didactic style of feminism that has a long and fraught colonial history.

Esfandiari adopts a similar position regarding the debt she perceives Iranian women owe the WOI in *Reconstructed Lives* (1997). Here, she argues that the feminist activities undertaken by Iranian women under the Islamic Republic have been made possible by the past efforts of the WOI. While this seems like a rather grandiose claim to make, it would be unwarranted and ungenerous to unequivocally condemn the work of the women of the WOI, and it is not my intention to do so here. What I am trying to grapple with is the history of colonial and imperial feminist interventions in the Iranian feminist arena. The intersection of an imperialist Western feminist discourse with that of (dominant and state-sponsored) Iranian feminist discourse needs to be articulated and analyzed. If we, as feminist scholars—whether Western or Iranian, diasporic or indigenous—hope to address the overdetermined relations between Western and Iranian feminisms, we need to come to terms with feminism's imperialist history and to recognize that "accountability begins with tracing relations of privilege and penalty. It cannot proceed unless we examine our own complicity" (Razack 1998, 170).

It is unfortunate that former members of the WOI and their advocates dismiss the voices of those who attempt to speak outside of the dominant discourse and tend to rebuff (and indeed to resent) criticisms made of them, illustrating the problems that emerge when "dominant groups . . . argu[e] from a point of subordination, a position of innocence and non-implication in systems of oppression" (Razack 1998, 169–70). Iranian feminist scholars who do articulate their differences from Pahlavi feminists are often dismissed as "cultural relativists" or as apologists for the Islamic regime, positions that are often portrayed as interchangeable.

Former state-sponsored feminists tend to dismiss the charges of elitism or "Westernization" out of hand by arguing that the WOI managed to stay attuned to the feminist movement in the West as well as to the needs of traditional Iranian women (Esfandiari 1997, 33). Their insistence that the WOI was sensitive to the need to create an indigenous feminism, one that would speak to the traditional cultural and religious practices of Iranian women, is part of the image that the WOI tried to project in the late 1970s.

In the early 1970s, however, members of the WOI went to great lengths to position themselves at the forefront of the "women's rights as human rights" movement along with their second-wave feminist colleagues in the West. In 1973, the Shahbanou (Empress Farah Pahlavi) and Princess Ashraf extended an invitation to noted second-wave feminists Betty Friedan and Germaine Greer, and to UN Assistant Secretary-General for Social Development and Humanitarian Affairs Helvi Sipila, "to visit Iran to advise Persian women on women's liberation" (Friedan 1975, 71).[7] Friedan subsequently wrote an article on her experiences in Iran in the *Ladies' Home Journal,* unwittingly disclosing one of the major problems that emerged out of 1970s Iranian and Western feminism.

During her stay in Iran, Friedan associated primarily with women of the elite class, whose concerns intersected more closely with her own and her global sisters in the United States than with those of the majority of working-class Iranian women:

> My first few days in Teheran were strictly caviar and jet lag and a sense of being strangely at home. Teheran, a Middle Eastern city, seems like an American Western boom town—buildings go up overnight, international banks next to Persian wimpy stands, and no beggars. We were all put up at the Teheran Hilton where I found real Iranian caviar on the menu. (98)

Friedan's awe-filled experience of Iran, a country notable for its wealth of caviar and lack of beggars, and her exposure to a glamorous Iranian feminism, informs her glowing portrayal of the state-sponsored feminist reforms in 1960s and 1970s Iran. Although she makes several token gestures to question the regime's notorious human rights record—its reputation for torture, censorship, internal corruption, and nepotism— the article is, for the most part, laudatory of the WOI:

> The Women's Organization of Iran is not exactly NOW. It doesn't have to fight for anything; the Shah gives it funds beyond our wildest dreams—a treasury of $50 million, a paid staff of 1,300, with 70 centers serving women and providing day care for children. (104)

The controversial Australian feminist Germaine Greer, however, offers a significantly different perspective on Friedan's days in Iran and on their hosts, the women of the WOI:

> When Betty Friedan arrived at the Hilton in Teheran, she announced that she would see nobody, nobody, not even the shah himself, until she had recovered from the flight. Our attendants, highborn Iranian damsels clad head to foot in Guy Laroche, begged Helvi and me to intercede on their behalf: there were formalities to be undergone, briefings, welcomes. We were helpless. Betty refused to take calls, and no one dared to pound on her door. (1988, 37–38)

When Friedan does eventually meet her hosts, she is impressed by the "very beautiful" Empress Farah Pahlavi, to whom Friedan presents a copy of *The Feminine Mystique* (Friedan 1975, 99). The empress informs her, "'I read it originally in French in paperback. . . . I agreed with it all'" (99). While Pahlavi's unequivocal endorsement of Friedan's book can be read as an example of *ta'aruf*, the elaborate and complex codes of deferential politesse in Iranian culture, it seems to me that her comment can be placed within the context of a specifically 1970s didactic feminist model. The women at the helm of the WOI, most of them royalists, dubbed "the haute couture" by Greer, aligned themselves with noted second-wave feminists in the West and adopted a similarly hierarchical relationship in relation to less prosperous Iranian women (Greer 1988, 38). The discourse of international sisterhood, while attempting to be egalitarian and humanitarian, has historically tended to reinforce class alliances across national borders.

Friedan is deliberate about including the shahbanou's praise of her book as well as the shah's flattery of her: "In a few years, I can see the women of Iran in whatever intelligent and right place the women of the advanced countries will be. In a few years, I hope the women of Iran will be just like you" (1975, 104). The insertion of the shah's unctuous comments has a twofold effect: first, they invoke the trite—and frustratingly tenacious—binary model of the East as traditional (read backward) and the West as modern (read advanced).[8] The unquestioned assumption here is that Friedan is one of the leaders of the second wave of feminism, and that as a model of advanced womanhood, she can now educate her retrograde Iranian sisters. Second, these comments reinforce Friedan's position as the woman who, in her own words, "is sometimes blamed for starting 'women's lib'" (72). The article was published in 1975, a period during which Friedan's star had fallen in Western feminist circles. As the rift between "liberal" and "radical" feminists grew stronger, Friedan's homophobic, elitist, and conservative vision for the future of feminism was becoming increasingly unpopular among her feminist colleagues in the West. Indeed, the woman who liked to take credit for starting the second wave was being led unceremoniously away from the podium. In response to a 1970 article in the *New York Times Magazine* that described Friedan as the mother of "women's liberation," dissenting feminists raised their voices in protest:

> If the women libbers needed a "mother," many of them told [Paul] Wilkes [author of the article], they would, thank you very much, choose their own. Betty, the writer Sally Kempton proclaimed, "misrepresents the case for feminism by making people believe that

reform is the answer. . . . She is not the movement mother; that is
Simone de Beauvoir." (Cohen 1988, 310)

Friedan's portrayal of her fawning reception by Iran's royalty and the
WOI serves to reposition her at the center of the second-wave feminist
movement. In a sense, Iranian feminism functions as Friedan's self-
consolidating other; she goes to the margins to secure her place in the
center.

Germaine Greer, who wrote her version of events in "Women's
Glib," published in *Vanity Fair* magazine, seems to be less enamoured of
the "Empress who is also a feminist" (Friedan 1975, 100). Greer also
appears to have a less glowing impression of Pahlavi feminists and of
state-sponsored feminism in general than does Friedan. Greer, who
distinguishes herself from her prominent American sisters by attending to class differences, is merciless in her description of the feminist
seminars:

> Helvi spoke first, delivering a seamless series of high-minded U.N.
> platitudes for the exact twenty minutes she was allotted. Then Betty
> arose. "The world will never be the same again," she barked. "Women
> want to make paḥlicy, naht coffee! A chicken in every home and a
> whore in every putt." The thoughts poured out higgledy-piggledy, and
> Betty's tongue ran after them, never quite capturing one before setting
> off in pursuit of another. The Iranian women, exhausted after a day of
> having their eyebrows and hair roots bleached and their arms and legs
> depilated in preparation for the meeting, had a fairly slender grasp of
> English at the best of times. They sat glassy-eyed as the torrent of
> unfinished sentences raced past. If they knew what TV dinners or
> waste-disposal units were, they gave no sign. (1988, 38)

Greer's comments, though quite ruthless and ungenerous, do make several effective points: that this sort of feminist gathering under the aus-
pices of global sisterhood often produces hollow, if well-intentioned,
platitudes; that the discourse of women's rights, as articulated by Friedan,
does not reach a universal audience; further, that the audience members
in attendance demonstrate a greater commitment to their personal
grooming than to the plight of their sisters around the globe. By the end
of their stay, Greer confesses that their trip to Iran accomplished little
for the feminist movement and that she had "long ago given up on the

shah's tame women's association" (38). On their last night in Tehran, Princess Ashraf threw a party in honor of the three Western feminists; suddenly, Greer reports, chaos erupted in the courtyard:

> Betty was standing screaming in front of our Cadillac. "Dammit! I want, I deserve, my own car. Get me my own car. I will not travel cooped up in this thing with two other women. Don't you clowns know who I am?"
>
> "Mrs. Greer," said the attendants, who were shaking with fright. "What shall we do? Please make her be quiet. She is very drunk."
>
> "In a manner of speaking," I said. Betty was drunk, but not with wine. She was furious that the various dignitaries and ministers of state had their own cars, while the women guests of honor traveled in a single car like a harem. She just stood there in her spangled black crêpe de Chine and kept on yelling. "No! No! I will nutt just be quiet and gettinna car. Absolutely nutt!" After a good deal of stifled giggling, it was decided that one of the ministers would lend his car for Betty. As the big car with the flag pulled out of the gateway, I saw Betty, small, alone, in the back, her great head pillowed on the leather. She had closed her eyes to rest after another important victory. (40)

Greer's harsh criticism of the inequities she sees within the global sisterhood movement emerges out of her own strong commitment to attending to class differences.[9]

Throughout the 1970s and 1980s, Greer maintained a persistent critique of the inequities and structures of domination within the global feminist movement, particularly as reflected at the level of the United Nations.[10] Shortly after the first UN International Conference on Women, Greer published an article in *Chatelaine* magazine, condemning the Mexico City conference, whose speakers' list was dominated by prominent Western feminists and the wives and sisters of male heads of state in third-world countries. According to Greer, the NGO conference, which took place alongside the UN conference, was a forum to which everyone except Mexican working-class women had access. State-sanctioned feminist discourse, as promoted by the UN International Year of Women and as was the case with the WOI, Greer suggests, only speaks to an elite group of women who have the luxury to discuss such issues as managing their roles as mothers and "career women."

Deploying her acerbic wit, Greer voices her anger at what she perceives to be the spurious feminist credentials and disingenuous commitment to women's rights espoused by state representatives at the Mexico conference:

> The next day began reasonably well, with an enormously long speech by Sirimavo Bandaranaike in which we were induced to believe that women in Sri Lanka had nothing further to ask for (except perhaps a living wage for picking tea, some form of industrial organization to represent them, and literacy and a decent diet, but on the statute books they were doing fine). Well. Mrs. Bandaranaike is a head of state so there was a reason for her being the first to address the third plenary session. The second speaker was Her Imperial Highness Princess Ashraf Pahlavi of Iran, twin sister of the man who repudiated a wife because she did not bear him a son. That was a little harder to understand, but Princess Ashraf had headed the Consultative Committee which had worked on the Draft World Plan of Action for IWY. Besides, she paid a million dollars for the privilege. (Greer 1975a, 102)[11]

Greer denounces the discrepancies between official feminist rhetoric and its relevance to the lives of the majority of working-class women. By openly critiquing Ashraf Pahlavi, Greer foregrounds questions of economic and social class, and calls attention to the problems perpetuated by state-sponsored feminist organizations that claim to strive for universal women's rights.

The idea of the universality of women's rights and experiences is an important part of the discourse of global sisterhood and has been actively promoted through second-wave feminist writings. In 1984, Valerie Amos and Pratibha Parmar argued that studies of third-world women conducted by privileged white women from the West are inherently imperialist and oppressive (6). By using a feminist anthropological text, *Women United, Women Divided: Cross Cultural Perspectives on Female Solidarity* (1978), as an example of feminist imperialist scholarship, they write:

> The authors defined feminist consciousness and then proceeded to judge other cultural situations to see if they are feminist or not. . . . [They assume] that pre-capitalist economies equal backwardness in both a cultural and ideological sense and in fact are responsible for the continued oppression of women in these societies. It is further implied that it is only when Third World women enter into capitalist relations will they have any hope of liberation. (6)

Amos and Parmar touch on a key issue here: that the discourse of universal women's rights is overshadowed by a colonial imperative that positions the West as a marker of liberal capitalism and humanitarianism against which other nations inevitably appear less civilized; this representation, in turn, is used as justification for first world intervention and domination in the third world.

The events of Mexico City highlighted the major problems with the global sisterhood movement—and its wholesale embrace of the language of women's universal rights—as it manifested itself on the international stage and as it played itself out on the domestic scene in Iran.[12] Indeed, the Iranian monarchy's superficial support of "women's rights" was directly related to the shah's sweeping plans for the industrialization and modernization of the country. The rhetorical support for women's rights was part of the image that he was trying to project to the West, an image of a civilized and modern country in which women were equal to men. As the shah's support of women's human rights was staged for the benefit of the West, much of the financial support for this project was channeled into visible international institutions such as the United Nations.

In *Ms.* magazine, Mim Kelber criticizes the Pahlavi regime's involvement in international women's organizations and specifically takes Ashraf's position on women's rights to task. Although she appears to support the project of international women's rights, Kelber criticizes the advantages the movement reaped from Ashraf's financial contributions:

> International women's projects "benefited" from the Princess' immense fortune—stolen from the people, charged critics; the illicit gains of heroin trafficking, hinted the European press. She helped to get Iranian funds for the United Nations' International Women's Year Conference in Mexico City in 1975. The government also hosted women's film and arts festivals (which were boycotted by many well-known international feminists) and was prepared to pick up the tab for the UN Women's Decade Conference in July 1980, originally scheduled to be held in Teheran. (In late 1978, the Shah backed out of Iranian sponsorship of the conference and the UN moved it to Copenhagen, much to the relief of feminists in the United States and around the world who had protested the plan to hold it in Iran). (1979, 96)

Spivak has argued that the UN programs for and conferences on women "have produced feminist apparatchiks whose activism is to organize the

poorest women of the developing world incidentally in their own image"
(1996b, 264, n. 8). Indeed, Ashraf Pahlavi and Farah Pahlavi portrayed
themselves as the saviors of Iranian women and as models of progressive, modern Iranian womanhood. In *My Thousand and One Days: An Autobiography*, the queen writes:

> In my country, I am considered, whether I like it or not, *the representa-*
> *tive of feminine emancipation*. My strength, the power I wield will, in
> one way or another, be passed on to all Iranian women. Already
> these women, formerly regarded as chattels, without the right to
> be heard, have increasingly more to say for themselves. (1978, 130–31;
> emphasis mine)

Farah Pahlavi adopts a position of benevolent "maternalism" here as she
relegates all Iranian women to the position of "chattels" before she arrived
to uplift and mold them in her own image. But, perhaps more insidi-
ously, she makes a rather transparent effort at reconstructing the history
of the Pahlavi regime and whitewashing its notoriously repressive and
violent reign. The title of her memoirs is meant to counter Orientalist
representations of Persia as the land of a *Thousand and One Nights*, put-
ting to rest any questions about the indolent and spendthrift ways of
the monarchy. By stressing her long days of work as the head of a number of organizations, as the wife of a monarch, and as a mother, Farah
Pahlavi takes special pains to portray her position as a difficult and arduous one, although one she accepts with resignation and dignity. She
ends her autobiography by expressing her sadness about what she claims
are false accusations of human rights abuses leveled against the Pahlavi
regime:

> What distresses me far more at this moment is the bad reputation of
> Iran abroad. This adverse publicity, based on political prisoners and
> tortures, is terribly unjust. It is truly dreadful to attack a country and a
> system so relentlessly. The accusations made against us are grotesque. . . .
> Nothing in life is easy, not even for a Queen, contrary to what many
> people think. I am very busy, I work very hard, often with great
> energy, joy and enthusiasm, but there are also moments when I am
> very tired, when so much injustice depresses me. Then I feel that
> everything is going wrong, that it is the end of the world and I am
> desolate. But I soon recover, I recall the immense progress we are
> achieving and tell myself that very soon no one will be able, without

appearing ridiculous, to pretend not to see. The attitude of Western intellectuals towards us will then be forced to change. (1978, 142)

Interestingly, she suggests that it is Western intellectuals who are criticizing the regime—and not the Iranian people themselves. By eliding the growing dissatisfaction and anger of Iranians with the regime's fraudulence and corruption, Farah Pahlavi reproduces her husband's agenda of censorship and repression. Although he uses the more violent method of the brute torture and murder of dissidents to secure their silence, she compounds their silencing by refusing to acknowledge their grievances.

By the mid- to late 1970s, there were a growing number of women who bristled at what they understood to be the royal women's fallacious self-representation as advocates of women's rights and human rights. On July 7, 1977, the shahbanou was invited to a luncheon sponsored by the Appeal of Conscience Foundation, an organization for the cause of religious freedom, at the Pierre Hotel in New York City to accept "an award for her efforts to raise the status of women" (Cummings 1977, B2). The guests at the luncheon included then governor Hugh Carey and mayor Abraham Beame, former governor W. Averell Harriman, and Andy Warhol. Journalist Judith Cummings writes:

> The luncheon at the Pierre Hotel was interrupted by a woman who was sitting at a press table. She rose to shout, "That's a lie," after the Empress, in an acceptance speech, spoke of changes by the Pahlevi regime that she said had enabled women "to participate in the overall development of their country." (B2)

According to the article, fifteen hundred demonstrators stood outside the hotel. Most of the demonstrators were Iranian students and the majority of them wore masks to conceal their identities. Opposition to the shah's regime was gaining increasing support from a wide spectrum of political groups whose diverse philosophies converged on one point only: the desire to end what they saw as the subjugation of the nation to a corrupt and repressive regime heavily influenced by the West, and by the United States in particular. The imperialist influence on prerevolutionary Iranian feminism was a point of contention for many Iranian women and some Western feminists, including Kate Millett, who was present at the demonstration in New York.[13]

In the opening pages of her political travelogue, *Going to Iran,* Millett writes:

Farah's unscheduled visit to New York City which cost two and a half
million dollars in police security, a figure we rejoiced in griping over in
the streets, a picket line I joined one cold winter night with Arthur
Miller, other literary folk who showed up, a few feminists who never
miss anything. And thousands of angry Iranian students in masks
in whose ranks I marched out of curiosity for an hour and because
I couldn't find my Caifi [Committee on Artistic and Intellectual
Freedom in Iran] friends. (1982, 19)

While Millett's political commitment is certainly laudable, one cannot
help but wonder at the incongruity between her self-representation
as a committed activist and her admission that she marched "out of
curiosity" with a group of angry demonstrators who were motivated by
a deep sense of social injustice. One can already detect in this statement
a certain ambivalent positioning of herself as located simultaneously in
the center of struggle and on the outside "looking in" as a curious but
disinterested observer.

Millett, a self-described "radical," explains her involvement with prerevolutionary Iranian opposition groups, specifically her work with
Caifi as follows: "I am in Caifi as a feminist. And I have always wished
for a greater interest on the part of feminists in the issue of Iran" (1982,
17). On the one hand, this statement gestures to Millett's recognition of
the complicity of some second-wave feminists with an elite group of
women in Iran who appropriated the term "feminist" and offered a narrow interpretation of what it might mean and to whom it might apply;
on the other hand, it betrays a prejudice that feminists are extrinsic to
Iran. There is no room here for a recognition of feminists who already
exist in Iran; feminism is represented as a Western phenomenon that
must be introduced to women of the third world.

In a *New York Times* article on March 11, 1979, describing the third
day of protests in Tehran, when fifteen thousand women marched for
their rights under the new regime, Millett declares, "I'm here because
it's inevitable.... This is the eye of the storm right now. Women all over
the world are looking here. It's a whole corner, the Islamic world, the
spot we thought it would be hardest to reach and, wow, look at it go!"
(7). There are Orientalist implications here as Iran is configured as an

unreachable, unknowable corner of the world and, as such, an object of desire for American feminism. Millett's excitement at the thought of Anglo-American feminists gaining some kind of control over "a whole corner" of the world, which they saw as "hardest to reach," betrays her fantasy of colonial appropriation and ownership. This fantasy remains unrealized, however, as she begins to recognize that not only is her presence superfluous to the feminist movement in Iran, but that it presents a possible threat to its very success.

During the revolutionary period of 1978 Iran, the majority of Iranian people from a wide spectrum of social classes came together to call for the overthrow of the Pahlavi regime. In February 1979, the monarchy was overthrown, and Mohammad Reza Shah and his family went into exile. One month after the revolution, Khomeini abolished the Family Protection Act of 1975, which had granted Iranian women the right to divorce under certain conditions and had restricted the practice of polygamy. Several days later, Khomeini issued a statement extolling the virtues of the veil, and Iranian women began to feel betrayed by the revolution they had worked hard to support.[14] Although a large body of outspoken Iranian women had marched against the oppressive practices of the monarchy during the revolutionary period, these same women, now at considerable risk to themselves, marched against the misogynist policies of the Islamic regime to the taunts and insults of supporters of the religious right who chanted, "Rusari ya tusari," which translates loosely as "Cover your hair or receive a blow to your head."[15]

Into this complicated state of affairs Kate Millett arrived in Tehran to speak at a rally scheduled on International Women's Day—the first time it was to be observed publicly in Iran. Under the Pahlavi regime, Iranian women were forbidden to celebrate International Women's Day on March 8. Instead, the state-sanctioned celebration of "women's liberation" was January 7, 1936, the day Reza Shah decreed the mandatory unveiling of all women.[16] According to Millett's own account, she was invited to speak at the rally and to participate in the Iranian feminist struggle by Khalil, one of the male members of Caifi, who declared, "'Kate, your sisters need you in Iran'" (1979, 25). Millett and her lesbian partner, Canadian photographer Sophie Keir, arrived in Tehran's Mehrabad Airport only to discover that Kateh Vafadari, one of the feminist leaders whom they had been led to believe would greet them at the airport, was nowhere to be found. The trip began unpromisingly as they were forced to find a hotel on their own; after a couple of days, their Caifi friends placed them in an abandoned apartment with no heat or food and much discomfort.

To her dismay, Millett finds that they are spending more time with the men than with the Iranian feminists with whom she was hoping to work:

> I hunger for female company as much as for lunch, a place to sleep, to study, to work and prepare my speech. . . . All the women are rushing about today, finding a hall, leafleting. As for Kateh, how busy can this young woman be? She might bother to find us and say hello sometime. Perhaps it is all a test, this waiting. Perhaps I have to establish my credentials all over again. And though Kateh and I know of each other through Caifi, we have not yet come to know each other. That takes time. I'm certainly aware it's her turf, however. In fact I feel *I am running after feminism in Iran;* despite their invitation, I have yet to meet even one sister. (1979, 68; emphasis mine)

This trip, unlike Friedan's in 1973, serves to decenter Millett from the international feminist scene. She feels increasingly frustrated with her position on the sidelines of the movement and begins to question her and Keir's presence in Iran during this volatile time. "Should we have come?" she wonders. "Was it all a mistake, Khalil's innocent miscalculation, our own naïve gratitude at an invitation that has merely become a burden on our hosts?" (73). Eventually, they do meet Vafadari, who tactfully suggests that Millett diffuse the potentially explosive reaction to her American identity by calling herself a "foreign" feminist. Since the International Women's Day rally was under attack by government officials as well as by other opposition groups who believed that women's rights were secondary to the greater question of national formation, Millett was forced to consider the possibility that she would not be able to speak at all. In response to her enthusiasm about reading messages of support from such prominent feminists as Gloria Steinem, Robin Morgan, and several European sisters, Vafadari appears "a bit nervous" and drops an obvious hint that there may not be enough time: "We now have a lot of speakers . . . and the program is long" (78). Her nervousness suggests a concern that according prominence to American feminists in the wake of a mass-mobilized, anti-imperialist revolution might jeopardize the future of a feminist movement in Iran.

The predicament of anti-imperialist Iranian feminists in 1979 arose out of the historical associations of feminism with "Westernization" as exemplified by the state-controlled WOI, as well as the association of the Pahlavi regime with "Westernization," since the shah cultivated a strong relationship with the West and with the United States in particular. Anti-imperialist Iranian feminists thus saw the presence of Millett and other European feminists in the midst of Iranian feminist demonstrations as a potential threat to the success of their movement.

The binary of Western (imperialist) feminism and Iranian (nationalist) tradition is one that resonates perhaps most strongly in Jalal Al-e Ahmad's 1962 book *Plagued by the West.* In this highly influential work, Al-e Ahmad identifies the continuity of the European and American presence in the "East" from the period during which they appeared as colonial officers to their more modern guise as political and economic "experts" and "advisers." He claims that the presence of the "West" has continuing detrimental social and political consequences in Iran, regardless of the various roles assumed by European and American foreign "representatives." Al-e Ahmad draws connections between the study of Persian poetry and culture by Orientalist scholars and the increasing political and economic influence of "Western" powers in Iran; this is a connection that Edward Said brought to the fore of Western consciousness sixteen years later in *Orientalism* (1978). Despite Al-e Ahmad's insightful comments about the unequal division of power between Western and Iranian officials, there is an uncomfortably misogynist tone to his analysis. His insistence that Iranian women should revert to their roles as guardians of Persian tradition and culture is a stereotype that legitimates an oppressive nationalist discourse that makes room only for a patriarchal anti-imperialist rhetoric and silences all feminist voices as the products of *gharbzadigi* (Westoxification).

.   The feminist demonstrations of March 1979 worked against the model of the traditional, patriotic Iranian woman as envisioned by Al-e Ahmad. Feminists in Iran were now seen as *gharbzadih* (Westoxified); thus, the news conference organized by "foreign" feminists, among whom were Kate Millett, Elaine Sciolino, and Claudine Moullard, came to represent the apogee of Western infiltration into the Iranian feminist arena.[17] In the midst of this highly precarious postrevolutionary period, Millett and her Western sisters in the international feminist struggle decide that the best way to help Iranian women is to hold a news conference and alert the world to their plight. When they convey their plans to Vafadari, she appears less than enthusiastic. To her credit, Millett's partner, Keir, remains skeptical about the benefits of staging a news conference on behalf of the very women who are not in favor of the idea (Millett 1982, 153). Millett's position in Iran is a contradictory one: on the one hand, her relationship to revolutionary Iranian feminists is marked by the hierarchies inherent to the discourse of global sisterhood. She goes to Iran as an "expert" on feminism and assumes that she will adopt a leadership role in a cultural and political milieu completely foreign to her—hence her surprise at the lackluster reception she receives upon her arrival in Iran. On the other hand, she makes repeated expressions of admiration for the independence and courage of Iranian feminists throughout her book. Millett's reaction to the tensions surrounding the imminent arrival of a contingent of French feminists into the fray is to write: "Are they fool enough to think they can 'organize' these women?—the Iranian feminists are the coolest and most self-possessed, seasoned and sophisticated political females I've ever run across—you don't 'organize' them" (152).

Regardless of tensions and resistance to the idea, the "international feminists" in Iran organized a news conference for March 11, 1979 (Millett 1982, 152). At this point, the tide had already begun to turn in favor of the nascent revolutionary government, and the news conference provided patriarchal nationalists with leverage to discredit the Iranian feminist movement and served as a catalyst for the antifeminist violence that was to ensue. On the morning of the news conference, only three of the panelists were present: Kate Millett and two French women, Claudine Moullard and Sylvina (whose last name is not mentioned). Eventually, one of the Iranian panelists, Vafadari, does appear, but late, while the other two Iranian feminists remain absent.[18] At this point, Millett is obliged to concede:

> We are looking a bit stupid now; the purpose of this farce was to introduce the world press to Iranian feminists, a few international feminists being done the honor of acting as go-between—and we can only produce one Iranian feminist. (157–58)

The news conference turns into a debacle, in which Millett is accused (by the Western press as well as by various Iranian feminists in the crowd) of interfering with an Iranian feminist cause. Others question Vafadari about the connection of the current feminist movement with the WOI:

> Another lady, very British accent, actually English and not Iranian: "What part have the old women's organizations played in this?" I imagine she means Ashraf's crowd. "As far as we know, none whatsoever," Kateh answers firmly. The lady thought they organized the one at the high school, our rally. Heavens no, Kateh's committee did—but if this were not clarified, we could be smeared. . . . "The Women's Organization of Iran that was here when the Shah was here is finished." Kateh pronouncing the word like a death sentence. Her hatred of the regime is complete and perfect. "I'm not talking about everyone who was in it; I'm talking about the organization itself. It was created by the Shah's sister, Ashraf. It is abolished and there is no voice of it remaining at all." (Millett 1982, 168)

Feminist activism in Iran was stigmatized domestically by the history of Western women's involvement in the Iranian feminist arena and by their close associations with the WOI; consequently, a news conference held by Western women about Iranian women was doubtless more harmful than helpful during that volatile political period. In response to criticisms leveled against them by Iranian women in the audience who objected to Western appropriation of the Iranian feminist cause, Millett and her colleagues made repeated offers to share the podium with them. Not surprisingly, their invitation was refused and served only to reinforce the structural inequities within the sisterhood movement. They remained, to borrow bell hooks's words, "totally unaware of their perception that they somehow 'own' the movement, that they are 'hosts' inviting us as 'guests'" (hooks 1986, 133).

The news conference encouraged the revolutionary regime's stratagem of conflating feminism with imperialism, and labeling all feminists as *gharbzadih* and thus as counterrevolutionary insurgents. The second factor that contributed to the disintegration of the news conference, and arguably precipitated the antifeminist violence of the following days, was due in part to Millett's politically naive response to a reporter who asked whether it would be germane to call the Ayatollah "a male chauvinist." She responds: "Yes, a male chauvinist would be a very simple and a very idiotic way to describe it, but certainly germane" (Millett 1982, 178). Her comment was published in a number of papers, quoting her accusing Khomeini of being a "male chauvinist pig" (*Washington Post,* March 12, 1979). By Millett's own account, she was baited by male journalists at the news conference, eager for a contentious statement from the "radical feminist."

Millett's inexpert handling of the question played into the hands of patriarchal nationalists, who claimed that Iranian feminists were Westoxified agents of imperialism. At the feminist march the day after the news conference, there was increased violence against the female demonstrators; their male supporters had to form a human chain to shield the women from the jeering and menacing crowd of antifeminist men marching alongside them. Millett confesses that this is the first time she has feared for her life during a demonstration for women's rights (1982, 197). Suddenly, it seems, she becomes aware of the high stakes involved in the Iranian feminist struggle:

> The attackers have climbed on top of cars and are haranguing us,
> exhibiting a page of what looks like Time magazine bearing a
> picture of the Shah, and another picture of what appears to be his
> sister, Princess Ashraf, dancing with someone indecipherable,
> probably one of the big parties of the Shah's ambassador, grand
> affairs attended by luminaries like Andy Warhol and Elizabeth Taylor.
> This decadence, they accuse us, is ours: we are in sympathy with
> the Shah; Ashraf called herself a feminist. Taunting us with the
> very thing to make us angry, a charge so transparently false yet an
> affront to our honour. "Death to the Pahlavi dynasty," we chant
> back. (201)

According to Millett, she and her European feminist friends narrowly escape a violent beating—if not certain death—by a group of angry revolutionaries at the demonstration (206–7).

Meanwhile, in New York City, prominent American feminists such as Gloria Steinem, Robin Morgan, and Betty Friedan staged a demonstration in support of Iranian women in front of the Rockefeller Center. The demonstration, they claimed, was part of a series of "international feminist" demonstrations across the United States and in Paris, London, and Rome (*New York Times,* March 16, 1979). Paradoxically, when Steinem and Morgan telephone Millett to apprise her of their activities, she appears judgmental of their long-distance involvement, and even comes across as occupying the moral high ground. Millett recounts her phone conversation with Steinem and Morgan, who inform her of the location of the demonstration:

> "In front of Rockefeller Center and St. Pat, the old corner, you know," Robin [Morgan] chimes in, chuckling from her end of the extension phone. "And then on down to the Iranian embassy to give 'em hell— like we used to do to the Shah." The New York battle cry; how odd it seems at this distance, a hotel room in Tehran with gunfire intermittently in the road outside. . . . But how still more complicated to explain without seeming to be smug—the thousands of differences that separate our experience, friends that we are, have been so long. Not just Uptown and Downtown differences, but differences of half a world away in an armed camp that has swiftly replaced an uprising— all the nuances of left and nationality and religion. (1982, 187)

The subtext of her narrative here is that Millett is the committed feminist who is helping Iranian women by her very presence in the country and by her participation in the demonstrations, whereas her American feminist colleagues are merely performing radical politics at a safe distance. On March 19, 1979, Kate Millett and Sophie Keir were expelled from Iran. They were arrested in the morning and held in police custody at the airport until they were placed on an airplane the following day:

> "It was a horrible experience," Millett told reporters at Orly Airport. "I have never been so terrified in my life." . . . She said, "We are afraid for our sisters there. The Iranian women are afraid of being arrested and for them it won't be someone saying: 'Please take an airplane and get out of here.'" (*Washington Post,* March 20, 1979)

During her stay in Iran, but particularly after her expulsion from the country, Millett becomes quite conscious of the very real dangers facing Iranian women struggling for their rights as women under the Islamic Republic; she is aware, it seems, that it is impossible to equate the experiences of Western sisters who demonstrate for several hours outside Rockefeller Center in New York with those of Iranian women who risk their lives when they march in the streets as feminists.

Shortly after Millett's and Keir's expulsion from Iran, seventeen European women and one Egyptian woman from le Comité international du Droit des Femmes, an organization presided over by Simone de Beauvoir, arrived in Iran to demonstrate *their* support for their beleaguered sisters.[19] Claude Servan-Schreiber, one of the French feminists in the delegation, writes:

> At the press conference in Paris, announcing the committee, an Iranian man protested the departure of the delegation: "This is not the time." But Simone de Beauvoir, president of the committee, replied with passion: "I've seen many countries, and I've seen many revolutions, and each time the question of defending women's rights came up, I was told it wasn't the time." (1979, 95)

The assurance with which this committee enters the fray at such a volatile and contentious time in Iranian political history is galling, but perhaps not entirely surprising, given the tendency of feminist leaders of the sisterhood movement since the nineteenth century to rescue their suffering sisters without attending to the concerns articulated by those very women.[20]

This contingent of self-proclaimed "international" feminists traveled to Qom, the religious center in Iran, and demanded an audience with religious leader Ayatollah Khomeini. Khomeini granted them a five-minute interview, during which he was confronted with a barrage of questions regarding the status of Iranian women. Khomeini responded, in the words of French feminist Katia Kaupp, with "le silence total" (1979, 49). Khomeini's symbolic silence during his interview with a group of Western feminists in Iran represents, at the most obvious level, a stubborn taciturnity regarding his position on Iranian women and an active participation in stifling the voices of these women. But this silence is also, I believe, produced by the historical alliance between second-wave and Pahlavi feminists. The unique position Iranian women carved for themselves as feminists and anti-imperialist nationalists was a precarious one that they were forced to abandon shortly after the arrival of Anglo-American and European feminists in Iran and the unwelcome host of associations evoked by their presence in the Iranian feminist movement.

Despite the fiasco of Western feminist participation during the feminist demonstrations in Iran, the myth of international feminism remained indestructible. Shortly after Millett's and the European feminists' catastrophic involvement in the Iranian feminist struggle, Mim Kelber wrote:

> Not until Kate Millett, the guest speaker invited for March 8 by the
> Iranian feminists, had arrived did press attention begin—and only then
> did police protection follow. The lesson was not lost: international
> attention could be helpful to the women's struggle to keep the anti-
> Shah revolution democratic. (1979, 90)

Kelber is mistaken on two points. First, it is not clear that Millett was
invited by Iranian feminists. By her own account in *Going to Iran,* Millett
was invited by Khalil, an Iranian man with whom she worked in Caifi
(1982, 25). Furthermore, it remains unclear who, if anyone, actually invited the French contingent. In fact, in *Going to Iran,* Millett describes
Kateh's apprehension about the arrival of the European feminists:

> Kateh is not that enthusiastic about the delegation. . . . What impression
> will it make among people here? Simone de Beauvoir is president of the
> delegation, but unwell and unable to come herself. The delegates are
> mainly French, but also German, Scandinavian: European feminists,
> writers, journalists. There is the question that members of the
> delegation may not be acceptable. . . . To Kateh, it's insufficiently
> political. They might just come for a story, as reporters, or as super-
> feminists, to colonize. I argue uselessly for sisterhood. (1982, 153)

Second, Kelber's article, published three months after the aborted anti-
imperialist Iranian feminist movement, shows that, contrary to Kelber's
belief, "the lesson" clearly *was* lost—at least on Kelber. Despite the fact
that the presence of Western feminists served to divide Iranian feminists
and make them even more vulnerable to physical attack by patriarchal
nationalists, Kelber celebrates the impractical idea of an international
women's movement.

Indeed, the Iranian women's movement was occluded at that time in
two ways. First, by appropriating the "cause" of Iranian women, Western
feminists interfered with an indigenous anti-imperialist feminist movement. Undoubtedly guided by the best intentions, Western feminists
tried to "direct" the Iranian feminist movement and transform the movement into something to which they could relate as "international sisters."
By turning Iranian feminist concerns into an international women's concern, the particularity and specificity of anti-imperialist Iranian feminism was elided. Second, by taking advantage of the Western (imperial)
versus Iranian (nationalist) binary, the conservative clerics successfully
defused the radical potential of the Iranian feminist movement. Thus,

despite the fact that there were many other Iranian feminist groups active before and during the revolution, their work was often overshadowed by the dominant (and overlapping) discourses of state-sponsored Iranian feminism and global sisterhood. The presence of Kate Millett and European feminists in Iran at that particular historical juncture allowed the ruling elite to argue that feminism was a Western phenomenon[21] and that all feminist activity in Iran would be perceived as "counterrevolutionary" behavior. Iranian feminist activists were thus forced to choose between the two sides of a false binary: the West and Iran. They found themselves choosing to support the tenets of the revolution; the choice was, of course, a spurious one, since to opt for what was seen as an "imperialist" feminism was to declare oneself a counterrevolutionary and a threat to the state.

Sisterhood in the Diaspora

Although a number of feminists have moved away from a second-wave model of global sisterhood, some prominent prerevolutionary Iranian feminists, such as Mahnaz Afkhami, former minister of women's affairs and secretary general of the Women's Organization of Iran, maintain that the project of "global sisterhood" remains a viable model for contemporary Iranian feminist work:

> The disparity in physical and material power between the developed and the less-developed countries forces Third World women to withdraw to reactive positions, formulating their discourse in response to the West and its challenge. Consequently, they fail to think globally, that is, move beyond the indigenous culture they have objectively outgrown. Their discourse remains nationalistic, parochial, fearful, tradition-bound, and rooted in the soil of patriarchy. (Afkhami 1994, 17)

Afkhami praises the benefits of international sisterhood and stresses the need for Iranian women to adopt a "global" way of thinking if they ever hope to advance their rights as women. The suggestion is, then, that any attempt at change from within Iranian cultures and traditions is an already defeated effort. By aligning "indigenous culture" and nationalism with a "parochial" and patriarchal discourse, she reintroduces the question of temporality into the debate. Her argument evokes the concept of linear and evolutionary development, representing some feminists as less evolved than others and therefore in need of guidance. Afkhami's article reproduces the same kind of divisive binary between (Western) global feminism and an indigenous Iranian feminism that foreclosed the possibilities of an anti-imperialist feminist movement in 1979 Iran.

Since the 1979 revolution, Afkhami and Robin Morgan, both of whom continue to uphold the notion of "universal sisterhood" as a working model for feminist activism, have had a close working relationship. *In the Eye of the Storm: Women in Post-Revolutionary Iran* (1994), one of Afkhami's many books to have attained canonical status in Iranian feminist studies, includes a foreword by Morgan. Afkhami's *Women in Exile* (1994) has an exuberant endorsement by Morgan on its back cover. Morgan's poem, "A Woman's Creed," written in collaboration with Afkhami and other members of the Sisterhood Is Global Institute,[22] is reproduced in Linda Christiansen-Ruffman's article in the "Post-Beijing" issue of *Canadian Women's Studies;* this poem rearticulates the universality of women's rights and the primacy of gender unity over class or cultural differences. It reproduces the romanticized language of 1970s global sisters who saw all women united in resistance to universal patriarchy. That this feminist document should be called a "creed" is doubly ironic, as the term suggests uncritical, catechistic learning and evokes the doctrinal Christianity of colonial missionaries. It is worth quoting here at length:

> We are female human beings poised on the edge of the new millennium. We are the majority of our species, yet we have dwelt in the shadows. We are the invisible, the illiterate, the labourers, the refugees, the poor. And we vow: *No more.* We are the women who hunger—for rice, home, freedom, each other ourselves. We are the women who thirst—for clean water and laughter, literacy, love. . . . For we are the Old Ones, the New Breed, the Natives who came first but lasted, indigenous to an utterly different dimension. We are the girl child in Zambia, the grandmother in Burma, the women in El Salvador and Afghanistan, Finland, and Fiji. . . . Bread. A clean sky. Active peace. A woman's voice singing somewhere, melody drifting like smoke for the cookfires. . . . A humble, earthy paradise, in the now. We *will* make it real, make it our own, make policy, history, peace, make it available, make mischief, a difference, love the connections, the miracle, ready. *Believe it. We are the women who will transform the world.* (reprinted in Christiansen-Ruffman 1996, 37; emphasis theirs)

The language of the creed presents a totalizing vision of what it means to be a woman and a feminist. It is formulated as a creed, which implies that the document is an article of faith demanding a dogmatic adherence; those who do not believe the creed cannot be good feminists. The result is a rhetorical position that automatically precludes the possibility of disagreement or dissent. In the tradition of the 1970s, the creed foregrounds gender as the essential similarity that overrides all differences. The discourse of universality enables privileged women in the West to align themselves with and speak for the aboriginals in North America, the girl child in Zambia, and the grandmother in Burma, thus occluding the colonial history of the very discourse they employ.

In *Sisterhood Is Global* (1984), an anthology edited by Morgan, Afkhami's contribution, "Iran—A Future in the Past: The 'Prerevolutionary' Women's Movement," implies that the Iranian women's movement was initiated by the WOI and that all feminist activism ceased once the new regime acceded to power. This view is stated quite explicitly by Ashraf Pahlavi in her autobiography, *Faces in a Mirror:*

> We had come such a long way since the days when Iran's women were almost invisible that it was hard for me to comprehend how women can relinquish those rights now with so little resistance. When I am optimistic, I think that the women of Iran have gone underground and are just waiting for an opportunity to surface and reassert themselves. In pessimistic moods, however, I think that perhaps our women have taken their freedom too lightly because they have not had to fight for it or go to jail for it, and that they will not realize how much they have lost until they have been effectively repressed again. (1980, 158)

Afkhami and the former princess reinscribe the state-sponsored feminism of the Pahlavi regime that advocated "top-down" feminist reform and education, a model that can only function within a hierarchical and rigid system that disregards other voices and other models of feminism. With a stroke of the pen, Afkhami and Ashraf effectively undermine the history—and the presence—of Iranian feminist consciousness and activism.

Nevertheless, it is important to recognize that Pahlavi feminists such as Afkhami did struggle to bring questions regarding women's legal, political, and social status to the fore of the Iranian political scene. In so doing, these feminists faced numerous obstacles and difficulties as they worked within a political system that was only superficially committed to gender equity. It is equally important to recognize, however, that those women who felt excluded from the ideals of Pahlavi feminism, and its endorsement of global sisterhood, had a legitimate concern. Spivak has argued that the desire for global feminist alliances is prevalent among women of the dominant social classes in third-world countries (1988, 288). Thus, women who are placed in a position of economic and social security can afford to celebrate international alliances. The women of what Spivak calls the "urban subproletariat," on the other hand, find themselves in a position complicated by their disadvantaged social position in relation to the elite feminist groups and to the dominant patriarchal power (1988, 288). Thus, the agential power and the subject position of the anti-imperialist Iranian feminist are elided in the moment of collusion between the two dominant discourses of international feminism and anti-imperialist patriarchy. Through the act of representation, then, the dominant classes affirm their own subject constitution by "cathecting" the figure (and the voice) of the subaltern woman. By transforming the subaltern into an object of study and, by extension, into an object of desire, the dominant classes impede the articulation of subaltern voices. Indeed, Iranian women expressed their demands vociferously and publicly during the anti-veil protests, but the cultural appropriation of the Iranian feminist movement by Western feminists and the cultural attacks against the West by anti-imperialist activists converged to shroud their voices.

Contemporary Iranian feminists face the challenge of maintaining significant and articulate feminist positions in Iran and in the diaspora. Postrevolutionary Iranian feminists need to move away from the dubious position of simply laying blame on the shortcomings of the state-sponsored Women's Organization of Iran. By the same token, former WOI members and other prerevolutionary Iranian feminists would benefit by recognizing the diversity of postrevolutionary Iranian feminist voices. A glance at some (diasporic) Iranian feminist scholarship reveals the reluctance of some Iranian feminists to do this. In "Émigré Iranian Feminism and the Construction of the Muslim Woman," Haideh Moghissi launches a severe attack on, in her words, "neoconservative" feminists. According to her, neoconservative feminists refuse to celebrate the work of secular Iranian feminists, but instead aggrandize the work accomplished by their more religious counterparts. After listing the numerous (presumably mistaken) beliefs held by Iranian feminists with whom she disagrees, Moghissi brings the paper to a close with the following counsel:

> For those of us who lived through the memorable experience of the revolution, and who have watched, in horror, the devastating consequences of the Islamization policies, and felt the clutches of the Islamists on our personal lives, the infatuation of academic feminists with "Islamic feminism," and their softening tone vis-à-vis Islamic fundamentalism, reminds one uncomfortably, of the self-negating actions and discourse of the traditional left when it was thrust into the frenzy of "anti-imperialist" populism during the post-revolutionary period. . . . In the writings of neoconservative, academic feminists one hears again, tragically, an echo of this same romantic confusion, surrendering, at the same time, their own vocation (and obligation) to act as critical intellectuals. (1999a, 201–2)

Moghissi's representation of the work of diasporic Iranian feminists who attempt to problematize dichotomies of enlightened secular feminism and backward Islamic—or indigenous—feminism is profoundly ungenerous and didactic. Not only does she accuse feminists with whom she disagrees of lacking political sophistication and acumen, but she also implies they are failures as "critical intellectuals."

The kind of feminist pedagogy embraced by Moghissi, a feminism that claims to instruct the ignorant masses of Iranian women, betrays a heritage of colonial feminism, one that is predicated upon a hierarchy of feminist enlightenment. Indeed, Moghissi maintains a scolding tone throughout her paper, lest Iranian women should forget their indebtedness to Pahlavi feminists. But, more significantly, this kind of feminist project unwittingly reproduces the moment of silence in 1979 Qom by contributing to the continued absence of Iranian feminist representations in Iranian nationalist as well as Western and diasporic Iranian feminist discourses.

Minoo Moallem cautions feminists to be aware of the discursive similarities between "fundamentalist" discourse and feminist discourse: "both Western egalitarian feminism and Islamic fundamentalism [are] regimes of truth with consistencies and inconsistencies in their desire for change and closure" (1999, 324). In *Feminism and Islamic Fundamentalism*, Moghissi also argues that the discourses of fundamentalism and feminism resemble each other, but, according to her, it is not easy "to draw a clear distinction between the position of fundamentalists and that of a large number of anti-representational post-colonial feminists" (1999b, 47). While Moghissi collapses the position of postcolonial feminists with that of "Islamic fundamentalists," Moallem's more nuanced argument aims to "problematize not only fundamentalism for—among other things—the construction of a false totality, but also feminism for its potential to construct rigidified categories" (1999, 325). In refusing to distinguish between the radically different positions adopted by post-colonial feminists and "Islamic fundamentalists," Moghissi discredits the work of feminists who are attempting to think outside the hierarchies of dominant discursive structures, and effectively precludes the possibility for social change. Her blithe dismissal of postcolonial scholarship aligns her with the fields of Iranian studies and Middle East studies in the United States, which have historically been marked by a suspicion of postcolonial and poststructuralist work. While it is important to recognize and confront, as Moghissi does, the limitations the Islamic Republic places on Iranian women's mobility and expression, reproducing the false binary of Islamic backwardness (or "neoconservative" support of it) and progressive Western feminism is not a productive path.

Spivak's apt warning against "an unexamined chromatism," since "there is no guarantee that an upwardly mobile woman of colour in the US academy would not participate [in the reproduction of colonialist structures]," is particularly germane to the current predicament of Iranian feminists who have to contend with the discursive control of Iranian feminist narratives by some diasporic Iranian feminists (1986, 237–38). Iranian and Western feminists need to be receptive to alternative models of feminism and we need to recognize the necessity of questioning what Razack refers to as our "position of innocence," a position that elides our participation in the subordination of others and the occlusion of their voices (1998, 10). Moving toward a politics of accountability compels us to acknowledge that "we are implicated in systems of oppression that profoundly structure our understanding of one another. That is, we come to know and perform ourselves in ways that reproduce social hierarchies" (10).

The future of oppositional feminist politics that aim to challenge and subvert cultural and political structures limiting women's freedom depends upon a recognition of the checkered history of feminism, particularly of the global sisterhood movement, from its nineteenth-century colonialist beginnings to its more contemporary imperialist manifestations. Further, it is incumbent upon us to examine our own participation in the abjection and subjugation of other women. Ziba Mir-Hosseini argues that we need to be "honest about our own personal, individual motives" when writing about third-world women and, in particular, about feminists in Islamic states (1999, 4). Academics who depict Muslim women as oppressed and submissive, or who dismiss Islamic feminists as misinformed or duped, Mir-Hosseini claims, often present their work under the guise of "objectivity," thereby stifling any possibility of debate (4). Thus, recognizing the ways in which we participate in and reproduce dominant discursive representations about "Other" women is crucial to the creation and development of a resilient feminist politics, one that moves away from the hierarchical model of compulsory sisterhood and makes room for disagreement and dissent.

CHAPTER 4

Female Homosocial Communities in Iranian Feminist Film

S INCE THE LATE 1980s, Iranian cinema has gained a privileged status on the international film festival circuit. Abbas Kiarostami, Mohsen Makhmalbaf, Dariush Mehrjui, and Jafar Panahi are among the most prominent Iranian male directors whose films have enjoyed international acclaim since the 1980s. But increasingly, the works of female directors such as Rakhshan Bani-Etemad and Tahmineh Milani (and a growing number of other directors such as Samira Makhmalbaf and Marzieye Meshkini) are being celebrated both in Iran and abroad. Milani's films in particular contribute to a significant and forceful expression of feminist voices from within an Iranian context.[1]

Representations of women in contemporary Iranian cinema offer us a glimpse into the challenges women face as they attempt to redefine gender roles from within the limitations imposed upon them by traditional cultural practices as well as by the restrictive laws of the Islamic Republic. These films, I believe, also contest Western and Pahlavi feminist representations of the veiled woman as voiceless and subjugated. As a way of moving outside the limitations of the discourse of sisterhood, this last chapter works in contrapuntal relation to chapter 1, which looks almost exclusively at Western representations of the Persian woman. Here, I focus exclusively on Iranian women's self-representations through the medium of cinema and examine the ways in which women and feminists in Iran are reconfiguring the terms of the debate about the place of women in postrevolutionary Iranian society.

This chapter is divided into two sections: the first section will look at the feature film, with a particular focus on Tahmineh Milani's *Two Women* (1999) and *The Fifth Reaction* (2003); the second section will look at the documentary form, focusing on Ziba Mir-Hosseini's and Kim Longinotto's *Divorce Iranian Style* (1998) and *Runaway* (2001), and Mahnaz Afzali's *The Ladies' Room* (2003). Although there are, of course, numerous differences between the films discussed here, I am especially interested in what I perceive to be a feature common to them all: the potential of female bonding to contest traditional cultural as well as current legislative prejudices against women. Female bonding presents a challenge to the cultural concept of *ghiyrat*, which sees women's behavior as a yardstick by which male honor and authority are measured. It also posits an alternative model to that of sisterhood, which, as I have argued throughout this book, has been historically predicated on a structure of inequality between women of different cultures and classes.

This chapter will draw on Eve Kosofsky Sedgwick's formulation of homosocial desire as "the affective or social force, the glue, even when its manifestation is hostility or hatred or something less emotively charged, that shapes an important relationship" in conjunction with Afsaneh Najmabadi's consideration of homosocial relations in Persia in order to discuss the changing landscape of Iranian gender relations (1985, 2). I suggest that it is through the rediscovery of homosocial spaces that Iranian women have been working toward a reconfiguration of gender roles in Iranian society.

In her work on Iranian modernity, Najmabadi has argued that the premodern (veiled) Persian woman existed in a female homosocial space. Women often communicated their poetry and prose to each other orally. In the face of a female audience, the language of the veiled Iranian woman was boldly eroticized and sexually explicit. The shift from an oral to a print culture, a shift required by a self-styled modern Iran, necessitated a concomitant transformation of women's discourse (Najmabadi 1993, 488). The growing popularity of print culture and state-enforced heterosociality meant that women's literary works, often bawdy, would now have a male and female audience. This movement out of homosocial and into heterosocial spaces, argues Najmabadi, compelled the self-regulation of women's literary expression:

> When the female voice found a public audience, it became a veiled voice, a disciplined voice. Erasing or replacing its sexual markers, it sanitized itself. . . . In the homosocial female space, language and body could be sexually overt; stepping into the heterosocial world of modernity was coterminous with the construction of a disciplined female language and body. (1993, 489)

According to Najmabadi, early twentieth-century discourses positioned the modern, unveiled Iranian woman as chaste and virtuous as opposed to the premodern, or "traditional," veiled Iranian woman, now represented as licentious.[2] Perhaps most threatening to the project of Iranian modernity, which sought to rethink the nation through European ideas of what constitutes "civilization," was the practice of women's veiling:

> A woman's veil was . . . not only a marker of cultural difference between Iran and Europe but also the most visible marker of gender separation, a key signifier of homosociality. It was explicitly linked to "unnatural love" among men (itself a sign of backwardness); "unnatural sex" among men, in turn, was held responsible for "unnatural sex" among women. (Najmabadi 2005, 150)

The Iranian woman's de-eroticized body and language through unveiling was thus a necessary precursor to the heterosexualization of nationalist discourse, a move which enabled the nation's entrance into "modernity," aligning it with (civilized) European nations.

Although Adrienne Rich's work is marked by the limitations of the second-wave feminist moment out of which it emerges, I believe that her term "compulsory heterosexuality," by which she refers to the naturalization and institutionalization of heterosexual relationships, is pertinent to the discussion of the shift from homosociality to heterosociality in discourses of Iranian nationalism and modernity. While heterosexuality remained the official state-sanctioned model of sexual relations during the 1970s revolutionary period, homosociality (but certainly not homosexuality) and sexual segregation reemerged as the preferred model of Iranian gender relations. The unveiled woman, previously an admirable symbol of modesty and self-restraint, was now denounced as the morally corrupt, Westoxified, "painted doll" of the Pahlavi regime, and the veiled woman resumed her place as the epitome of chastity and virtue.

I am interested in exploring an altogether different configuration of the Iranian woman here. The women portrayed in contemporary Iranian cinema, particularly those in the feature films and documentaries I discuss in this chapter, are veiled, but they are neither modest nor unchaste. They mobilize their voices to articulate their demands for inclusion—as equals to men—in the Iranian national conscience and under Islamic law. What these movies in particular seem to convey is that women's well-being is contingent upon the absence of men.[3] The regime of compulsory heterosexuality, claims Rich, ensures that "female friendship and comradeship have been set apart from the erotic, thus limiting the erotic itself" (1980, 650). I believe that we can see the potency of women's homosocial communities in postrevolutionary Iranian films, and that the return to women's homosocial spaces, ironically mandated by the laws of the Islamic Republic, enable women to draw on the possibilities of female bonding as a way of negotiating a disciplinary masculine culture.

The Feature Film: Tahmineh Milani

Female bonding and women's friendships as a site of potential subversion form a strong subnarrative in Tahmineh Milani's unapologetically feminist films, *Two Women* and *The Fifth Reaction*. Afshin Molavi writes that Milani submitted *Two Women* to the Iranian film censorship board in 1995 and "the predominantly male commission showed her the door. . . . 'I think many of the men on the board saw themselves in the movie and it was too sensitive for them,' Milani later reflected" (2002, 217). *Two Women* was finally released in 1999 and became "the biggest box office hit in Iranian history" (Sciolino 2000, 265).

The story of *Two Women* follows the lives of two university students: the brilliant and ambitious Firishtih, from the rural laboring classes, and Roya, a bright, middle-class Tehrani. The women meet at Tehran University in the 1978–1979 revolutionary period, shortly before the universities shut down during the government's purging of "Westoxified" intellectuals from the academy.[4] Some critics have chosen to read Firishtih and Roya as two sides of the same woman;[5] I believe, however, that the intimacy in the two women's relationship deserves closer examination.

The film traces the trajectory of the women's friendship. Firishtih tutors her fellow students, one of whom is Roya, to finance her way through the university. Soon the two women become close friends. In one scene during which the women are studying together, Roya gazes at Firishtih with open admiration, saying, "You truly are a genius. I swear to you I am being honest. You are a genius. You're lovely—and lovable."[6] Roya uses the language of courtship to express her feelings to Firishtih, who brushes off her lavish compliments, although she appears to enjoy the attention. When Roya discovers that Firishtih has taught herself to speak English, she crosses the room, leans towards her, and asks her to say a few words. Firishtih responds coyly (in English): "I'm going to ask you something. Let's get out of here." Playing the coquette, Firishtih steps away from Roya, who continues to marvel at her and to move closer to her. As with other scenes throughout the movie, the sexual tension between the two women is difficult to ignore. The suggestions of homo-eroticism in the film are particularly radical as same-sex relationships are seen as inherently threatening to the hierarchical organization of heterosexuality in Islamic Iran.

The playful banter between Firishtih and Roya and the evident plea-sure they derive from each other's company are foregrounded in the movie, and work as one of the primary motivations for male violence in the film. In her queer reading of mainstream cinema, and her analysis of the "hypothetical lesbian" in straight films, Chris Straayer contends that "female bonding and the exchange of glances between women threaten heterosexual and patriarchal structures" (1994, 350). There is an added dimension to this threat in the Islamic Republic, where same-sex relationships are crimes punishable by death under the current regime.[7] The lighthearted, flirtatious exchange mentioned above is followed by a violent reestablishment of patriarchal authority. In one scene, Firishtih and Roya ride the bus home together; they are standing facing each other in the center aisle when Firishtih's stalker emerges. He places himself behind Roya so that he is directly opposite Firishtih. Visually, this scene enforces the subtext of the movie: the disruption of a male heterosexual fantasy of dominance by the possibility of lesbian desire between the two women. The stalker sees Roya's presence as an impediment to his union with Firishtih, and later, Firishtih's husband regards Roya as a threat to his and Firishtih's marital happiness.

Following the scene on the bus—during which Roya has the stalker ejected for harassing them—Firishtih stops to play hopscotch as the two women walk companionably along a street. Roya watches her with undisguised affection and exclaims, "Oh, you are so lovely!" The modest Firishtih blushes in the face of Roya's compliment, and Roya insists: "I swear to God, I am being truthful. You do everything right. You are mischievous at the right time. You are graceful at the right time. And I can't believe it—how do you manage to read so many books?" After showering Firishtih with compliments, Roya turns to find herself face-to-face with the stalker. He brandishes a knife in front of her and threatens to kill her. He then issues an ultimatum: "This had better be the last time you hang around [Firishtih]. If I see you with her one more time, I will disfigure your face with this," waving a bottle of acid in the air.

Given the historical period in which this film is set, the mention of acid throwing is particularly significant. Shortly after the overthrow of the Pahlavi regime, the morals police and Islamic vigilantes patrolled the streets, throwing acid on women who behaved or dressed in what they perceived to be an immodest fashion. Under a regime in which same-sex relationships are punishable by one hundred lashes, or even execution, the violent threats of Firishtih's stalker are particularly chilling.[8] He eventually seizes the opportunity to splash his bottle of acid on Firishtih's (male) cousin, imagining him to be a rival. After this incident, Firishtih's father, horrified by what he perceives to be the damage done to his honor, orders her to return home to her village. The stalker, however, follows her home. In one chase scene, he races her car with his motorcycle and they run over two children, killing one and injuring the other. The charges against Firishtih are dismissed, while her stalker is sentenced to thirteen years in jail; he vows, however, to return and avenge himself on her. In the meantime, Firishtih's father, who continues to fret about his honor, forces her into a marriage to "save face." As Molavi has observed:

> The issue of honor is central to the problems the film explores—In
> Iranian society a woman is still too often cast as the symbol of a man's
> honor. . . . In mosques across Iran, conservative clerics preach the
> perverted patriarchy of honor regularly, urging their all-male audiences

to "control your women." Even in downtown Tehran mosques, clerics
may be heard delivering hour-long rants against men who fail to control
their women, with exhortations such as: "Do not let your women wear
make-up and Western clothing. This is against your honor." (2002, 218)

Indeed, the story of Firishtih's unrelenting misery revolves around the
ghiyrat, or honor, of the men in her life: her father, her stalker, and her
husband. When Firishtih is bailed out of jail after the accident involv-
ing the two young boys, her father is beside himself with anger at the
besmirching of his honor. He decides that it would be more honorable
to murder Firishtih and her sister than suffer the indignity of his injured
ghiyrat. "I will kill both of them tonight. I am not my father's son if I
don't send their corpses out of this house tonight," he yells. When Firishtih pleads her innocence, her father tells her to "silence [her] voice," to
which she finally responds in anger, "I will not be silent! I want to speak!"
Firishtih's indignation here can be productively read, I believe, within
the context of the increasingly defiant voices of contemporary Iranian
feminists. She insists on having her own voice, challenging the state's
entrenched patriarchy. At the same time, I believe we can read the articulation of Firishtih's position as a contestation of the regulatory impulse
in some Western and diasporic Iranian feminist discourses, as the feminism expressed in this film does not conform to Western or prerevolutionary state-sponsored feminist models.

Despite Firishtih's insistence that she complete her degree when universities reopen, her father forces her to get married. Initially, her husband promises to support her academic and professional goals. Shortly
after their wedding, however, he begins to control her movements, eventually confining her to the home and even denying her access to the
telephone. When she goes to court to request a divorce, the official
asks her whether her husband is impotent, physically abusive, mentally
ill, or destitute. She responds in the negative to his questions, and then
states, "He insults my intelligence. I am living with a man whom I did
not choose. This man is destroying my identity as a human being." When
she realizes that these are not legitimate grounds for divorce under the
Islamic Republic, she pleads with the official:

Haj Aqa,[9] look at me. *Haj Aqa,* I want you to see me. I am human. I
want to live like a human being. How can you think that if a husband
does not provide for me financially, he is a bad man, but if he insults

my intelligence, if he destroys my identity as a human being, he is not a bad man? I just want to be a partner in a relationship. . . . Am I expecting too much?

Haj Aqa evidently seems to think that she *is* expecting too much, since Iranian divorce laws do not make allowances for women who want to make decisions about their lives as independent subjects.

While Firishtih's relationships with men (her father, her husband, her stalker) are vilified in this movie, her relationship with Roya is idealized and, I would argue, eroticized. Throughout the movie, the friendship between Firishtih and Roya is perceived as a threat to the male authority figures in their lives, since "the primary threat of female bonding is the elimination of the male" (Straayer 1996, 18). Initially, their relationship is interrupted by Firishtih's stalker; later, Firishtih's husband goes to great lengths to keep the two women apart. When Firishtih wants to invite Roya to visit them, her husband sulks and expresses his dislike of her, although he has never met her. To keep Firishtih isolated, away from Roya as well as from the numerous lovers he imagines her having, he keeps the telephone under lock and key. The ever-resourceful Firishtih, however, manages to make a duplicate key and telephones Roya in secret. When Firishtih's husband returns to find her speaking to Roya on the telephone, he flies into a jealous rage. In another scene, we see Firishtih's husband at the front door of their home, urging Roya, who has come to find Firishtih, to leave them alone so that they can enjoy their married life without disruption. Unlike previous scenes that feature the two women taking pleasure in each other's company, the camera focuses on Firishtih's husband, showing only the back of Roya's head. She is effectively cut out of the scene—and out of Firishtih's life. Straayer makes the point that

> the focus on two women together threatens to establish both asexuality and homosexuality, both of which are outside the heterosexual desire that drives mainstream film and narrative. Therefore, simultaneous actions take place in the text to eroticize the women's interactions and to abort the resulting homoerotics. These very contradictions and opposing intentions cause the gaps and ambiguous figurations that allow lesbian readings. (1996, 21–22)

It is through such gaps and ambivalences in the visual and narrative text that we can read suggestions of an eroticized relationship between

Firishtih and Roya. The two women seem happiest when they are to-gether, which is, perhaps, the ultimate threat to the heteropatriarchal imperative. Even Firishtih's family conspires against their friendship; Roya's letters to Firishtih are consistently intercepted by her parents. These elaborate efforts to destroy the two women's friendship suggest the extent of the taboo against same-sex relationships in Iran; it demon-strates, as well, an anxiety over the transformative potential of female bonding.

Eventually, Firishtih's stalker is released from prison and he returns to find her. In a melodramatic scene, her stalker and her husband engage in a violent argument and end up killing each other, ostensibly leaving her free to pick up the pieces of her life. At the end of the movie, Firishtih summons Roya to her aid and their friendship resumes. Thir-teen years of an abusive marriage, however, leave Firishtih unrecogniz-able; she has lost her independent and resourceful spirit. There is no longer any suggestion of sexual tension between Firishtih and Roya when they are reunited after the death of Firishtih's husband. This is partly due to Firishtih's shattered sense of self, but more important, I believe, it points to a recuperation of the dominant heterosocial narrative. The film's radical representation of the early stages of their eroticized friend-ship is contained by Roya's successful marriage, thus affirming Straayer's contention that "one way to interfere with female bonding is to insert references to men and heterosexuality between women characters" (1994, 351). Nevertheless, Straayer says, the recuperation of the hetero-sexual narrative "remain[s] a feeble attempt to undermine the visual impact that the women together make" (1994, 351).

The recognition and affirmation of female homosocial communities from within an Iranian feminist context disrupts not only the patriar-chal structure of traditional Iranian gender relations, but also the regime of heterosexuality imposed by the discourse of modernity. If the proj-ect of secular Iranian modernity, as Najmabadi has argued, discouraged female homosociality and necessitated the construction of the disci-plined, heterosexualized, and unveiled body of the Iranian woman, then how can we read the ensuing discourse of Islamic modernity? The model of Islamic womanhood as advocated by Ali Shariati in the 1970s re-quired, much like secular modern discourse, a woman modest in dress and language who subsumed her own desires for the good of the nation.

The role of the Muslim Iranian woman, not unlike that of her secular predecessors, entailed the reproduction and nurturing of the nation's future men.

Thus the language of modernity, in its secular and Islamic manifestations, is one of enforced heterosexuality and cultivated homophobia. To be lesbian or gay in Iran is, in effect, to renege on your duty as a citizen of the modern nation by not participating in the procreation of its future subjects. While the modern secular Iranian nation enforced the heterosexualization of Iranian citizens through the desexualization of their bodies, modern Islamic discourse resexualized them. Indeed, the enforcement of sexually segregated spaces and rigid sartorial regulations under the Islamic Republic inadvertently facilitated the establishment of homosocial communities and enabled their transformative potential. Najmabadi states that one of the effects of the heterosexualization of modern Iran was that

it provided homosexuality a homosocial home for masquerade. Formation of homosexuality through denial and disavowal becomes its condition of possibility and reproducibility. The denial of any overlap between the now separate domains of homosociality and homosexuality paradoxically provides a shelter, a masqueraded home, for homosexuality. (2005, 38)

Najmabadi's argument about masqueraded homosexuality could also be made about the reestablishment of homosocial spaces in contemporary Iran, paradoxically enforced by segregation laws under the Islamic Republic.

As I have been suggesting in my reading of *Two Women,* one area in which a camouflaged form of homosocial/homosexual desire appears is through the medium of Iranian cinema. Postrevolutionary cinematic codes of modesty, for instance, appear to have enabled coded representations of homosocial desire in a country where gay and lesbian relationships are explicitly outlawed. As Jonathan Dollimore has argued, "Dissidence may not only be repressed by the dominant (coercively and ideologically), but in a sense actually produced by it, hence consolidating the powers which it ostensibly challenges" (1991, 26). For example, film censorship guidelines that prohibit physical contact or intimacy between men and women allow the representation of affection between two women or two men. As with all the laws governing the lives of people in the Islamic Republic, the censorship regulations for cinema are arbitrary, and their enforcement often depends upon the whim of the authority figure in charge.[10] Because of the censorship guidelines that prevent any visual representation of affection or love between a man and a woman, Iranian film directors have had to develop creative ways of working around them. This is a good illustration of how the exercise of state power can produce effects opposite to its explicit intentions. In this case, the enforcement of a regime of compulsory heterosexuality and simultaneous repression of public expressions of heterosexuality by the Islamic Republic unwittingly enables the strengthening of the very homosocial/homosexual communities it deems immoral and unlawful.

By disrupting established Iranian gender hierarchies, female homosocial networks enable women to move outside of the heterosexual and patriarchal family units that position them as mere extensions of their fathers, their brothers, and eventually, their husbands. As I have suggested above, contemporary Iranian movies seem to imply that women's happiness and sense of fulfillment requires the absence of men—and the presence of women. In *Two Women,* Firishtih's freedom, and the rekindling of her friendship with Roya, is achieved at the expense of her husband's life. In *The Fifth Reaction,* the only good husband is the one who dies a premature death. In other movies, such as Rakhshan Bani-Etemad's 1998 film *The May Lady,* the protagonist's male lover is represented in a positive light, but he is physically absent during the entire film, thus raising the question of whether it is his absence that enables her to pursue a fulfilling and independent life.

While husbands and fathers remain, for the most part, background figures in *The May Lady* and *The Fifth Reaction,* the plight of women and mothers figures prominently. These films trouble the category of Iranian motherhood by recognizing women's desires to occupy more than just maternal roles; they address women's rights as independent, self-sufficient individuals. Perhaps most controversially, they address women's right to love. In fact, women's right to love and happiness is a constant refrain in both these films. In *The May Lady,* the female protagonist muses, "Love belongs to human beings. Why doesn't it belong to a mother? Isn't a mother a human being?" Ziba Mir-Hosseini has observed that the subject of love has always formed a central theme of Persian poetry, but

> it is seldom clear whether the writer is talking about divine or earthly
> love, or (given the absence of grammatical gender in Persian) whether
> the "beloved" is male or female. Both the Persian language and the
> poetic form have allowed writers to maintain and even work with
> these ambiguities. . . . But such ambiguity cannot be sustained in the
> performative and graphic arts, where both the language and the form
> demand greater transparency and directness in the depiction of
> women and love. (2001a, 2)[11]

Shortly after the revolution, the representation of women and
romantic love in Iranian cinema became the subject of much contro-
versy and restricted the representation of women in film. According to
Hamid Naficy, however, "the incorporation of a complex system of modesty (*hejab* in its widest sense) at all levels of the motion picture industry and in the cinematic texts" transformed Iranian cinema in such a
way that "both the industry and the screens became open to women as
never before as long as women abided by very specific and binding
Islamic codes of modesty" (560). Not only have Iranian women film
directors and actors claimed a prominent place for themselves in contemporary Iranian cinema, but the subject of love, albeit veiled with
specific codes of Islamic modesty, also entered this medium. Thus, directors such as Milani have created powerful and controversial work even
while abiding by contemporary cinematic codes of modesty.

The Fifth Reaction, for example, is framed by women's call for love and
respect: the film begins with a playful discussion about romantic love
by a group of women friends and ends with a tearful plea for an understanding of maternal love by an elderly woman, Zir Madinih. The film
opens with a pleasant scene in a restaurant where five women friends
have gathered: Firishtih (played by Niki Karimi, who also stars as Firishtih in *Two Women*), Taranih, Maryam, Nasrin, and Faridih. The subject of
discussion is initially their meager salaries as teachers, but the conversation turns quickly to their husbands and their various qualities. Of the
five women there, Firishtih and Maryam are the ones without husbands;
Firishtih is a recent widow and Maryam has never married. The others
describe, with good-natured humor, the various ways in which their husbands communicate their amorous intentions and declare their love for
them. This fantasy of emotionally and physically satisfying marriages is
shattered by the appearance of Taranih's husband at the restaurant with

his young, attractive secretary. Upon seeing her with her friends, he marches over in indignation and verbally abuses his wife and her friends for neglecting their duties as wives and mothers, and frequenting restaurants like loose, irresponsible women.

The interruption of the fantasy of loving and harmonious relationships serves to elicit confessional narratives from each of the women there: Taranih's husband has just publicly demonstrated his inability to love and respect his wife; Nasrin divulges the fact that her husband, who fought in the Iran-Iraq war and became a prisoner of war, returned home as a complete stranger after a twelve-year absence, leaving her trapped in an unhappy and loveless marriage; Faridih admits that her husband has taken a second wife, a young woman half his age, and that he has not come home in a year; Maryam, the unmarried woman, regrets not having experienced love. Despite not being married, she too suffers under patriarchal Iranian law; she raised her brother's children, only to have them taken away from her with no recognition of her role as surrogate mother; Firishtih is the only one among them who loved her husband and had a happy marriage, but her husband's untimely death has left her at the mercy of her tyrannical father-in-law, Haj Safdar, who is determined to secure custody of her children.

Throughout the film, we see the formation—and constant interruption—of women's homosocial networks. The movie opens with Taranih's husband's disruption of the women's gathering; however, the character of Haj Safdar, a caricature of oppressive patriarchy, poses the greatest threat to the women's bonding. He is relentlessly suspicious of the women's friendships, and by the end of the film manages to effect the group's complete dissolution. The movie's central narrative rests on the trials of Firishtih as she attempts to escape the clutches of Safdar and keep custody of her children. Safdar is incapable of understanding Firishtih's love and loyalty to her deceased husband, and insists she can remain in his home and raise her children on one condition only: she must marry his son—her dead husband's younger brother—so that she can remain in Safdar's home without becoming *namahram*, which, under Islam, refers to people who are not related, and thus risk entering into an inappropriate relationship. Firishtih adamantly refuses his request, and then faces the prospect of losing her children. She turns to her own family, but her mother refuses to help her as she, in Firishtih's words, "is like a robot that can only bow in obeisance to members of the opposite sex." She appeals to her brother, Farid, a university student in Bushehr, who also refuses to help her, prompting her to exclaim, "By God—I'm a human being. A human being. Look at this [hand]. It is made of flesh, skin, and bone. I have feelings. I am not a rock. Believe me, Farid, sometimes I think I am going crazy."

Where her immediate family fails her, her extended family of women friends rally round and offer her their support. Scenes of Firishtih's misery and oppression at the hands of Safdar, and the unwillingness of her family to interfere on her behalf, are interspersed with optimistic and compassionate meetings with her women friends, during which they plan various escape routes for Firishtih and her children. Most dramatically, Taranih offers to drive Firishtih out of town to a temporary safe location arranged by her friends, but they are forced to continuously revise their plans and alter their destination, as Safdar repeatedly obstructs their success. Haj Safdar, a wealthy, influential man who owns a large truck-driving company, orders his employees to track Taranih and Firishtih's movements; as well, he and his son, Majid, pursue them by car. This leads to some memorable Iranian-style "Thelma and Louise" chase scenes; these are two women on the open road, clearly enjoying each other's company and reveling in their flagrant violation of the state's laws. The state, in this case, is literally embodied by Safdar, who declares at various moments throughout the film that he is himself the law, further driving home one of Milani's principal points in almost all of her films: that there is no space for women at the macro-level of the state. This is an argument I will develop further in the second half of this chapter.

Eventually, Safdar manages to coerce Firishtih and Taranih's separation by threatening Taranih with arrest: Taranih returns to Tehran on her own, and discovers that Safdar has lodged official complaints against their group of friends. The women face a prison sentence if they interfere in his affairs again; thus, by using the law to his full advantage, he disrupts the emotional and physical space of female bonding.

The movie ends in Bushehr, where Firishtih has gone to seek her brother's help. Safdar catches up with her and throws her in jail while her children clamor for their mother's release. Zir Madinih, the elderly woman with whom her brother lives, and who represents a strong and nurturing maternal figure in the film, confronts Safdar and condemns his callous behavior. The prison official tells her that she may be justified in her anger, but that she "cannot stand in the way of the law," to which she replies: "When they wrote the law, did they consult mothers? Your mother? Me? *His* mother?" (she gestures to Haj Safdar with a disdainful toss of her head). Here again, the film emphasizes the lack of women's participation in legal and nationalist discourses.

Zir Madinih's words seem to have an effect on Safdar, since he softens in his resolve to keep Firishtih locked up. He returns to her jail cell and tells her that she has his permission to return to his home and raise her children. The final scene is a powerful one, as we see Firishtih crouched down on the floor of her cell in a position of total abjection; upon hearing his words, she turns her tear-stained face toward him slowly in disbelief and hope. But as Safdar informs her that she can return to his home and to her children, he leans over and thunders, "But on one condition!" The final scene is a freeze-frame shot of Firishtih's fearful face and the shadow of Safdar's admonishing finger raised above her head on the wall behind her. While he never names his condition, we get the oppressive sense that we are back at the beginning of the film, when Safdar tells her she can stay in his home on condition that she marry his son, Majid. The film thus ends by drawing us into Firishtih's cycle of despair, and her utter helplessness in the face of legal, national, and cultural discourses that do not enable women to exercise their rights: the right to choose whom to love, the right to raise their children, the right to make their own choices in life. It also provides us with a view of what happens to women when they lose the company of women; the movie thus underscores the fact that the heterosocial imperative disrupts homosocial female bonding and enforces an oppressive and hierarchical model of social relations.

The Documentary Film: Ziba Mir-Hosseini and Mahnaz Afzali

The themes of female homosocial bonding and motherhood remain dominant in feminist documentary films. This section explores the ways in which the dynamics of a transient network of women at the microlevel works against a relative absence of women at the macrolevel. In other words, the transient, homosocial women's space works as an alternative to a fixed and heteronormative nation-state.[12] My focus here is on three documentary films: *Divorce Iranian Style* and *Runaway,* both collaborative projects by London-based Iranian anthropologist Ziba Mir-Hosseini and documentary filmmaker Kim Longinotto, and *The Ladies' Room,* by Iranian actor and documentary filmmaker Mahnaz Afzali.[13] I will explore the configuration of women's spaces in these documentaries as alternative sites of community and belonging, as well as potential sites of the contestation of restrictive gender roles imposed through state legislation as well as through determining cultural practices. These films offer us a glimpse of the socially transformative possibilities of female bonding through the creation of temporary homosocial spaces in, ironically, three state-owned facilities: a family court, a women's shelter, and a women's public washroom. Further, I will explore the implications of the participation of the women filmmakers in these communal women's spaces. Does the genre of the documentary compromise these women's spaces by disclosing what is private to the public sphere, or does their presence strengthen the political potential of women's spaces?

The 1998 documentary *Divorce Iranian Style* was filmed almost entirely in an Iranian family court, and chronicles the divorce proceedings of six couples, with a particular focus on four cases. This documentary portrays the ways in which Iranian wives, surrounded by a support network of women, strategically work within the limits of divorce laws to get what they want. The film features four subjects: Massy, a coquettish young woman seeking to divorce her husband on grounds of his impotence; Jamilih, who threatens her philandering husband with divorce, and even has him jailed overnight, to teach him a lesson about the consequences of his waywardness; sixteen-year-old Ziba, who desperately seeks a divorce from her thirty-eight-year-old husband (whom she was forced to wed in an arranged marriage) and who resorts to lies and blackmail to achieve her goal; and last, Maryam, who lost custody of her eldest daughter after divorcing her first husband and who fights to retain custody of her youngest child, whom she stands to lose since her remarriage.

In "Negotiating the Politics of Gender in Iran: An Ethnography of a Documentary," director Mir-Hosseini writes that during the making of the documentary, she spent a considerable amount of time discussing women's legal rights and sharing her own views on divorce and child custody rights in Iran with the petitioners between court sessions:

> The fact that I took an active role in these discussions, speaking my
> mind and talking about my own divorces, broke down the barriers and
> made women feel at ease with the camera. The informality of the
> court also allowed people to talk to us. When shooting, we always
> stood together—I with my face at the same level as the camera—and
> were treated as one person. Kim, too, was open and did not hide her
> feelings, making it clear where her sympathies lay— though she could
> not follow the details. Many times during the proceedings she was
> moved to tears. (2002a, 188–89)

The overwhelming, and sympathetic, presence of women in the courtroom (in large part due to an all-female film crew) seems to afford women
claimants the courage and the strength to fight for their rights, thus
posing a not-insignificant threat to the established patriarchal order.
Throughout the documentary, the women petitioners engage with the
filmmakers by turning to the camera and sharing confidences with
Longinotto and Mir-Hosseini, whom they see as allies in their disputes.
While the women with whom Mir-Hosseini spoke between sessions
were, for the most part, supportive of her project and of her position
regarding women's rights in Iran, many of the men present took the
opposite stance. One of the most outspoken opponents to Longinotto's
and Mir-Hosseini's presence in the courtroom was a trainee judge "who
tried unsuccessfully to convince Judge Deldar to stop [their] work" (Mir-
Hosseini 2002a, 188).

Nasrin Rahimieh uses the phrase "packing the court" to describe
the transformation of the divorce court into an arena in which Iranian
women can discuss their problems and fight for their legal rights:

> The presence of a sympathetic judge, the court secretary, her daughter
> and a female camera crew are part of what I see as packing the court.
> While the laws destined for implementation in the courtroom rest on
> a fundamental inequality between the sexes, the courtroom itself
> becomes a space populated by the very constituency its enactment of
> the law is meant to restrict. In fact, the balance is tipped against men,
> who coincidentally often emerge as frustrated and powerless. (8–9)[14]

Thus, the courtroom—ordinarily dominated by patriarchal laws and the
language of Islamic allegiance—is transformed into a productive homosocial space. The power of women's collective and supportive presence
enables the women petitioners to fight for their rights and for their

dignity. Jamilih's situation brings the possibilities of female bonding into specific focus.

Her husband is represented as an irresponsible philanderer who mistreats his wife and children. Jamilih, who turns to the camera and whispers confidentially into the lens that she truly loves her husband and only wants to teach him a lesson, uses the concept of *female* honor—a direct inversion of *ghiyrat*—as justification for her legal actions. Rahimieh observes:

> Supported by Judge Deldar and a receptive female film crew, Jamilih combines her attempt to make her husband agree to the terms of a renewed legal contract between husband and wife with a self-affirmation in terms of her own honor. . . . Quoting her sister-in-law, Jamilih insists that women, like men, are entitled to *ghiyrat*. Her use of the law and dominant cultural values endows her with an agency in which she clearly revels. (11)

Jamilih's appropriation and feminization of *ghiyrat* is inherently threatening to the gendered hierarchy in Iranian culture, in which woman is positioned as the embodiment of male honor. By seeing women as a reflection of masculine dignity, Iranian culture fails to acknowledge women's individual needs and desires. Jamilih's demand that women have access to *ghiyrat* challenges Iranian familial, cultural, and legal structures that limit women to occupying roles in the service of others—as daughters, as wives, and as mothers. Although Iranian men are also understood to have responsibilities within the family, they are at greater liberty than women to pursue their individual goals and desires.

Describing Jamilih's divulgence of her emotions to her ally, the camera, Rahimieh writes:

> This can be seen as an instance when the presence of the camera and the female film crew changes the dynamics of the courtroom. Beyond the filmmakers' desire to lay bare the process that brought them into close interaction with those they filmed, I think the awareness of the camera and the filmmakers allows the women to offer opinions they would otherwise not voice in a courtroom. (11)

Mir-Hosseini herself recognizes that "the presence of an all-woman crew changed the gender balance in the courtroom, and undoubtedly gave several women petitioners courage" (2002a, 185). Female bonding and the transformation of patriarchal space into a female homosocial space in *Divorce Iranian Style* destabilizes conventional gender and power relations. Women's demands to be treated as individuals with specific needs and wants is fundamentally challenging to the secondary position relegated to them both within traditional Iranian culture and under the Islamic Republic. It is thus the communal quality of the homosocial space that allows for the articulation of a woman's individual will.

Mockery is one of the devices used by women to enable the dismantling—and demystification—of *ghiyrat* as the quintessence of Iranian masculinity. In one of the early scenes of *Divorce Iranian Style,* Massy launches a fervent appeal to the judge, asking him to grant her divorce. Using her husband's alleged sexual impotence as the main issue of contention, she attempts to persuade the amiable Judge Deldar:

> [My husband] has sexual problems. I found out on our wedding night,
> but I kept quiet not to shame my family. I cried all through our
> honeymoon. Everywhere we went, I was in tears. . . . I'm ashamed
> to say it: we didn't do anything on our wedding night. Afterwards,
> I always had to make the first move.

As her husband and his brother vehemently protest her claims, she turns to her husband and asks repeatedly: "Do you or do you not have sexual problems?" She chases him out of the courtroom, hounding him for a response. The camera shows the judge struggling to contain his mirth at the comical scene unfolding before him. Shortly afterward, there is a ruckus in the hall and the unhappy husband returns, with Massy in hot pursuit. He breaks down in hysterics and pleads for the judge's sympathy for his plight. This episode is a humorous instance of the ways in which women like Massy take advantage of the restricted avenues available to them when seeking divorce. By using one of the few provisions available to her for divorce (male impotence), she undermines her husband's cherished *ghiyrat* by emasculating him. He cannot satisfy her sexually, complains Massy, since she is always the one who initiates sexual intercourse. Most shamefully, he is incapable of performing one of the most valued masculine duties: ensuring his progeny.

One of the most effective moments in the documentary involves Paniz, the young daughter of the court secretary, Mrs. Maher. When the judge leaves the courtroom, Paniz takes her seat at his desk, places a makeshift turban (a white ski hat) over her braided pigtails and proceeds to call the court to order. Her admonishment of the (imagined) wayward, abusive husband before her is simultaneously painful and delightful to watch. In a culture where children, especially girls, are instructed not to question authority, and given a legal system that prohibits women from becoming judges, Paniz's spirited parody of the divorce court leaves viewers with a powerful image.

The female homosocial space of the court addresses the issue of *ghiyrat* by performing a mockery of the entire judicial system as Paniz demonstrates in her clever parody, by reappropriating it as does Jamilih, or by public humiliation as Massy manages so effectively. One of the paradoxes of current Iranian legislation under the Islamic Republic is that the climate of rigorous morality is enforced through a sexualization of language and legal discourse. While Iranian cultural traditions and the elaborate discursive ritual of *ta'aruf* require tact, subtlety, and ambiguity, the legal loophole enabling women to initiate divorce proceedings necessitates the foregrounding of explicit and straightforward language.[15] Currently, an Iranian woman can apply for divorce on very limited grounds. She must be able to prove that her husband is physically abusive or mentally ill. Alternatively, she can argue that her husband is unable to support his family financially or that he is impotent. Massy's sexually explicit language can thus be attributed to the gender imbalance in the courtroom. The presence of a supportive female community lends her courage to air her concerns with candor to a judge who, in his official capacity in an Islamic family court, is the arbiter of moral and restrained conduct.

Another petitioner, Maryam, who battles against losing custody of her youngest daughter, claims that she will divorce her second husband to keep her child. She later retracts that statement and asks defiantly why Iranian child custody laws must force her to choose between her love for her (new) husband and her love for her child. Maryam allows Longinotto and Mir-Hosseini to film her and her husband in their home, and speaks openly about the rights of women in marriage: "A woman wants love and affection," she says to the camera.

The documentary follows Maryam's case closely and reveals the cruel impact of child custody laws on the lives of divorced women. Although Judge Deldar chastises Maryam's ex-husband for his elder daughter's deteriorating scholastic performance since leaving her mother's care, Iranian law is unequivocal in denying Maryam custody of her children. The documentary ends by showing Maryam's utter devastation when she realizes that all avenues are closed to her and that she will lose both her children.[16]

Maryam demands a radical revisioning of marriage and love as they are currently configured within an Iranian legal and cultural context. This is a position with which Mrs. Maher, the court secretary, cannot sympathize: "This woman has no maternal feelings. She gave up her children for lust," she tells Mir-Hosseini. Mir-Hosseini then asks her: "Must only mothers suffer? Women want happiness too." According to Rahimieh:

> The terms Mrs. Maher uses to describe motherhood as founded upon self-sacrifice resonate deeply in twentieth-century Iranian discourses about women's place in the nation. . . . What Mrs. Maher's views about Maryam point up is the need to ask why a good or responsible mother is necessarily contingent on women abandoning their own desires and needs. (9, 10)

If *Divorce Iranian Style* is about mothers desperate to break away from the heteropatriarchal family and to hold on to their children, *Runaway* focuses on the effects of dysfunctional domestic situations on the lives of children. Rayhaneh House, the shelter for runaway girls featured in this documentary, provides young girls a temporary refuge from sometimes extremely abusive domestic situations. *Runaway* offers a look at the tragic circumstances of young women who escape (if only temporarily, in some cases) their oppressive families. Afzali's *The Ladies' Room* is filmed entirely in a women's public washroom in Laleh Park, a large public park in downtown Tehran. To put it bluntly, *The Ladies' Room* shows us where the most unfortunate subjects in *Runaway* may end up. These documentaries provide us with a glimpse into dynamic, although transitory, communities of women; these spaces offer women the support that is often denied them at the macrolevel of the state.

In *Runaway,* we are introduced to a self-contained and productive homosocial space: this is a center run by women for women, but from within the parameters of the state.[17] The documentary begins immediately by presenting us with an unusual act: the camera focuses on a young girl singing the *Azan,* the call for prayer, which is a special privilege usually reserved for a man. This is not an entirely unimaginable situation: when no men are around, a woman has the right to step in and announce the beginning of prayers, but it remains an unconventional circumstance. Most important, however, this introductory scene highlights the absence of men in this space and in this context.

The fact that the movie begins with the image of a young girl singing the *Azan* and ends with the voice of another girl singing a famous ballad, "Du Panjirih" (Two Windows), by the darling of Iran's popular music world, Googoosh, make for remarkable bookends to this film.[18] As we hear the singing of this melancholy pop song, the camera focuses on the retreating backs of another reunited family leaving the center; this is a particularly tragic reunion (and one the counselors at the center did not encourage), as the departing girl is almost certainly going to relive the abuses inflicted upon her by her tyrannical and drug-addicted father and brother. As they leave Rayhaneh House, we hear the first two stanzas and the first two lines of the sixth stanza of "Du Panjirih":

> In a stone wall
> Two windows are imprisoned
> Both tired and lonely
> One of them you, one of them me
> The wall is made of black stone
>
> Cold, hard, granite stone
> The lock of silence
> Is placed on our lips
>
> We must remain confined
> We stay alive only while captive.[19]

This is a powerful, and in many ways, disheartening song about an impossible and paradoxical state of being: on the one hand, these two windows are contained by the heaviness, the restrictive quality of a cold, hard, granite wall; on the other hand, the only way for these windows to exist, to stay intact is for the wall to hold them up. In other words, the very system that oppresses them is also what keeps them alive.

At the same time, the last two stanzas of this song (not sung in the film) are about imagining alternatives, and creating spaces of possibility in severely constrictive circumstances:

Oh that this wall would crumble
You and I could die together
In another world, we will hold each other's hands

Perhaps there in people's hearts
There will be no more malice
Between their windows
There will be no more walls.

Thus, while this song posits a bleak view of a current system of oppression and confinement, it offers a kind of popular utopianism, a projection of desire for better things. It also illustrates the ways in which women imagine other possibilities, other ways of being in the face of what might appear to be impossible circumstances.

As I observed earlier, *Runaway* is framed by two radical moments: the singing of the *Azan* by a young girl and the singing by another young girl (whom we do not see) of Googoosh's song about a system, or a life, of oppression. The fact that we do not see the young girl singing is worthy of note because Googoosh herself has been banned from singing in Iran since the 1979 revolution;[20] the young girl's physical absence on the screen draws particular attention to the silencing of Googoosh and other women singers who are not permitted to perform under the current regime. In this way, the documentary begins and ends by defying several restrictions against women's public self-expression.

A further challenge to the discourse of the patriarchal and Islamic state is the film's focus on Rayhaneh House as a space that lends itself to homosocial female bonding. At the same time, the ultimate goal of the center is to return the young women to their families, if at all possible, because the place of a traditional Iranian woman's place is understood to be with her family. The young girls who chafe under severe restrictions to their mobility, those who are kept locked up at home and even prevented from going to school, are encouraged to return home and endure these hardships until they are old enough to take care of themselves. As the film documents reunion after reunion, we are left with a sense of despondency that nothing will ever change for these women. One of the most striking aspects of this film is that the violence of the patriarchal nation-state is mirrored at the microlevel within the Iranian family.

Despite the potential containment of the film's radical possibilities for the reconfiguration of Iranian gender roles (through the center's ultimate upholding of the status quo as it returns girls to their families), the most effective challenge to this possible containment is the homosocial bonding between the women. One of the stories *Runaway* traces is the developing friendship between Sitarih and Parissa. Sitarih's father forced her, as well as her now dead mother and sister, into a life of prostitution to support his heroin addiction. For three years after her mother's death, Sitarih lived and worked on the streets until she came to the center for help. Parissa initially tells a convoluted tale about her mother's death and other family problems that have led her to escape her home, and Sitarih sympathizes with the fabricated plight Parissa describes. Eventually, Parissa confesses that she does have a family; they appear to be a traditional and oppressive family in many ways, but without the obvious drug and physical abuse problems from which most of the runaways have escaped. Despite these radical differences between them, and despite Parissa's earlier deception, Sitarih remains her close friend and tries to give her courage to return to her family, the explicit mandate of the center. There is an instant bond and affection between the two women, who repeatedly declare their deep affection for each other, and an undeniable homoerotic undercurrent to the women's friendship.

In one poignant scene, Sitarih tries to lend her support to Parissa, who must return to the heteropatriarchal family fold: her father, her uncle, and her fiancé have come to take her home with them. Sitarih stands next to Parissa's chair, remaining close to her and speaking on her behalf about her devotion to her family. In this scene, Sitarih speaks for Parissa and while doing so, strokes her fondly as a husband or a lover might. The men pointedly avoid looking at Sitarih. Parissa's father shifts uncomfortably in his seat as Sitarih's inappropriate presence clearly makes the men uneasy; this is a woman whose dubious life experiences place her beneath the radar of the state. This is a woman absent at the national level, but whose obvious existence and noticeable presence in the room and in Parissa's life create a tension between the heteronormative discourse of family duty and the potential erotics of women's homosocial bonding. This tension is defused, however, as the film's subtle representation of the women's eroticized friendship gives way to Parissa's family reunion and her impending marriage.

This family reunion is an important moment in the film for several reasons: first, it challenges what we might presume to be the very premise of the film—that family reunions are the desired outcome for these young women. The scene with Parissa's family contrasts what appears to be a relatively healthy women's community, which Parissa clearly does not want to leave, with an oppressive and traditional family structure. When in the presence of the patriarchal family, represented by the presence of the three principal male figures in her life, Parissa can assume only one posture: that of abjection and apology; however, we see from her previous interactions in the female community that this is not her necessary posture. Second, Parissa's virginity is the focus of her father's, and presumably her fiancé's, concern. In the reunion scene in which Parissa's family drinks tea and eats sweets with the director of the women's center in celebration of her impending marriage, Parissa's father takes pains to repeat, presumably for the benefit of the ever-present camera, his future son-in-law, and his brother, that Parissa is still a virgin (lest there be any doubt about the honor of his family name). Third, the idea that home is the woman's natural place is ironized by the obvious comfort Parissa has when not at home. Sitarih's final comment to Parissa, "Cheer up, you're going home," necessarily invites doubt. Finally, this scene underscores female homosociality as a disruption not only of the structure of traditional Iranian gender relations, but also of the regime of heterosexuality imposed by the discourses of modernity and nationalism.

How, then, do such women's homosocial communities work? Rather than reproducing familiar (and unsuccessful) models of sisterhood, they offer temporary models of community and support. Afzali's *The Ladies' Room* is another fascinating example of the ways in which a transient, temporary space can be turned into a productive, transformative space. In this case, the public washroom, a physical structure and space owned by the state, which is guided by patriarchal laws and the language of Islamic allegiance, is paradoxically transformed into a dynamic homosocial space. The fundamental tension of the film is that the *The Ladies' Room* is a site of both filthiness and cleanliness. The opening scene of the documentary shows a woman sweeping the floor as the camera then pans to another woman washing her hair in the sink. This scene is followed by the cleaning woman performing *vusu:* washing herself, purifying herself for her prayers. The prayer rug is rolled out on the washroom floor and she performs her religious duties. These introductory scenes, then, highlight the paradox of this community and of the film itself: the ritual of purification in preparation for prayer and the act of praying itself are acts of physical and moral cleanliness, but these purifying acts are taking place in a site associated with dirtiness. Furthermore, the women gathering in this washroom are from the lower echelons of society: they are, for the most part, drug addicts or prostitutes. At a symbolic level, then, these women are not clean or pure.

The washroom, a site of state-sponsored cleanliness, thus becomes a gathering place, a meeting place for transient women who would, culturally, be perceived as unclean and impure, and who do not belong to a recognizable or respected group. Throughout the documentary, there is much discussion of virginity, another measure of cultural and state-policed cleanliness for women. The public washroom as the site of the women's gathering is significant as it is a venue that carries out the state function of public sanitation and health. Similarly, the morals police in Iran function as guardians of public and national health; thus both are state tools for the policing and enforcing of the nation's health and morals.

In an early moment in the film, a group of women gather in the washroom to drink tea and chat. The subject of discussion is a woman known to all of them and whom they are savaging in her absence for her false claims of virginity. The women in the washroom disparage her for a number of reasons: First, she seems to be in a more comfortable economic position than the women in the washroom. They claim that she prostitutes herself only to feel young, not because she is in need of money. This lack of financial need divides her at the level of economic class from this community. It also allows women who are regarded as immoral by their betters to criticize the morality of another. Second, according to the women's suspicions, she has ties to the state, as they claim she offers her sexual services to the state authorities in order to evade their official censure. This is particularly noteworthy because not only is this community of women outside of state control, but also it is directly antithetical to its official ideals of femininity. So, this woman's consorting with the enemy, as it were, makes her the target of the women's savagery. Further, this public space of the women's washroom in a city park is technically under state control. In other words, this transient and potentially subversive women's community is operating right under the state's nose. Finally, the group mocks this woman's false claims to virginity, the very attribute upon which the state's concept of female virtue rests. There is a long tradition in nationalist discourses of the strength and future of the state residing in the virtue of the nation's women, and this notion is clearly challenged not just in this scene, but in the film as a whole.

Throughout the documentary, the nastiness among the women is, at times, confounding, making this film both intriguing and extremely challenging. *The Ladies' Room* presents a model of female bonding very different from the one we see in *Divorce Iranian Style* or *Runaway,* which offer a much more recognizable model of community. The women in *The Ladies' Room* actively challenge and ridicule the cultural ideal of the demure, modest Iranian woman who embodies the concept of *sharm,* a culturally and gender-specific ideal to which all Iranian women are expected to aspire.[21]

The ways in which this transient population in *The Ladies' Room* talks openly and caustically about other women's claims to virginity suggest a real challenge to the concept of *sharm* upon which *ghiyrat,* or male honor, is predicated. These ideal feminine and masculine attributes are inherent to the discourse of heterosexuality upon which official state rhetoric rests. As in *Divorce Iranian Style,* women use mockery to interrogate established notions about women's *sharm* and men's *ghiyrat.* But unlike *Divorce Iranian Style,* mockery in *The Ladies' Room* is not just turned against men, but against the women who presumably submit to the conservative cultural demands made of them. This is a place where traditional gender roles and expectations, as embraced by women, are not only questioned but mercilessly ridiculed. This presents a significant challenge to a feminist viewer: how can we understand a form of women's community and bonding that relies upon often cruel and vicious verbal exchanges?

As viewers in the West, we experience a disconnect from the subjects of the film. It is difficult to have any sympathy for the subjects here as their model of community support and "female bonding" is so radically alien from the more recognizable model of women's community with which presumably most Western audiences are familiar: one of a celebratory and emotive sisterhood characterized by harmony and mutual support. The model of sisterhood in *The Ladies' Room* emphasizes and maintains hierarchies between women, and bonding seems to take place through the exchange of caustic commentary rather than through the expression of generosity and kindness to all sisters. I am not suggesting, of course, that a Western model of 1970s sisterhood is unproblematically predicated upon the promise of equality between all sisters. Rather, I am trying to make a distinction at the level of discourse and representation: the discourse of sisterhood promises the collapse of hierarchies and equality for all. The discourse of this alternative "washroom sisterhood" makes no such promises. It highlights inequalities; it reinforces difference; and it sustains itself through sarcasm and mockery.

But there is a further reason for the disconnect between audience and subject here, and this has to do with the problems inherent to the genre of the documentary. All three documentaries discussed here are examples of the mode of participatory documentary, which "involve[s] the ethics and politics of encounter" (Nichols 2001, 116). This style of participatory documentary highlights the power dynamics between those behind the movie camera and the subjects fixed in its lens. All three share the strategy of structuring their narratives through the interview form, which depends on a hierarchical model of information exchange (Nichols 2001, 51).

Despite Nichols's valid claim that the interview is already compromised by its form, as it immediately posits an unequal relationship and hierarchy between interviewer and subject, in *Divorce Iranian Style* and *Runaway,* viewers get the sense that these subjects are willing participants. Although there are notable differences between *Divorce Iranian Style* and *Runaway,* it seems to me that Mir-Hosseini's and Longinotto's approach and sensitivity to their subjects remain the same. In her article on the making of *Divorce Iranian Style,* Mir-Hosseini makes it clear that the women in the documentary were approached beforehand and agreed to be filmed:

> We never filmed without consent. . . . Before each new case, I
> approached the parties concerned in the corridor, explained who we
> were and what our film was about and asked whether they would agree
> to participate. Some agreed, others refused. Perhaps unsurprisingly,
> most women welcomed the project and wanted to be filmed. (2002a, 186)

Their experience of filming *Runaway* is similar to their work on *Divorce Iranian Style* in that the women and young girls in the film all consented to be filmed and appear to engage easily with the filmmakers behind the camera. According to Mir-Hosseini, "The girls accepted us almost immediately; as they began to trust us with their stories, we—the three women in the film crew . . . soon became part of the healing process" (2002b, 23). In both *Divorce Iranian Style* and *Runaway,* the women interviewed often turn to the camera as to an ally or a confidante; the eye of the camera appears to be a sympathetic one, which, as Mir-Hosseini states above, participates in the women's "healing process."

In contrast, in *The Ladies' Room,* we are left with the distinct impression that permission to film the women has not been secured ahead of time, and that the camera's intrusion into their lives is perpetuating the violence to which these women have been already subjected. Afzali cajoles the most vulnerable members of society—drug addicts, prostitutes, the mentally ill—into answering her probing questions. At various points in the documentary, she appears literally to chase some of her subjects around the washroom, badgering them to be interviewed. For example, one of the first women Afzali interviews initially ducks for cover and then runs away from the camera when she realizes she is being filmed. Afzali pleads with her to answer a few questions and the resulting interview is extremely disturbing: the woman has clearly been scarred by years of drug abuse and a life of prostitution. Her response is both tragic, as she relates the events of her life, and confusing, as she relays a contradictory jumble of conflicting events. This interview foregrounds some of the most crucial problems with the documentary form: how do we watch a scene in which a filmmaker, from a privileged class as suggested by her enunciation and accent, let alone her profession, insists on painful testimony from a clearly damaged woman? The discursive context here is already "overdetermined" by the structure of the interview, which "testifies to a power relation in which institutional hierarchy and regulation pertain to speech itself" (Nichols 2001, 50).

While the three documentaries appear to differ in their motivations and approach, they share certain similarities: they all demonstrate the importance of women's homosocial communities, and they function as radical contestations of the dominant discourse of heterosociality that guides Iranian social relations. Although the feature films discussed above have played to much popular acclaim to audiences in Iran, *Divorce Iranian Style, Runaway,* and *The Ladies' Room* have yet to be screened in public cinemas in the country. However, all three documentaries have been shown at independent film festivals in Iran: *Divorce Iranian Style* and *Runaway* were screened at the Forough Film Festival, a festival for women documentary filmmakers, as well as at a number of universities and in Khaneh-ye Film (Film House).[22] Similarly, *The Ladies' Room* has been screened at several Iranian film festivals, including the Forough Festival, and won best film award in March 2004 at the Kish International Film Festival.[23] After several screenings at film festivals in Iran, however, *The Ladies' Room* was unable to secure a government permit for further participation at Iranian festivals, although it has not been officially banned by the state.

In the West, all three documentaries have been actively promoted and celebrated on the international film festival circuit, and *Divorce Iranian Style* in particular has sparked much discussion on the status of Iranian women. The popular reception of these documentaries in the West is, perhaps, not surprising since the nature of the genre is such that it promises to offer a glimpse into an otherwise forbidden world. In their own way, these documentaries offer Western viewers the long-desired glimpse behind the veil. In a review of *Divorce Iranian Style,* Nick Poppy invokes the familiar image of the veiled woman as invisible and silent: "Don't let their veils fools you; these are *outspoken* women" (1999, 1; emphasis mine). Poppy's article begins by evoking stereotypical images of postrevolutionary Iran as impenetrable, unknowable, and threatening. He then remarks: "But there are signs, too, that Iran is starting to open itself up to foreign eyes, or allowing at least access to a keyhole to peep through" (1). Poppy's language invokes the notion of concealment and emergence, veiled mysteries and unveiled truths, discussed in previous chapters. It is precisely this assumption of gaining "access to the truth"—an assumption inherent to the genre of the documentary—that appeals to Western audiences and repels (some) Iranian viewers.[24]

In his analysis of the genre of the documentary, Paul Wells observes that "[i]t is often the case that documentary is believed to be the recording of actuality—raw footage of real events as they happen, real people as they speak, real life as it occurs, spontaneous and unmediated" (1996, 168). Indeed, these documentaries create the illusion of "raw footage of real events." In *Divorce Iranian Style,* the camera enters into the private space of women's cloakrooms, taking the audience with it. In some ways, the film undermines its own achievements by reinscribing Western voyeurism as it affords the viewer a glimpse into women's private space. The cloakroom scene promotes the sense of the "real" as an undoctored, unedited version of life in Iran by affording an intimate view of the effects of Iranian law on women's bodies. The cloakroom functions as an in-between space, mediating between the outside world and the world of the courtroom. This is the space where the arm of Iranian law extends, demanding that women conform to its regulations. But at the same time, the official discourse of authority is subverted by the eye of the camera that shows most women disobeying the Islamic Republic's rigorous dress codes. One by one, women who enter the cloakroom are asked to remove their makeup in order to be permitted access to the courthouse. There are boxes of Kleenex on hand for women to remove their heavy makeup; one woman even asks to borrow a chador from the female clothing inspectors, the implication being that spare chadors are regularly kept on hand for the numerous *bad-hijabi. Divorce Iranian Style* thus reveals women's continuous subversion of the laws regulating their behavior and clothing.

For the Western reader and viewer, what makes these documentaries so palatable is that they perhaps deliver, on one level, comfortable notions of what it means to be an oppressed Iranian woman through the perspective of "authentic" others. But more important, I believe, these films disclose a model of women's liberation that has the potential to undermine the very patriarchy (the *ghiyrat* or male honor) that informs Iranian cultural and political traditions, and the state that sustains it and is sustained by it. *Divorce Iranian Style, Runaway,* and *The Ladies' Room* provide us with a glimpse into alternative communities of women; these spaces offer women the support that is denied them at the macrolevel of the state. In these documentaries, the women are faced with the task of imagining their own limited and temporary communities as an alternative site of belonging. These female homosocial communities enable women to move outside of the heterosexual and patriarchal family units that position them as extensions of their fathers, their brothers, and, eventually, their husbands.

In *Divorce Iranian Style,* we see women having to choose between motherhood (maintaining custody of their children by remaining in an unhappy marriage) and their desire for independence; in *Runaway,* most of the young women are sent back to their (often abusive) families; in *The Ladies' Room,* the prostitutes and drug addicts roam the streets of Tehran and the public park, subject to the whim of their male clientele. Despite these distressing scenarios, there is nevertheless a sense that the patriarchal family order—and by extension, the state—is constantly being, if only temporarily, disrupted. These moments of disruption can become productive sites of contestation and change for a resilient Iranian feminism that works within the limits of a constrictive system, a feminism that, to borrow from de Certeau, is "always on the watch for opportunities that must be seized 'on the wing'" and forced to "continually manipulate events in order to turn them into 'opportunities'" (1984, xix).

Communicating across Disciplines Post 9/11

I N THIS STUDY, I have attempted to trace the ways in which a certain truth about the abject Muslim (specifically Iranian) woman in need of rescue has become consolidated in liberal feminist discourse. As I tried to establish in the introduction and throughout this book, my argument is not predicated upon an East/West binary division; rather, I am interested in the cementing of certain stereotypes of the Muslim woman in a type of liberal feminism to which some "Western" as well as Muslim/Iranian feminists subscribe. I have endeavored to gesture to the ways in which discourses reproduce themselves, and thus have strived to "tear away . . . their virtual self-evidence, and to free the problems that they pose; to recognize that they are not the tranquil locus on the basis of which other questions . . . may be posed, but that they themselves pose a whole cluster of questions" (Foucault 1986, 26).

This book has been concerned first with critiquing a history of feminism and a discourse of sisterhood in Iran. By undertaking such a study, I have also attempted to bring to bear the critical tools and analytical strategies of postcolonial theory on the Middle Eastern context. The fact that I felt such an enterprise was necessary highlights both the extent to which the Middle East has been absent from postcolonial debates, and the postcolonial absent from scholarship on the Middle East. But I will return for a moment to my critique of feminism.

For feminist scholars interested in cross-cultural or transnational feminist alliances, David Scott's query regarding the future direction of postcolonial studies is an important one to consider, "whether the moment of normalization of a paradigm is not also the moment when it is necessary to reconstruct and reinterrogate the ground of questions themselves through which it was brought into being in the first place" (1999, 8). A similar reinterrogation of feminism has become particularly pressing in a post-9/11 context, in which Western liberal feminists champion once again the rescue of their Muslim sisters from beneath the brutalizing weight of Islam. The "normalization of [the] paradigm" of sisterhood requires a persistent and continuous critique by feminists who no longer see it as a strategic metaphor of resistance to an overarching and amorphous patriarchy and who recognize the imperialist and regulatory impulses inherent to the discourse.

One of the disturbing transformations of the discourse of sisterhood is, particularly since the events of 9/11, its alliance with a chauvinistic nationalism predicated upon a xenophobic and fundamentalist religious rhetoric propagated by both the U.S. mainstream media and the government. There is an increasing and unsettling shift in the West from what, traditionally, has been understood as a tension between feminist and nationalist discourses to a merging of interests between liberal feminism and a xenophobic nationalism. This conflation of feminist and nationalist energies drives a further wedge between a liberal feminist discourse that works with the state to perpetuate its own agenda and an antiestablishment feminism that works from within the parameters of the state, but against its antifeminist aims. (My reading, in chapter 4, of transient homosocial spaces within state-controlled and monitored spaces in Iranian documentary films is an example of the latter model of feminism.)

A productive and egalitarian transnational feminist network remains a challenge for feminists today, as historically and now, the language of feminism has been successfully co-opted by an antifeminist state rhetoric that promotes and supports what Minoo Moallem has called "civilizational thinking": "a powerful modern discourse influenced by the Enlightenment and the idea of progress dividing the civility of the

'West' from the barbarism of the 'Rest'" (2005, 161). Judith Butler rightly cautions, though, that despite its most recent co-optation by the Bush administration,

> it would surely be a mistake to gauge the progress of feminism by its success as a colonial project. It seems more crucial than ever to disengage feminism from its First World presumption and to use the resources of feminist theory, and activism, to rethink the meaning of the tie, the bond, the alliance, the relation, as they are imagined and lived in the horizon of a counterimperialist egalitarianism. (2004, 41–42)

The problem, however, is not just the appropriation of a discourse by an antifeminist state; the manipulation of feminist discourse in the service of colonial aims is not novel. What is distressing in the post-9/11 context is the unnuanced and uncritical support of the Bush and Blair administrations' rhetoric of the "us/them" divide, the "civilized world versus the terrorists" by liberal feminists in the West. The work of the Feminist Majority Foundation on behalf of Afghan women is one such example. On the one hand, their work has been extremely effective, as they were instrumental in drawing the world's attention, before 9/11, to the courageous resistance work of RAWA (Revolutionary Association of the Women of Afghanistan) in the face of the atrocities committed by the Taliban. On the other hand, one of their most public and problematic fund-raising campaigns was the selling of mesh fabrics symbolizing the burka, which American women pinned to their clothes in solidarity with their Afghan sisters. Another recent example of the overlap between liberal feminism and imperialist goals is the public unveiling of Zoya, a representative of RAWA, at a gala performance of Eve Ensler's *The Vagina Monologues* at Madison Square Garden in February 2001. After Oprah Winfrey's reading of Ensler's "Under the Burqa," she literally unveiled a burka-clad Zoya in front of a crowd of eighteen thousand people.[1] This reproduction of the nineteenth-century missionary drive to rescue Muslim women suffering "under the yoke of Islam" is all the more alarming as it is now almost indistinguishably aligned with current Anglo-American imperialist objectives.

I have raised here the specter of 9/11, as the repercussions of that day continue to be felt and make it incumbent upon us as feminists, as postcolonialists, and as scholars who work on the Middle East, to critique the legacy of colonial discourse in the rhetoric and foreign policies of Western states, most recently demonstrated by the "liberation" of Afghanistan, the occupation of Iraq, and the threats of regime change leveled against Iran. We need also to consider carefully how feminist discourse participates in, indeed enables, colonial interventions through the perpetuation of such representations as the suffering Muslim sister in need of rescue or enlightenment. Adopting a critical position in relation to the established discourse of the "civilized" world, however, has become increasingly difficult. In September 2002, Daniel Pipes established his notorious Web site Campus Watch, which critics have described as a modern-day McCarthy-ite witch hunt against university professors who dare to criticize U.S. foreign policy in the Middle East. The Pipes Web site epitomizes the climate of fear and silencing around any criticism of the Bush administration. Voicing her own opposition to the now heavily regulated realm of public debate, Butler has argued:

> Dissent and debate depend upon the inclusion of those who maintain critical views of state policy and civic culture remaining part of a larger public discussion of the value of policies and politics. To charge those who voice critical views with treason, terrorist-sympathizing, anti-Semitism, moral relativism, postmodernism, juvenile behavior, collaboration, anachronistic Leftism, is to seek to destroy the credibility not of the views that are held, but of the persons who hold them. . . . It is precisely because one does not want to lose one's status as a viable speaking being that one does not say what one thinks. (2004, xix–xx)

In light of the not-so-subtle forces of censorship, we need to recognize the ways in which the (potentially) political charges of Middle East, feminist, and postcolonial studies can complement each other and how an interdisciplinary scholarship might enable a rigorous rethinking of established truth claims about, for example, the violent Muslim man and the abject Muslim woman, or about "civilized" and "barbarous" nations.

I make an argument for disciplinary openness at the beginning of this book, and think it is important to return to it here. Afsaneh Najmabadi, whose work has greatly influenced my own thinking, suggests that a postcolonial perspective on Iranian history belies a type of continued colonial mentality: "That we worry about the question of agency in one direction but never consider the impact of 'the East' on 'the West' as an issue of denial of agency for Europe is a colonial/anticolonial legacy that continues to inform our current thinking" (2005, 6). Mohamad Tavakoli-Targhi, another eminent scholar, begins his influential book *Refashioning Iran* by stating:

> Said's *Orientalism* provided the foundation for immensely productive scholarly works on European colonial agency but these works rarely explore the agency and imagination of Europe's Other, who are depicted as passive and traditional. This denial of agency and *coevality* to the "Rest" provided the ground for the exceptionality of the "West." (2001, 33–34)

Although Najmabadi and Tavakoli-Targhi are not the openly hostile critics of postcolonial theory that others in Middle East studies are (indeed, I have immense respect for their careful scholarship), even their more thoughtful questioning of postcolonialism's value misses a critical point. What both Najamabadi and Tavakoli-Targhi overlook is the regulatory and continuing impact of discourse on the subject-constitution of the Muslim other in Western thought. In fact, Said states explicitly that only by understanding Orientalism as a discourse can one come to terms with the way in which the West was able to produce and control the Orient (3).

Whether there was a two-way cultural exchange in the nineteenth-century between the Persians and the British, for instance, is immaterial. What matters is that certain "truths" about Persia became sedimented, circulating broadly, and gaining widespread legitimacy in a range of contexts: popular, literary, academic, economic, and military. Foucault stresses that not every utterance can achieve the status of discourse; for instance, a Persian traveler to Britain who records his impressions of the country and its people in his journal will not have a notable effect on the ways in which the British or "the West" circulates broadly, as discourses gain legitimacy and power through a complex system of institutional authority. Thus, while representations of the West by Eastern travelers, for instance, were certainly articulated, recorded, and circulated, discourse authorizes which views are most "true" and have the most power. It seems to me that the resistance to Said's theory of Orientalism in Middle East studies often hinges on an oversight of the Foucauldian view of how discourse works.

While I certainly do not want to suggest that the *only* way to conduct anti-imperialist, political scholarship is via postcolonial studies, I *do* want to create a space for it in Middle East studies, just as I want to create a space for the Middle East in postcolonial studies. It is vexing that postcolonial studies continues to ignore the significance of the Middle East to the discipline; perhaps the reason for this oversight can be partly attributed to the fact that colonization did not take the same shape or force in the Middle East as it did, for example, in South Asia or Africa. At the same time, postcolonialists appear to have little difficulty integrating analyses of settler societies such as Australia, Canada, and New Zealand, whose postcolonial status is highly fraught, into the field. In the United States, most of the scholarship on the Middle East is relegated to history departments, or to area studies, itself a colonial hangover from the days of Orientalist studies. In Canada, scholarly interest in the region has escalated since 9/11; this is reflected in the expansion of Middle East studies departments at Canadian universities, but this expansion of interest remains bound within the same disciplinary strictures: predominantly history and religious studies. This is an egregious oversight that needs to be redressed by those who claim social and political commitments in their work.

One way of challenging homogeneous representations of the Muslim world as backward and in need of civilizing, and of breaking down colonial stereotypes of the Middle East, is to bring together perspectives and methodologies from various disciplines, thereby opening a space for a rethinking of existing social and political paradigms. Butler reminds us, in the context of her critique of the current climate of fear and censorship in the United States, that "the foreclosure of critique empties the public domain of debate and democratic contestation itself, so that debate becomes the exchange of views among the like-minded, and criticism, which ought to be central to any democracy, becomes a fugitive and suspect activity" (2004, xx). This is an apt statement that also can be leveled against the guardians of disciplines who believe that the integrity of their particular field might be in some way compromised by looking outside of itself.

In an era during which insularity and self-censorship are encouraged, an interdisciplinary scholarship encourages scholars to speak to each other, rather than at cross purposes, through respectful debate. This type of healthy dissent can, I believe, offer alternative representations of the Middle East and the Muslim subject in Western popular, intellectual, and political discourses. And such a destabilization of firmly established representations can present a challenge to an imperialist agenda in which the world is divided simply into civilized nations that act to protect democracy, and rogue nations that act out of a bloodthirsty allegiance to a primitive and barbarous faith.

Acknowledgments

THIS BOOK HAS BEEN IN GESTATION for a long time; it has received the support of numerous people whom I would like to take the opportunity to thank. I am grateful to Stephen Slemon for his insights on how to bring Iran into postcolonial debates and for his constant encouragement of my work. Nasrin Rahimieh has been an invaluable intellectual and emotional resource, offering me her expertise on Iranian feminism, most recently reading and offering her keen insights on chapter 3, "Global Sisters in Revolutionary Iran." Patricia Clements's constructive criticism on an early version of this chapter inspired me to rethink my approach and my framing of the confluence of events that led to the fraught intersection of Iranian and Western feminist activism during the revolutionary period. I would also like to thank my former colleague in the English department at the University of Winnipeg, Mavis Reimer, for providing her thoughtful comments on chapter 3. Ali Behdad has been an immeasurable source of support and inspiration for me; he read this manuscript in its early form with remarkable care and offered extraordinarily detailed and helpful suggestions for the revision process. While all of these people have assisted in shaping this book with their valuable comments, any errors or shortcomings are, of course, mine.

I am also indebted to Neil Besner, dean of humanities at the University of Winnipeg, who very generously granted me the six-month research leave I needed to complete revisions.

There are a few people on whom I have imposed with numerous questions, big and small, and I am obliged to them all for taking the time to respond to my various e-mail queries and for pointing me in the right direction: Mohammad Atebbai, Hamid Dabashi, Ziba Mir-Hosseini, and Hamid Naficy. At *Women Make Movies,* Christie George, Olivia Newman, and Sarah Reynolds offered me tremendous support by providing me access to films and film stills and by answering a host of film-related questions.

At the University of Minnesota Press, I would like to extend my gratitude to my editor, Richard Morrison, for finding merit in this project and for helping to bring it to fruition; Adam Brunner for graciously providing answers to my numerous queries; and Michele Hodgson for her meticulous copyediting. I would also like to thank my former student, Dana Landry, for help in formatting this manuscript and Eileen Quam for preparing the index.

The presence of my family can be felt everywhere in this book: my grandmother, Effat Shegefti, a model of a strong Iranian woman; my parents, Safidokht Safipour and Iradj Naghibi, who endured the travails of life in the diaspora to provide a brighter future for their daughters; and my sister, Mana, for her unwavering emotional support.

Finally, I would like to thank Andrew O'Malley for his remarkable versatility. He is my most careful and critical reader, and his thoughtful comments and insights have gone a long way to strengthening the argument in this book. I am grateful to him for consistently placing my needs before his in the final stages of this book's completion. And last, but certainly not least, I thank my spirited daughter, Safianna, who daily reminds me that cross-cultural and intergenerational feminist work is an ongoing process and not an abstraction, and my son, Cyrus, who was considerate enough to wait until after the manuscript was completed before arriving.

Notes

Introduction

1. Throughout this study, I will on occasion use the name "Persia" and on others "Iran" for reasons of historical accuracy. In 1934, as part of his program to reinvent the nation as modern and to emphasize a break from previous dynasties, Reza Shah changed the name of the country from Persia to Iran. Some historians have suggested that Iran, derived from the word "Aryan," appealed to the shah because it echoed the suggestions of racial purity formulated by Nazi German ideology. Reza Shah's close ties to Germany were, in large part, due to his deep distrust of both Britain and Russia and their long history of imperialist intervention in Iran. But as Nikkie Keddie has stated, Reza Shah was certainly "not averse to Nazi phrases and methods, as they suited his dictatorial and nationalistic inclinations" (1981, 110).

Some Iranian academics prefer to employ the term "Persia" in their works because of their perception of the racist roots of the word "Iran." The word Persia, on the other hand, is derived from the Greek, *Persis,* referring to the southwestern province of Parsa, or Fars (Morgan 1988, 1). According to Keddie, however, Reza Shah did not rename the country by calling it Iran; he was, in fact, proposing a return to the country's indigenous name: "The word 'Iran' is a cognate of 'Aryan'; these words were used by that branch of the Indo-European peoples who migrated southeast before 1000 B.C., the Iranians staying in Iran and the Aryans going on to India" (1981, 2).

In more recent years, Iranians have had other reasons to reject the name Iran. After the events of the 1979 revolution, and the establishment of an Islamic Republic, many Iranians in the West, particularly in North America, where there was heightened anti-Iranian sentiment during the 1980 American hostage crisis, chose to revert to the use of "Persia" as a way of dissociating themselves from the policies of the Islamic Republic of Iran. I have chosen to refer to both Persia and Iran according to official nomenclature in the historical record. I will speak of "Persia" in the pre-1930s period and of "Iran" in the post-1930s.

2. See, for example: A. Blunt and G. Rose, eds., *Writing Women and Space: Colonial and Postcolonial Geographies* (New York: Guilford Press, 1994); Jayawardena 1995; Grewal 1996; Indira Ghose, *Women Travellers in Colonial India: The Power of the Female Gaze* (Oxford: Oxford University Press, 1998); Yeğenoğlu 1998; McEwan 2000; Hsu-Ming Teo, "Femininity, Modernity, and Colonial Discourse," in *In Transit: Travel, Text, Empire,* ed. Helen Gilbert and Anna Johnston (New York: Peter Lang, 2002); Susan Bassnett, "Travel Writing and Gender," in *The Cambridge Companion to Travel Writing,* ed. Peter Hulme and Tim Youngs (Cambridge: Cambridge University Press, 2002).

Despite these works, there remains a tendency among some feminists to glorify the intrepid woman traveler as exemplified by the collection of essays in *Travel Writing and the Female Imaginary* (Bologna: Pàtron, 2001), edited by Vita Fortunati, Rita Monticelli, and Maurizio Ascari. In the introduction to this collection, the editors claim that, "for women travellers, the relationship with *otherness*—represented both by nature and the natives—emphasizes a complex movement of identity, which reveals the marginal position of women in the social order of their mother country as already 'others.' Their journey thus becomes a tool to investigate women's social constraints as well as an instrument to acquire awareness of their 'self'" (6; emphasis theirs).

Thus, according to Fortunati et al., travel affords women the opportunity to explore their inner selves and to "find themselves." Such work pays scant attention (if any at all) to the position of these writings within colonial discourse and to the women travelers they discuss as colonizing subjects.

3. In missionary and feminist writings of the nineteenth century, women's quarters in countries of the Middle East have been referred to as the "heart of Empire." It was generally believed that the colonial project depended on the support (and the conversion) of women in the colonies as they were the carriers of culture and religion. Chapter 1 discusses this concept in further detail.

4. Antoinette Burton calls this particular dilemma "the white woman's burden"—also the title of her important essay published in *Western Women and Imperialism,* edited by Nupur Chaudhuri and Margaret Strobel (Bloomington: Indiana University Press, 1992).

5. This volume, *Western Women in Eastern Lands,* was issued by the Central Committee on the United Study of Missions. The committee was formed at a special session for women at an ecumenical conference held in New York in May 1900. The Baptist, Congregational, Methodist, Presbyterian, Protestant Episcopal, Dutch Reformed, and Lutheran boards each appointed a member to the committee, whose goal was to publish works on foreign missions, primarily written by and for women: "While these studies were primarily for the use of women, they have all been along broad lines, not confined to woman's work nor unduly magnifying it. *[Western Women in Eastern Lands],* therefore, meets a real need, as there has never been an adequate presentation of this department of Foreign Missions" (1987, xiii).

6. In Janaki Nair's instructive essay on the representations of the Indian Zenana in British women's discourses, she writes: "In 1881, *The Englishwoman's Review* had even suggested that the segregation of women in India was a useful 'prejudice' since it provided Englishwomen doctors and lawyers an opportunity to exercise their newly won skills, an opportunity largely denied them in Britain" (1990, 24).

7. bell hooks makes a similar critique against 1970s global sisters in "Sisterhood: Political Solidarity between Women." hooks believes that one of the main problems with the sisterhood of the second-wave feminist period was the insistence of white, bourgeois women that they lead the movement: "Racist socialization teaches bourgeois white women to think they are necessarily more capable of leading masses of women than other groups of women. Time and time again, they have shown that they do not want to be part of the feminist movement—they want to lead it" (1986, 132).

8. Chapter 3 examines the development of "global sisterhood" in second-wave feminist discourse and its application in a prerevolutionary Iranian feminist context.

1. Enlightening the Other

1. The second phase, Paidar claims, takes place "during the 1920s to 1940s as the era of nation building" (1995, 78). The third phase saw the "transformation of the era of nation building into the era of nationalism" (118), and the fourth phase of the discourse of modernity takes place during the 1960s and 1970s, "which was characterized by a rapid process of diversification and disintegration" (147).

2. As I explain in the introduction, I am not making the claim that all the women I discuss here are feminists. Indeed, some, like Gertrude Bell, most vociferously were not. However, these very differently positioned women share

similar discursive strategies: the use of the concept of sisterhood in their representation of the Persian woman. This notion of sisterhood later metamorphoses into a feminist rallying cry during the 1970s.

3. Some Iranian historians strongly object to the discussion of Iran from a postcolonial perspective because the country was never officially colonized. I disagree with this opposition to the use of postcolonial theory and borrow here the words of David Scott: "As a political-theoretical project . . . postcoloniality has been concerned principally with the decolonization of representation; the decolonization of the West's theory of the non-West" (1999, 12). Thus, as one of the aims of this book is to "decolonize," or at least destabilize, established representations of Iranian women in Western discourses, it seems to me entirely necessary to turn to postcolonial theory as one of the tools that would enable this project.

4. For more detailed historical analysis of this period, see the works of historians such as Janet Afary, Nikkie Keddie, and Parvin Paidar.

5. Ironically, this declared neutral zone was later discovered to be rich in oil, and despite its "neutrality," the British were not deterred from extending their sphere of influence to that region. The Anglo-Persian Oil Company, of which the British government eventually gained majority control, formed two subsidiary companies: one was the aptly named First Exploitation Company and the other, the Bakhtiari Oil Company. Both subsidiaries offered 3 percent of their shares to the Bakhtiari Khans and leased land directly from the Bakhtiaris instead of negotiating with the shah (Wright 1977, 109).

6. Robert Bruce was not the first Anglican missionary in Iran. He was preceded by Henry Martyn, who went to Persia in 1811 after five years of work as a translator and an evangelist in India. Martyn spent ten months in Shiraz revising a translated version of the New Testament into Farsi. During that time, he debated the virtues of Protestant Christianity with the Muslims who came to see him, but his main goal was to leave behind literary works that could be used as tools in the evangelical project (Addison 1942, 179).

7. See Monica Ringer's *Education, Religion, and the Discourse of Cultural Reform in Qajar Iran* (Costa Mesa, Calif.: Mazda, 2001) for an informed account of missionary education in Iran.

8. According to Adele Schreiber and Margaret Mathieson's history of the International Alliance of Women for Suffrage and Equal Citizenship in *Journey Towards Freedom* (1955), the organization held biennial meetings until World War I. After the war, the meetings were held triennially.

9. Mary Wollstonecraft makes a strong argument along these lines in *The Vindication of the Rights of Woman* (1792). In this foundational work of Western feminism, the "Eastern" woman is associated with the incomplete state of

childhood and the dependent state of slavery, both states that the modern British woman, as a symbol of the nation's modernity and progress, needs to escape. Indeed, the health of the modern nation depends upon women because, as future mothers, they must be educated accordingly so that they are capable of raising an enlightened (and rational) generation worthy of the modern British nation. Thus, educated British women become associated with future progress, and their Eastern sisters with a stagnant past. Interestingly, this same discourse of progress and evolution, and the argument that mothers as the progenitors of the new generation should have access to better education, becomes a central part of the discourse of Iranian modernity and Iranian feminism in the early twentieth century. I will be discussing these connections at further length in chapters 2 and 3.

10. In 1911, Sykes went to Canada disguised as a woman seeking domestic employment on behalf of the Colonial Intelligence League for Educated Women, an organization interested in investigating employment opportunities in the colonies for the educated and single British woman. According to Scott Christianson, Sykes's book on Canada "offers the kind of 'keen' descriptions of scenery and places she delivered in *Through Persia on a Side-Saddle*. She also displays the same condescending sympathy for Canadian women less fortunate than herself that she showed toward Persian women" (1997, 174). He describes her charade as ridiculous and condescending: "It is also colonialist: a daughter of the empire goes to the Dominion to discover how it may be exploited to solve England's problem of rampant unemployment of single women. Sykes' straightforward narrative lays bare the workings of imperialism—its hierarchy, its exploitation of its own working-class people and its colonies, even its exploitation of upper-class women, such as herself, drafted to 'do their bit' for colonization" (174).

11. After her first trip to Persia, Sykes established herself as an unofficial authority on the subject. In addition to *Through Persia on a Side-Saddle* and *Persia and Its People*, she published *The Story-Book of the Shah; or, Legends of Old Persia* (London: Macqueen, 1901). The late nineteenth and early twentieth centuries seem to have been the "honeymoon" period of her relationship with the country. She wrote and presented papers on Persian folklore, but after the publication of *Persia and Its People*, and during the time of the Constitutional Revolution, Sykes hardened her position on Persia. The country was no longer the romantic and exotic locale that provided her with quaint anecdotes to relate; rather, it became a hopelessly backward and primitive country with a barbarous religion responsible for the imprisonment of the nation's women. Her paper at the National Geographic Society in October 1910, "A Talk about Persia and Its Women," is a condensed version of *Persia and Its People*, in which she reiterates

one of her favorite statements: "From the moment of his entrance into the world, throughout his entire life and even in the hereafter, the Persian man has decidedly the best of everything and the woman the worst" (853).

12. Iran declared neutrality during World War I, but because of its strategic geographical location, it became a battleground for English, German, Russian, and Turkish forces. The Germans capitalized on Iranians' distrust of England and Russia, and they organized a tribal revolt against the British in the South.

13. I am indebted to Ali Behdad for urging me to consider this moment of subaltern agency in the exchange between Baji and Sykes. He also encouraged me to recognize the usefulness of de Certeau's theorization of the art of "making do" here and at other moments in my argument.

14. For a fascinating study of the connection between soap and Empire, see the chapter titled "Soft-Soaping Empire: Commodity Racism and Imperial Advertising" in Anne McClintock's *Imperial Leather* (1995).

15. After visiting a "Europeanised Persian" woman who "poured out tea, handing round milk and sugar quite *à l'Anglaise*," Sykes expresses pity for her because "her lot was by no means a happy one, and [Sykes was] reminded of the caged starling in the Bastille that all day long kept crying, 'Let me out! let me out!'" (1901, 22).

16. When describing the culture of the bazaar, Bell refers to a story from *A Thousand and One Nights* about a shopkeeper who waives the price of his wares in exchange for a kiss from a beautiful female customer: "So reckless a disposition is no longer to be found among Eastern merchants; shopping is now conducted purely on business principles, though not without a charm which is absent from Western counters" (1894, 134–35).

17. This tension between nationalist and feminist allegiances continues to haunt Iranian politics; the thwarted feminist demonstrations of March 1979 (discussed in chapter 3) epitomize this particular tension.

2. Scopophilic Desires

1. Examples of accounts of the Orient that are simultaneously sexualized and menacing include *The Book of the Thousand Nights and a Night: A Plain and Literal Translation of the Arabian Nights Entertainments*, 6 vols., trans. and notes Richard F. Burton (New York: Limited Editions Club, 1934); Charles-Louis De Secondat Montesquieu, *Lettres Persanes, 1721* (Paris: Société des Belles Lettres, 1949); Pierre Loti, *Aziyadé* (Paris: Calmann-Lévy, 1879) and *Vers Ispahan* (Paris: Calmann-Lévy, 1927); Gustave Flaubert, *Salammbô* (1862; Paris: Garnier Flammario, 1961); Alexander William Kinglake, *Eöthen* (1844; London: J. M. Dent and Sons, 1908); Thomas Moore, "Lalla Rookh: An Oriental Romance" (1817), in

The Complete Poetical Works of Thomas Moore (New York: Thomas Y. Crowell and Company, 1895); James Morier, *The Adventures of Hajji Baba of Ispahan* (New York: Random House, 1937); Gérard de Nerval, *Voyage en Orient* (Paris: Garnier-Flammarion, 1980).

2. I am grateful to Andrew O'Malley for his insights into eighteenth-century discourses of domestic and middle-class ideologies. For further reading on eighteenth- and nineteenth-century discourses of maternity and domesticity, see Leonore Davidoff and Catherine Hall, "'The Nursery of Virtue': Domestic Ideology and the Middle Class" and "'The Hidden Investment': Women and the Enterprise," in *Family Fortunes* (1987); and Mary Poovey, *The Ideological Work of Gender in Mid-Victorian England* (Chicago: University of Chicago Press, 1988).

3. The gendered discourse of protection was mobilized by representatives of colonizing nations to justify their presence in the "Orient" and served to conceal the economic and political motivations of colonizing nations. For discussions of how British and French colonial discourses of protection operated in relation to veiling in Egypt and Algeria, see Leila Ahmed's "The Discourse of the Veil," in *Women and Gender in Islam* (1992), and Marnia Lazreq's "Nationalism, Decolonization, and Gender," in *The Eloquence of Silence* (1994).

4. The veil, worn quite differently in a number of Muslim countries as well as in many other regions, has come to embody various meanings at different historical moments in diverse national contexts. For the purposes of my argument here, I am focusing on its manifestations in the Iranian context.

5. Susynne McElrone has observed that the tobacco protests often falsely stand in for the originary moment of Iranian women's activism and urges scholars to recognize earlier evidence of Iranian women's political agency. See "Nineteenth-Century Qajar Women in the Public Sphere" in *Comparative Studies of South Asia, Africa, and the Middle East* (2005) for her full argument.

6. I will address this apparent contradiction below.

7. In *The Women's Rights Movement in Iran* (1982), Eliz Sanasarian notes that the Iranian feminist movement in the early part of the twentieth century was composed of upper- and upper-middle-class women, but she takes pains to argue that the movement was characterized by the "classless nature of [the women's] ideological stands" (46). This seems to me a dubious proposition, as much of the rancor among women in 1970s revolutionary Iran appears to stem from a history of imposing a particular classist and elitist feminist vision on the lives of rural and working-class Iranian women.

8. For a more nuanced and critical view of Taj al-Saltanah's writings, see Nasrin Rahimieh's *Missing Persians* (2001).

9. In "Negotiating Women's Rights," Mana Kia criticizes Iranian feminist scholars for denying the agency of (mostly upper-class) women, the women I

discuss here as "Pahlavi feminists," who worked from within the limits of state-sponsored feminism. While Kia rightly observes that "feminist activism within state institutions cannot be dismissed as a direct extension of state policies," I find it curious that she feels compelled to champion the agency of privileged women who mostly benefited from their close ties to the state (2005, 228). Kia ends her essay by recognizing the problems that haunted the Iranian feminist movement, namely the class prejudices of the very women whose agency she wishes to recognize. I am not suggesting that the very fact of their privilege justifies a denial of their agency, but rather, that in the larger terrain of Iranian feminist politics, the paternalism of elite Iranian women, which manifested itself as a type of noblesse oblige in relation to their lower-middle-class and working-class counterparts, demands more rigorous critique.

10. Under the Islamic Republic, "Women's Day" is celebrated on the birthday of Prophet Mohammad's daughter, Fatimih.

11. Bamdad's sycophantic praise of Reza Shah's policies characterizes much of Pahlavi feminism. In state-sponsored Iranian feminist discourse, the Pahlavi shahs and their immediate family were the saviors of Iranian women; they were represented as progressive rulers who forged ahead, even in the face of women's resistance, with the project of women's enfranchisement. Bamdad expresses her appreciation at the containment of Iranian feminist activism and the state co-optation of feminist organizations in the late 1950s by stating: "The Iranian women's movement owes much to the support of H.I.H. Princess Ashraf Pahlavi, who has always devoted much time to social guidance with a view to fulfilment of the lofty aims of her brother, H.I.M. Mohammad Reza Shah Pahlavi. She has given particular attention to mothercraft training and to winning equality of women's rights with men's" (1977, 112).

12. The configuration of Iranian women as having "false consciousness," and thus requiring guidance by their more worthy sisters, is an unfortunate (and consistent) theme in Pahlavi feminist discourse. In an article published in Robin Morgan's *Sisterhood Is Global* (Garden City, N.Y.: Anchor Press/Doubleday, 1984), prominent prerevolutionary Iranian feminist Mahnaz Afkhami celebrates the achievements of the Women's Organization of Iran, of which she was secretary general, and its efforts to enlighten and educate Iranian women. However, she dismisses women's active participation in the 1979 revolution as indicative of their lack of political sophistication: "The degree of political awareness reached by the masses of Iranian women became strikingly apparent during the antigovernment marches of 1978–79. In a meeting of the secretaries of the WOI we asked the Secretary of Kerman Province about the veiled women who had taken part in a recent demonstration. 'Who were they?' we asked. 'Our own members,' she said. 'You kept saying "Mobilize them." Now they are mobilized,

and they shout "Long Live Khomeini."' Yet to this day we are all still in agreement that what is important is that they marched and shouted their will. *That it was in support of a destructive force came from political naïveté which only time and experience can correct*" (Afkhami 1984, 335–36, n. 3; emphasis mine).

13. See chapter 3 for a closer look at the intersection of 1970s Iranian feminism with second-wave American and European feminism.

14. In Germaine Greer's caustic account of her 1973 trip to Iran with Betty Friedan and Helvi Sipila, she paints Friedan as a ludicrous and insular figure who refuses to see or understand those women who do not belong to the elite membership of the Women's Organization of Iran: "One day, as we rolled in majesty through the chaotic Teheran traffic, past women holding huge semicircles of black nylon georgette in their teeth, with a toddler on one hand and a shopping bag in the other, I said to Betty, 'Strange how coquettish the veil is in Iran, and so uncomfortable and unmanageable.'

"'What veil?' barked Betty. 'Don't you know anything? The veil was abarlished [*sic*] in 1936.' No one could ever say that Betty was not well briefed. She had learned the 'facts' in the official handout sheet by heart. 'Betty, if you would only open your eyes and look out of the car, you would see that every woman on the streets of Teheran is veiled.' Betty looked, grunted, and closed her eyes again. She had succeeded in getting an interview with the shah through the American glossy that had her on the masthead as a contributing editor [*Ladies' Home Journal*], and she was convinced that everything in Iran must be fine" (1988, 38).

While Greer is right to point out Friedan's willful ignorance of her host country, her righteous assertion that all the women were veiled is clearly an exaggeration, considering that the early 1970s were the peak of Iran's emulation of Western fashions.

15. Khomeini's contemptuous statement is a direct response to Reza Shah's proclamation on "the day of women's emancipation," or, in the opinion of Islamic clerics, "the day of women's shame." On January 7, 1936, at the Teacher Training College in Tehran, Reza Shah told the (coercively unveiled) graduating female class, "We must never forget that one-half of the population of our country has not been taken into account, that is to say, one-half of the country's working force has been idle" (qtd. Mackey 1996, 182).

16. See chapter 3 for a more detailed account of these events.

17. The segregation laws demonstrate the absurd and somewhat surreal quality to life under the Islamic Republic; while men and women have to comply with segregated seating on city buses and in government offices, they find themselves literally sitting on each other's laps in the overcrowded taxis that people hail on the streets of Tehran. Later in this chapter, I will discuss how young people regularly subvert the laws of public segregation.

18. An example of Western feminist configurations of the *hijab* as the ultimate sign of women's subjugation can be found in Merle Hoffman's "Iran: Notes from the Interior." Hoffman, editor-in-chief of the feminist magazine *On the Issues,* traveled to Iran in 1998 and described her experience of wearing the mandatory *hijab:* "From the very beginning, Iran challenged my vanity. In order to conform to Islamic *hejab,* I was expected to cover my hair and neck, wear a long, loose dress, dark stockings or trousers, and forego cosmetics in public. . . . The scarf made my long hair, which is so much a part of my female self and self-definition, situationally unavailable to me. I felt neutered, de-sexualized. But that was the point. The associations I began making were brutal: Auschwitz, where the first thing done to the women—before the dogs and the gas—was to shave their heads in an attempt to dehumanize them; female collaborators during World War II being shamed by having their heads shaved" (1998, 2).

Hoffman does moderate her tone by the end of her article and acknowledges that her visit helped her rethink some of her preconceived notions about women's oppression in Iran. Nevertheless, the associations she makes between veiled Iranian women and Holocaust victims seem, at the very least, inappropriate.

19. For productive analyses that move beyond these binaries, see work by such scholars as Homa Hoodfar, Ziba Mir-Hosseini, and Zohreh T. Sullivan.

20. For more on current debates between contemporary Iranian feminists, see chapter 3.

21. Gauri Viswanathan has most notably written about the role of the English literary canon in the British colonial project. See, for example, *Masks of Conquest: Literary Study and British Rule in India* (New York: Columbia University Press, 1989).

22. I am grateful to Stephen Slemon for making this point.

3. Global Sisters in Revolutionary Iran

1. There were, of course, other types of feminism in the 1970s, but I am focusing here, and throughout the manuscript, on a type of liberal feminism that I believe remains dominant even today.

2. My thanks to Afsaneh Najmabadi for recommending Jakobsen's work to me.

3. This is not to say that "difference" and "diversity" emerged only in the 1980s, but these are among the prominent works that take issue with what their authors perceive as the narrow vision of liberal feminism. It is also not my intention here to trace the history of the sometimes fractured second-wave feminist movement, as there have been many informed accounts of that period. Keeping in mind that this is not an exhaustive list, but rather a sampling from

a substantial body of work, here are some noteworthy critical engagements with global feminist politics: hooks 1981, 1984; Amos and Parmar 1984; Spivak 1985, 1986; Carby 1982; Ware 1992; Frankenberg 1993; Burton 1994; and Midgley 1998.

4. For intergenerational debates between Western feminists, see Gubar 1998, 1999; Wiegman 1999, 1999/2000; and Chow 1999/2000. For debates between diasporic Iranian feminists on the merits and/or shortcomings of pre- and post-revolutionary Iranian feminism, see Mir-Hosseini 1999; Moghissi 1999a, 1999b; and Najmabadi 1997.

5. For an excellent discussion of the problems of the Women's Organization of Iran's project of educational reform and "modernization" of the rural classes, see Sullivan 1998.

6. This description intimates that the Woodrow Wilson Center's purpose is to serve the interests of the U.S. government. A cursory glance at the speeches of its current director, Lee H. Hamilton, offers an indication of his right-leaning politics. In his September 15, 2005, speech on "The Lessons of 9/11," Hamilton claims that "everything" has changed since 9/11 and perpetuates the alarmist rhetoric favored by the Bush administration that the nation must remain ever-vigilant because it is perpetually under threat of attack (2005, 1).

7. Although Kate Millett does not mention the date of her invitation to Iran, it seems likely that she was invited at the same time as Friedan, Greer, and Sipila. In response to the trepidation Iranian feminists feel at Millett identifying herself at anti-imperialist Iranian feminist demonstrations in 1979, she writes, "I find it odd I should ever have been mentioned in women's magazines under the Shah, *having refused Farah's invitation to a feminist meeting which others accepted.* I should be known in Iranian circles only as a resolute opponent of the last regime" (1982, 78; emphasis mine).

8. Chapters 1 and 2 provide a closer look at the ways in which the concept of modernity has been mobilized within Western and state-sponsored Iranian feminist discourses to position women of less privileged classes and nations as objects in need of rescue and guidance.

9. Lest Greer come out looking beyond reproach, it should be noted that her often judgmental observations sometimes lead her into dubious political terrain. Her account of her time in Iran is often marred by a self-congratulatory description of her own "true" brand of revolutionary feminism. After mocking Sipila's and Friedan's speeches, she describes her own: "With five minutes of our hour left to go, the leader of the world's women would sit down, panting with triumph. For five minutes, I would try to say something about the truth of women's lives in the shah's Iran in terms that the women might understand. This was not easy, as I had been specifically requested not to refer to abortion

or contraception, or Islam or the passport law, against which my friend Mehrangiv Manouchehrian had struggled in vain" (1988, 38). Nevertheless, despite her occasional tendency to position herself as the authentic and knowing feminist subject, Greer's behavior in Iran is importantly different from Friedan's. Greer seems genuinely committed to a model of feminist activism that, at least in principle, includes a partnership of women from across social and economic classes.

10. Greer is vociferous about the hypocrisy of the United Nations on the subject of women's rights. In May 1975, she published an article in the *New York Times*, launching a scathing critique of the UN-sponsored International Women's Year: "The decision to have a women's year was simply a belated recognition of the fashionableness of feminism in the West, whose lifestyles dominate the UN self-image despite their manifest irrelevance to most of the people living on the planet. . . . International Women's Year is a simple extension of Madison Avenue feminism: The agricultural labourers of Asia and Africa might as well lay down their hoes and light up a Virginia Slim" (1975b, 35).

11. According to the shah's unauthorized biography, Princess Ashraf "offered $500,000 to help defray the costs of the conference, $500,000 for an Economic and Social Commission for Asia and the Pacific, and $1 million for an international institute for research on the status of the world's women. Enthusiasm for this last plan sagged when it was learned that the institute would be based in Tehran" (de Villiers 1976, 298).
This privilege cost her as much as $2 million.

12. Gayatri Spivak's critique of the fourth world conference on women held in Beijing in 1995 suggests that the problems that emerged out of the 1975 conference on women have continued to plague subsequent UN conferences on women: "We are witnessing the proliferation of feminist apparatchiks who identify conference organizing with activism as such. . . . They often assume that altogether salutary debate in the conference will have necessary consequences in the lifeworld of oppressed and super-exploited women" (1996a, 4).

13. Like Germaine Greer, Millett distinguishes herself from her second-wave feminist colleagues (such as Betty Friedan) by her criticisms of what she understands to be the corrupt practices of the state-controlled Women's Organization of Iran and of the Pahlavi regime in general. Like Greer, she appeared to be driven by a deep-seated commitment to addressing social injustice. Millett writes: "Ashraf, the Shah's hideous twin sister, went around pretending to be a feminist, her representation alone enough to discredit the idea if she were not so cleverly fraudulent; actually got herself appointed head of a UN commission on women's rights years ago. A disgraceful event in itself. Then tried to invite world feminism to Tehran for the second International Women's Year

meeting following that in Mexico City. An invitation declined even before history intervened" (1982, 24).

14. Chapter 2 provides a more detailed analysis of the politics of veiling in twentieth-century Iran.

15. Western media coverage of the repercussions of the postrevolutionary feminist demonstrations was extensive. An article worth citing is Mim Kelber's "Five Days in March": "When the [Iranian] women tried to gather for planning [feminist] meetings, they were menaced and sometimes stopped by young men with knives—religious extremists who felt that the role of Ayatollah Khomeini as the symbol of the revolution, and the promise of an Islamic republic, meant that women must return to the seclusion of the veil and the status of chattel. 'We have faced the tanks of the Shah,' said one of the brave women, one of many who had worn the chador, a head-to-toe covering, as a symbol of defiance to the Shah. 'Do you think we can be frightened by boys with knives?'" (1979, 90). Kelber offers an insightful summary of the historical trajectory of Iranian feminist struggles which makes this piece well worth reading. Although the article plays on Western fears of the threat of a growing "religious fundamentalism," Kelber does manage to convey the strength and commitment of Iranian women in the face of naked violence.

16. Under the Islamic Republic, the birthdate of Hazrat-i Fatimih, the daughter of Prophet Mohammad, was declared the new Women's Day. The day of "Women's Liberation" under the Pahlavi regime was now demoted to the "Day of Shame."

17. Elaine Sciolino, now a well-known correspondent on Iranian affairs for the *New York Times* and author of *Persian Mirrors* (1999), was working for *Newsweek* magazine at that time. Millett is effusive in her descriptions of Sciolino and her feminist commitments. She also portrays her as being very involved in helping to organize the news conference: "a press conference, we had thought of it even before Elaine came up to the room, the men gone now and a sister in the media to put it on the line—the need for one—and offered to do the arrangements for us" (1982, 152). And as the news conference descends into chaos and the panelists are attacked for appropriating the voices and the cause of Iranian women by people of various political stripes, Millett writes: "An American woman's voice, our angel—Elaine. 'As a woman and a journalist I should like to take some responsibility for this press conference. No one knew Kate Millett was in town, several people wanted to interview her and asked for this press conference. Kate is representing certain feminists in New York, Kateh is representing her own committee, in no way representing every Iranian woman—if you don't want to listen to it, fine'" (176).

Although Millett's portrayal of Sciolino is laudatory, the admiration does not seem to be mutual—at least in recent years. In her book, Sciolino devotes one brief paragraph to Millett's participation in the Iranian feminist struggle: "During the revolution in February 1979, women could go bareheaded in Iran, but within a month, Khomeini ordered all women to wear Islamic dress. At first, Iran's women resisted. I walked through the streets of Tehran as thousands of women marched—bareheaded—to protest Khomeini's order. Men hurled stones, bottles, and insults. Soldiers fired shots in the air. The American feminist Kate Millett showed up, branding Khomeini a 'male chauvinist' and marching with Iranian women. She was expelled" (2000, 134). Sciolino's tone is a dismissive one, and contains a not-too-subtle criticism of Millett's presence and behavior in Iran during that time. She also does not mention her own involvement with Millet's group and her participation (according to Millett's account) in organizing the disastrous news conference that led to Millett's expulsion from the country.

18. The following day, the Iranian women apologize to Millett for their absence and claim they were arrested and held in custody for several hours—which is highly probable, but there is room for doubt as they had been resistant to the idea of a news conference in the first place.

19. See Nasrin Rahimieh's chapter, "A Double Dilemma: Oriental Women's Encounter with the West," in *Oriental Responses to the West* (1990), for a discussion of the fraught position of Egyptian feminist Laila Said, who went to Iran as a member of the European feminist contingent.

20. Janet Afary and Kevin Anderson offer a different perspective on the participation of Millett and Western feminists in Iran during the March demonstrations. As much as I respect Afary's work, her celebratory rhetoric of international feminist participation at that historical juncture in Iran disregards the problems of that participation (as well, her condemnation of Foucault's writings about the Iranian Revolution seems somewhat unfair): "Where Foucault had stressed the totally unified character of the revolutionary movement, Millet focused on the multiplicity of forces involved. Millett's Iran was more varied than Foucault's. It was secular and religious, female and male, gay and straight, non-Islamic and Islamic. Where Foucault saw an undifferentiated totality united behind Khomeini, Millett saw deep contradictions within the movement that had overthrown the shah. Where Foucault had supported the anti-shah movement only to become silent when these contradictions emerged, Millett, who had been even more active than Foucault in the anti-shah movement, plunged into those contradictions, seeking to deepen them in a way that meant supporting the rights of women, of gay men, of workers, of religious and ethnic minorities" (2005, 112). See the chapter "Debating the Outcome of the Revolution, Especially on Women's Rights" for Afary's and Anderson's 2005 analysis of those events.

21. The assumption that feminism originates in the West is implied by

second-wave feminist discourse as well, thus constituting an ironic "meeting point" between two opposing positions.

22. Sisterhood Is Global Institute (SIGI) is an international feminist organization founded upon the publication of Robin Morgan's 1984 anthology by the same name. Mahnaz Afkhami served a five-year term as president of SIGI in Bethesda, Maryland, until January 2000, when the organization moved to Montreal, Canada, under the direction of Greta Hoffman Nemiroff. As of March 2004, SIGI began the transition to a permanent home in New York City.

4. Female Homosocial Communities in Iranian Feminist Film

1. After the 2001 release of *The Hidden Half*, which addresses controversial issues such as women's political activism during the revolutionary period, Tahmineh Milani was arrested on charges of "supporting those waging war against God" and "misusing the arts in support of counterrevolutionary and armed opposition groups" (Scott 2001, 2). She faced the death penalty, but after the high-profile intervention of the international and Hollywood film community, as well as numerous supporters both inside and outside of the country, the charges against her were eventually dropped.

2. See chapter 2 for a more detailed look at representations of veiling in twentieth-century Iran.

3. Norma Claire Moruzzi has made this observation in her discussion of *Two Women* and Fereydoun Jayrani's *Red:* "In both films the heroine is only released from the misery of her marital bondage by the eventual violent death of her husband.... In *Two Women,* the heroine is a perfect overachiever who is reduced to absolute passivity by her husband's jealous control. Her release only comes when her stalker murders her husband. In *Red,* the heroine is a strong-minded nurse and devoted mother who insists on her independence all through the film; when her crazed and violent husband eventually tries to gain ultimate control by killing her, she kills him in self-defense" (2001, 92).

4. Universities in Iran remained closed for approximately three years after the toppling of the shah's regime.

5. Milani herself seems to encourage this reading, according to Chandrahas Choudhury's "Hitchcock in Hijab": "In an interview Milani has provocatively said: 'The two female characters in my film are a single person with two personalities—the heroine's actual personality and her potential personality, what she is and what she wants to be but can't because of society and its mores'" (2005, 2). To Holly Morris of *Adventure Divas*, Milani states: "*Two Women* means every woman. I think the friendship between *Two Women* in Iran is like that anywhere else, although maybe a little stronger in Iran" (1992, 2).

6. The English translations of the dialogue in *Two Women* and *The Fifth Reaction* are mine.

7. Article 131 of the Islamic penal law states: "If the act of lesbianism is repeated three times and punishment is enforced each time, [the] death sentence will be issued the fourth time." Under Article 109: "Punishment for sodomy is killing; the sharia judge decides on how to carry [out] the killing" (Islamic Penal Law).

8. Article 112 of Islamic penal law stipulates the following about sexual relations between men and boys: "If a mature man of sound mind commits sexual intercourse with an immature person, the doer will be killed and the passive one will be subject to ta'azir of 74 lashes if not under duress." Lesbians, however, are subjected to one hundred lashes each, and after the third offense, they are sentenced to death (Islamic penal law).

9. *Haj Aqa* is a title of respect used to address Muslim men who have made the pilgrimage to Mecca. The use of this title confers an esteemed status on men by acknowledging their devoutness as Muslim subjects.

10. In an article about an international seminar on women in contemporary cinema held in Iran in January 2001, Rose Issa lists the censorship regulations for Iranian cinema published in a booklet by the Ministry of Culture in the summer of 1996. Issa writes that the following are "at random, . . . forbidden: tight feminine clothes; the showing of any part of a wom[a]n's body except the face and hands; physical contact, tender words or jokes, between men or women; jokes either [about] the army, police or family; negative characters with a beard (which could assimilate them with religious figures); foreign or coarse words; foreign music, or any type of music which brings joy!; showing favourably a character who prefers solitude to collective life; policemen and soldiers badly dressed or having an argument" (1997, 3).

11. See Najmabadi's *Women with Mustaches and Men without Beards* (2005) for a detailed analysis of gender ambiguities in classical Persian art and poetry.

12. Feminist theorists such as Jacqui Alexander (1997), Zillah Eisenstein (2000), V. Spike Peterson (2000), and Gayatri Spivak (1993) have addressed the ways in which women's rights are always and necessarily in tension with the interests of a heteropatriarchal nation-state.

13. My thanks to Christie George from *Women Make Movies,* who has provided me generous access to these films.

14. I am grateful to Nasrin Rahimieh for generously sharing with me her unpublished article, "Packing the Court in *Divorce Iranian Style.*" All page numbers cited in this chapter are from Rahimieh's original manuscript (Summer 2001).

15. This in itself might be a way of discouraging women's petition for divorce. Culturally, women's speech and behavior are regulated through linguistic and

physical codes of modesty. Since the language of the court necessitates a more direct and unnuanced speech, some women may automatically feel discouraged from asserting their rights through legal channels.

16. Women's limited divorce and child custody rights under Iranian law are recurring themes in postrevolutionary Iranian movies. In Dariush Mehrjui's 1990 film *Hamoun,* the female protagonist, Mahshid, argues with a court official who is reluctant to grant her permission to divorce her husband: "My concern here is about women's rights. The main issue is that the right to divorce only belongs to men. Do women have any rights at all? Each aspect of women's rights has been trampled upon in this society. They are never allowed to make decisions, even regarding their own divorce, but men can get divorced whenever they please. Women are obliged to suffer and put up with unworthy husbands for an entire lifetime."

17. Ziba Mir-Hosseini very kindly provided me with the longer version of her article on the making of *Runaway* (2001b), in which she states, "Rayhaneh House opened its doors to runaway girls in October 1999. It had its origin in a 1998 project funded by Tehran municipality . . . to deal with the problem of street children. . . . Two centers were created in 1998; Green House for boys and Rayhaneh for girls between the ages of 12 and 19" (3).

18. I am indebted to Ziba Mir-Hosseini for identifying the title of this song for me.

19. The translation of this song is mine.

20. In 2000, however, Googoosh went on a concert tour throughout North America and Europe, singing for the first time since the revolution for nostalgic diasporic Iranian audiences.

21. See chapter 2 on *sharm.*

22. My thanks to Ziba Mir-Hosseini for providing me with this information.

23. I am grateful to Mohammad Attebai for this information.

24. In an article on the making of the documentary, Mir-Hosseini discusses the varied reactions of Iranians—both in exile and at home—toward the film. At issue is the question of the *truth* of representation. Despite their radically different political and social positions, Mir-Hosseini observes the similarity between the reactions of Iranian government officials and a select group of diasporic Iranians to the film. Both groups continue to obsess about the country's negative image in Western media; *Divorce Iranian Style,* they believe, contributes to this unfavorable characterization. The documentary, they argued, "gave a distorted image of the reality of women's life in Iran and was not representative" (2002a, 194). Mir-Hosseini describes the reaction of the Iranian diasporic community that objected to the film as falling into three separate categories: "First are those who identify politically with elements of the Iranian opposition abroad:

they saw the film as propaganda for the Islamic Republic. . . . Second are non-political Iranian expatriates, largely middle-class in background, who said that the film made them feel ashamed in front of foreigners. . . . A third group of people, between these two extremes, not only dismissed conspiracy theories but also took issue with objections that the film is not representative. They saw the film as an indictment of Islamic law and the Islamic Republic" (194). Iranian officials objected to the film because it "undermined the image of the strong family that is the foundation of the Islamic system by showing women fighting for release from unwanted marriages" (197).

Conclusion

1. See Whitlock 2005 for a wonderful interpretation of the imperialist overtones of this moment of public unveiling.

Works Cited

Addison, James Thayer. [1942] 1966. *The Christian Approach to the Moslem: A Historical Study*. New York: AMS Press.

Afary, Janet. 1996. *The Iranian Constitutional Revolution, 1906–1911: Grassroots Democracy, Social Democracy, and the Origins of Feminism*. New York: Columbia University Press.

———. 2004. "Seeking a Feminist Politics for the Middle East after September 11." *Frontiers* 25, no. 1: 128–37.

Afary, Janet, and Kevin B. Anderson. 2005. *Foucault and the Iranian Revolution: Gender and the Seductions of Islamism*. Chicago: University of Chicago Press.

Afkahmi, Mahnaz. 1984. "Iran—A Future in the Past: The 'Prerevolutionary' Women's Movement." In *Sisterhood Is Global: The International Women's Movement Anthology*, ed. Robin Morgan, 330–38. Garden City, N.Y.: Anchor Press/Doubleday.

———. 1994a. *Women in Exile*. Charlottesville: University of Virginia Press.

———. 1994b. "Women in Postrevolutionary Iran: A Feminist Perspective." In *In the Eye of the Storm: Women in Post-Revolutionary Iran*, ed. Mahnaz Afkhami and Erika Friedl, 5–18. Syracuse: Syracuse University Press.

Ahmed, Leila. 1992. *Women and Gender in Islam: Historical Roots of a Modern Debate*. New Haven: Yale University Press.

Al-e Ahmad, Jalal. [1962] 1982. *Plagued by the West* [Gharbzadegi], trans. Paul Sprachman. Biblioteca Pesica: Modern Persian Literature Series 4. Delmar, N.Y.: Caravan.

Alexander, Jacqui. 1997. "Erotic Autonomy as a Politics of Decolonization: An Anatomy of Feminist and State Practice in the Bahamas Tourist Economy." In *Feminist Genealogies, Colonial Legacies, Democratic Futures.* New York: Routledge.

Amanat, Abbas. 1993. Introduction to *Crowning Anguish: Memoirs of a Persian Princess from the Harem to Modernity,* by Taj Al-Saltana, ed. Abbas Amanat, trans. Anna Vanzan and Amin Neshati. Washington, D.C.: Mage Publishers.

Amos, Valerie, and Pratibha Parmar. 1984. "Challenging Imperial Feminism." *Feminist Review* 17 (Autumn): 3–19.

Anderson, Max. 2001. "The Iranian Revelation: A Welcome behind the Veil." *Sunday Times,* 17 June. http://www.sundaytimes.co.uk.ti/2001/06/17/stitrltrlo3o18.html?1007000.

"Appeal from the Women." 1911. *Times* (London). 7 December, 5.

Arberry, A. J. 1947. Preface to *Persian Pictures,* by Gertrude Bell, 5–8. London: Ernest Benn.

Babcox, Deborah, and Madeline Belkin. 1971. *Liberation Now! Writings from the Women's Liberation Movement.* New York: Dell Publishing.

Bahramitash, Roksana. 2005. "The War on Terror, Feminist Orientalism, and Orientalist Feminism: Case Studies of Two North American Bestsellers." *Critique: Critical Middle Eastern Studies* 14, no. 2 (Summer): 221–35.

Bamdad, Badr ol-Moluk. 1977. *From Darkness into Light: Women's Emancipation in Iran,* ed. and trans. F. R. C. Bagley. Hicksville, N.Y.: Exposition Press.

Bassett, Rev. James. 1890. *Persia: Eastern Mission.* Philadelphia: Presbyterian Board of Publication and Sabbath-School Work.

Bayatt-Philipp, Mangol. 1978. "Women and Revolution in Iran, 1905–1911." In *Women in the Muslim World,* ed. Lois Beck and Nikkie Keddie, 295–308. Cambridge: Harvard University Press.

Behdad, Ali. 1994. *Belated Travelers: Orientalism in the Age of Colonial Dissolution.* Durham, N.C.: Duke University Press.

Bell, Gertrude. [1894] 1947. *Persian Pictures.* London: Ernest Benn.

Bhabha, Homi K. 1994. "Conclusion: 'Race,' Time, and the Revision of Modernity." In *The Location of Culture,* 236–56. London: Routledge.

Bird, Christiane. 2001. *Neither East nor West: One Woman's Journey through the Islamic Republic of Iran.* New York: Pocket Books.

Bird, Mary R. S. [1899] 1908. *Persian Women and Their Creed.* London: Church Missionary Society.

Burton, Antoinette. 1991. "The Feminist Quest for Identity: British Imperial Suffragism and 'Global Sisterhood,' 1900–1915." *Journal of Women's History* 3, no. 2 (Fall): 46–81.

———. 1992. "The White Woman's Burden: British Feminists and 'The Indian

Woman,' 1865–1915." In *Western Women and Imperialism: Complicity and Resistance,* ed. Nupur Chaudhuri and Margaret Strobel, 137–57. Bloomington: Indiana University Press.

———. 1994. *Burdens of History: British Feminists, Indian Women, and Imperial Culture, 1865–1915.* Chapel Hill: University of North Carolina Press.

Butler, Judith. 2004. *Precarious Life: The Powers of Mourning and Violence.* London: Verso.

Caplan, Patricia, and Janet Burja, ed. 1978. *Women United, Women Divided: Cross Cultural Perspectives on Female Solidarity.* London: Tavistock.

Carby, Hazel V. 1982. "White Woman Listen! Black Feminism and the Boundaries of Sisterhood." In *Third World Women and the Politics of Feminism,* ed. Chandra Talpade Mohanty, Ann Russo, and Lourdes Torres. Bloomington: Indiana University Press, 1991.

Chaudhuri, Nupur, and Margaret Strobel, ed. 1992. *Western Women and Imperialism: Complicity and Resistance.* Bloomington: Indiana University Press.

Choudhury, Chandrahas. 2005. "Hitchcock in Hijab." *Tehelka: The People's Paper,* November 12 and 15. http://www.tehelka.com/story_main14.asp?filename=hub111205hitchcock.asp.

Chow, Rey. "When Whiteness Feminizes . . . : Some Consequences of a Supplementary Logic." *differences: A Journal of Feminist Cultural Studies* 11, no. 3 (Fall 1999/2000): 137–68.

Christiansen-Ruffman, Linda. 1996. "Pages from Beijing: A Woman's Creed and the NGO Declaration." *Canadian Woman Studies/les cahiers de la femme: "Post-Beijing"* 16, no. 3 (Summer): 35–41.

Christianson, Scott R. 1997. "Ella C. Sykes." In *Dictionary of Literary Biography,* vol. 174, *British Travel Writers, 1876–1909,* ed. Barbara Brothers and Julia Gergits, 289–93. Detroit: Gale Research.

Cohen, Marcia. 1988. *The Sisterhood: The Inside Story of the Women's Movement and the Leaders Who Made It Happen.* New York: Fawcett Columbine.

Cooke, Joanne, Charlotte Bunch-Weeks, and Robin Morgan, ed. 1970. *The New Women: Motive Anthology on Women's Liberation.* Indianapolis: Bobbs-Merrill.

Cummings, Judith. 1977. "Lunch for Empress Interrupted by Shout of 'Down with Shah.'" *New York Times,* July 8, B2.

———. 1979. "Demonstrators in City Back Iranian Women's Rights." *New York Times,* March 16, A7.

Da Silva, Ginger. 2001. "Women in Iran." *Radio Netherlands,* May 17 and 18. http://www.rnw.nl/development/html/iranwomen010516.html.

Davidoff, Leonore, and Catherine Hall. 1987. *Family Fortunes: Men and Women of the English Middle Class, 1780–1850.* Chicago: University of Chicago Press.

Davis, Angela. [1981] 1983. *Women, Race, and Class.* New York: Vintage Books.

————. 1989. *Women, Culture, and Politics*. New York: Random House.

de Certeau, Michel. 1984. *The Practice of Everyday Life*, trans. Steven Randall. Berkeley: University of California Press.

de Villiers, Gérard, Bernard Touchais, and Annick de Villiers. 1976. *The Imperial Shah: An Informal Biography*, trans. June P. Wilson and Walter B. Michaels. Boston: Little, Brown.

Dollimore, Jonathan. 1991. *Sexual Dissidence: Augustine to Wilde, Freud to Foucault*. Oxford: Clarendon Press.

Eisenstein, Zillah. 2000. "Writing Bodies on the Nation for the Globe." In *Women, States, and Nationalism: At Home in the Nation?*, ed. Sita Ranchod-Nilsson and Mary Ann Tetreault. London: Routledge.

————. 2004. *Against Empire: Feminisms, Racism, and the West*. London: Zed Books.

Ensler, Eve. 1998. *The Vagina Monologues*. New York: Villard.

————. 2004. *The Good Body*. New York: Villard.

Entekhabi-Fard, Camelia. 2001. "Behind the Veil." *Mother Jones*, August, 68+.

Esfandiari, Haleh. 1997. *Reconstructed Lives: Women and Iran's Islamic Revolution*. Washington, D.C.: Woodrow Wilson Center Press.

————. 2003. *Middle Eastern Women on the Move: Openings for and the Constraints on Women's Political Participation in the Middle East*. Washington, D.C.: Woodrow Wilson International Center for Scholars. http://www.wilsoncenter.org.

Fabian, Johannes. 1983. *Time and the Other: How Anthropology Makes Its Object*. New York: Columbia University Press.

Faludi, Susan. 1991. *Backlash: The Undeclared War against American Women*. New York: Crown Publishers.

Fanon, Frantz. [1959] 1965. "Algeria Unveiled." In *A Dying Colonialism*, trans. Haakon Chevalier, 35–67. New York: Grove Press.

Felski, Rita. 1995. *The Gender of Modernity*. Cambridge, Mass.: Harvard University Press.

Foucault, Michel. [1972] 1986. *The Archaeology of Knowledge*. London: Tavistock Publications.

————. [1975] 1979. *Discipline and Punish: The Birth of the Prison*, trans. Alan Sheridan. New York: Vintage Books.

————. 1980. *Power/Knowledge: Selected Interviews and Other Writings, 1972–1977*, ed. Colin Gordon. New York: Pantheon Books.

Frankenberg, Ruth. 1993. *The Social Construction of Whiteness: White Women, Race Matters*. Minneapolis: University of Minnesota Press.

French, Marilyn. 1992. *The War against Women*. New York: Summit Books.

Friedan, Betty. 1975. "Coming Out of the Veil." *Ladies' Home Journal*, May 20, 71+.

Gikandi, Simon. 1996. *Maps of Englishness: Writing Identity in the Culture of Colonialism.* New York: Columbia University Press.

Greer, Germaine. 1975a. "Germaine Greer on Women's Year." *Chatelaine,* September, 4+.

———. 1975b. "At the U.N., Women's Year of Disgrace." *New York Times,* May 9, 35.

———. 1984. *Sex and Destiny: The Politics of Human Fertility.* New York: Harper and Row.

———. 1988. "Women's Glib." *Vanity Fair,* June, 32+.

Grewal, Inderpal. 1996. *Home and Harem: Nation, Gender, Empire, and the Cultures of Travel.* Durham, N.C.: Duke University Press.

Gubar, Susan. 1998. "What Ails Feminist Criticism?" *Critical Inquiry* 24, no. 4 (Summer): 878–902.

———. 1999. "Notations in Medias Res." *Critical Inquiry* 25, no. 2 (Winter): 380–96.

Haeri, Shahla. 1980. "Women, Law, and Social Change in Iran." In *Women in Contemporary Muslim Societies,* ed. Jane I. Smith, 209–34. Lewisburg, Pa.: Bucknell University Press.

Haggis, Jane. 1998. "White Women and Colonialism: Towards a Non-recuperative History." In *Gender and Imperialism,* ed. Clare Midgley, 45–75. Manchester: Manchester University Press.

Hamilton, Lee. 2002. "Combating Terrorism and Protecting Our Homeland." Speech delivered to Women's National Democratic Club, Washington, D.C., September 10. Available at http://www.wilsoncenter.org/index.cfm?fuseaction=director.speeches.

———. 2005. "The Lessons of 9/11" (September), http://www.wilsoncenter.org/index.cfm?fuseaction=director.speeches.

Heitlinger, Alena. 1999. "Émigré Feminism: An Introduction." In *Émigré Feminism: Transnational Perspectives,* ed. Alena Heitlinger, 3–16. Toronto: University of Toronto Press.

Hoffman, Merle. 1998. "Iran: Notes from the Interior." *On the Issues* (Spring), http://www.echonhyc.com/-onissues/sp98hoffman.html.

Holton, Sandra Stanley. 1996. *Suffrage Days: Stories from the Women's Suffrage Movement.* London: Routledge.

Hoodfar, Homa. [1993] 1997. "The Veil in Their Minds and on Our Heads: Veiling Practices and Muslim Women." In *The Politics of Culture in the Shadow of Capital,* ed. Lisa Lowe and David Lloyd, 248–79. Durham, N.C.: Duke University Press.

hooks, bell. 1981. *Ain't I a Woman? Black Women and Feminism.* Boston: South End Press.

———. 1984. *Feminist Theory: From Margin to Center.* Boston: South End Press.

———. 1986. "Sisterhood: Political Solidarity between Women." *Feminist Review* 23 (June): 125–38.

Howe, Marvine. 1977. "Iranian Women Return to Veil in a Resurgence of Spirituality." *New York Times,* July 30, 20.

Huber, Mary Taylor, and Nancy C. Lutkehaus. 1999. "Introduction: Gendered Missions at Home and Abroad." In *Gendered Missions and Men in Missionary Discourse and Practice,* ed. Mary Taylor Huber and Nancy C. Lutkehaus. Ann Arbor: University of Michigan Press.

Hull, Gloria T., Patricia Bell Scott, and Barbara Smith, ed. 1982. *All the Women Are White, All the Blacks Are Men, But Some of Us Are Brave.* Old Westbury, N.Y.: Feminist Press.

Islamic Penal Code. 2001. *Homan,* July 16. http://www.homan.cwc.net/english/Islamic_penal_law.htm.

Issa, Rose. 1997. "'Re-Orienting Our Views': A Rediscovery of Iran through Its Cinema and Women Filmmakers." *N. Paradoxa,* no. 5, May. http://www.nima3.com/IranMedia2/women.htm.

Jakobsen, Janet R. 1998. *Working Alliances and the Politics of Difference: Diversity and Feminist Ethics.* Bloomington: Indiana University Press.

Jayawardena, Kumari. 1995. *The White Woman's Other Burden: Western Women and South Asia during British Rule.* New York: Routledge.

Jaynes, Gregory. 1979a. "Bazargan Goes to See Khomeini as Iran Rift Grows." *New York Times,* March 9, A1+.

———. 1979b. "Iran Women March against Restraints on Dress and Rights." *New York Times,* March 11, 1+.

Kahf, Mohja. 1999. *Western Representations of the Muslim Woman: From Termagant to Odalisque.* Austin: University of Texas Press.

Kaupp, Katia. 1979. "Les visiteuses de l'ayatollah." *Le Nouvel Observateur,* March 26, 49.

Keddie, Nikkie. 1981. *Roots of Revolution: An Interpretive History of Modern Iran.* New Haven, Conn.: Yale University Press.

———. 1991. "Iran under the Later Qajars, 1848–1922." In *The Cambridge History of Iran: From Nadir Shah to the Islamic Republic,* ed. Peter Avery et al., 174–212. Cambridge: Cambridge University Press.

Kelber, Mim. 1979. "Iran, Five Days in March: Was the Revolution a Beginning of Women of the World United?" *Ms.,* June, 90–96.

Khomeini, Ayatollah Ruhollah. 1981. *Islam and Revolution: Writings and Declarations of Imam Khomeini,* trans. and annot. Hamid Algar. Berkeley: Mizan Press.

Kia, Mana. 2005. "Negotiating Women's Rights: Activism, Class, and Modernization in Pahlavi Iran." *Comparative Studies of South Asia, Africa, and the Middle East* 25, no. 1: 227–44.

Lazreq, Marnia. 1994. *The Eloquence of Silence: Algerian Women in Question*. New York: Routledge.

Mackey, Sandra. [1996] 1998. *The Iranians: Persia, Islam, and the Soul of a Nation*. New York: Plume.

McClintock, Anne. 1995. *Imperial Leather: Race, Gender, and Sexuality in the Colonial Conquest*. New York: Routledge.

McElrone, Susynne M. 2005. "Nineteenth-Century Qajar Women in the Public Sphere: An Alternative Historical and Historiographical Reading of the Roots of Iranian Women's Activism." *Comparative Studies of South Asia, Africa, and the Middle East* 25, no. 2: 297–317.

McEwan, Cheryl. 2000. *Gender, Geography, and Empire: Victorian Women Travellers in West Africa*. Adlershot, England: Ashgate Publishing.

Melman, Billie. 1992. *Women's Orients, English Women, and the Middle East, 1718–1918: Sexuality, Religion, and Work*. Ann Arbor: University of Michigan Press.

———. 1996. "Transparent Veils: Western Women Dis-Orient the East." In *The Geography of Identity*, ed. Patricia Yeager. Ann Arbor: University of Michigan.

Midgley, Claire, ed. 1998. *Gender and Imperialism*. Manchester: Manchester University Press.

Milani, Farzaneh. 1992. *Veils and Words: The Emerging Voices of Iranian Women Writers*. Syracuse, N.Y.: Syracuse University Press.

Millett, Kate. 1979. "Millett Says Iran Arrest Frightening." *Washington Post*, March 20, A12.

———. 1982. *Going to Iran*. New York: Coward, McCann, and Geoghegan.

Mills, Sara. [1991] 1993. *Discourses of Difference: An Analysis of Women's Travel Writing and Colonialism*. London: Routledge.

Mir-Hosseini, Ziba. 1996. "Veiling and Politics in Post-Khomeini Iran: Divorce, Veiling, and Emerging Feminist Voices." In *Women and Politics in the Third World*, ed. Haleh Afshar, 142–70. London: Routledge.

———. 1999. *Islam and Gender: The Religious Debate in Contemporary Iran*. Princeton, N.J.: Princeton University Press.

———. 2001a. "Iranian Cinema: Art, Society, and the State." *Middle East Report* (Summer). http://www.merip.org/mer/mer219/219_ziba-mir-hosseini.html.

———. 2001b. "Iran's Runaway Girls Challenge the Old Rules." Manuscript version.

———. 2002a. "Negotiating the Politics of Gender in Iran: An Ethnography of a Documentary." In *The New Iranian Cinema: Politics, Representation, and Identity*, ed. Richard Tapper, 167–99. London: I. B. Tauris.

———. 2002b. "Iran's Runaway Girls Challenge the Old Rules." *ISIM (International Institute for the Study of Islam in the Modern World) Newsletter* 9 (January). http://www.isim.nl/.

Moallem, Minoo. 1999. "Transnationalism, Feminism, and Fundamentalism." In *Between Woman and Nation: Nationalisms, Transnational Feminisms, and the State,* ed. Caren Kaplan et al., 320–48. Durham, N.C.: Duke University Press.

———. 2005. *Between Warrior Brother and Veiled Sister: Islamic Fundamentalism and the Politics of Patriarchy in Iran.* Berkeley: University of California Press.

Moghissi, Haideh. 1999a. "Émigré Iranian Feminism and the Construction of the Muslim Woman." In *Émigré Feminism: Transnational Perspectives,* ed. Alena Heitlinger, 189–207. Toronto: University of Toronto Press.

———. 1999b. *Feminism and Islamic Fundamentalism: The Limits of Postmodern Analysis.* London: Zed Books.

Mohanty, Chandra Talpade. 1991. "Under Western Eyes: Feminist Scholarship and Colonial Discourses." In *Third World Women and the Politics of Feminism,* ed. Chandra Talpade Mohanty, Ann Russo, and Lourdes Torres, 51–80. Bloomington: Indiana University Press.

———. 2002. "'Under Western Eyes' Revisited: Feminist Solidarity through Anticapitalist Struggles." *Signs: Journal of Women in Culture and Society* 28, no. 2: 499–535.

Molavi, Afshin. 2002. "A Tale of Two Women." *SAIS Review* 20, no. 2: 217–21.

Montgomery, Helen Barrett. [1910] 1987. *Western Women in Eastern Lands.* New York: Garland Publishing.

Moraga, Cherríe, and Gloria Anzaldúa, ed. 1981. *This Bridge Called My Back: Writings by Radical Women of Color.* Berkeley, Calif.: Third Woman Press.

Morgan, David. 1988. *Medieval Persia, 1040–1797.* London: Longman.

Morgan, Robin, ed. 1970. *Sisterhood Is Powerful: An Anthology of Writings from the Women's Liberation Movement.* New York: Random House.

———, ed. 1984. *Sisterhood Is Global: The International Women's Movement Anthology.* Garden City, N.Y.: Anchor Press/Doubleday.

Morris, Holly. 2005. "Tahmineh Milani: Activist/Filmmaker." *Adventure Divas,* November 12. http://www.pbs.org/adventuredivas/iran/divas/milani.html.

Moruzzi, Norma Claire. 2001. "Women in Iran: Notes on Film and from the Field." *Feminist Studies* 27, no. 1 (Spring): 89–100.

Naficy, Hamid. 2000. "Veiled Voice and Vision in Iranian Cinema: The Evolution of Rakhshan Banietemad's Films." *Social Research* 67, no. 2 (Summer): 559–76.

Nafisi, Azar. 1999. "The Veiled Threat." *New Republic,* February 22. http://www.thenewrepublic.com/magazines/tnr/archive/0299/022299/nafisi022299.html.

———. 2003. *Reading Lolita in Tehran: A Memoir in Books.* New York: Random House.

Nair, Janaki. 1990. "Uncovering the Zenana: Visions of Indian Womanhood in Englishwomen's Writings, 1813–1940." *Journal of Women's History* 2, no. 1 (Spring): 8–34.

Najmabadi, Afsaneh. 1991. "Hazards of Modernity and Morality: Women, State, and Ideology in Contemporary Iran." In *Women, Islam, and the State,* ed. Deniz Kandiyoti, 48–76. Philadelphia: Temple University Press.

———. 1993. "Veiled Discourse—Unveiled Bodies." *Feminist Studies* 19, no. 3 (Fall): 487–518.

———. 1997. "Feminisms in an Islamic Republic." In *Transitions, Environments, Translations: Feminisms in International Politics,* 390–99. New York: Routledge.

———. 1998. "Crafting an Educated Housewife in Iran." In *Remaking Women: Feminism and Modernity in the Middle East,* ed. Lila Abu-Lughod, 91–125. Princeton, N.J.: Princeton University Press.

———. 2005. *Women with Mustaches and Men without Beards: Gender and Sexual Anxieties of Iranian Modernity.* Berkeley: University of California Press.

Nichols, Bill. 2001. *Introduction to Documentary.* Bloomington: Indiana University Press.

Pahlavi, Ashraf. 1980. *Faces in a Mirror: Memoirs from Exile.* Englewood Cliffs, N.J.: Prentice-Hall.

Pahlavi, Farah. 1978. *My Thousand and One Days: An Autobiography,* trans. Felice Harcourt. London: W. H. Allen.

Paidar, Parvin. [1995] 1997. *Women and the Political Process in Twentieth-Century Iran.* Cambridge: Cambridge University Press.

Peterson, V. Spike. 2000. "Sexing Political Identities/Nationalism as Heterosexism." In *Women, States, and Nationalism: At Home in the Nation?,* ed. Sita Ranchod-Nilsson and Mary Ann Tetreault. London: Routledge.

Philip, Marlene Nourbese, ed. 1992. *Frontiers: Selected Essays and Writings on Racism and Culture, 1984–1992.* Ontario: Mercury Press.

Poppy, Nick. 1999. "Irreconcilable Differences: 'Divorce Iranian Style.'" *indieWIRE,* November. http://www.indiewire.com/people/int_Longinotto_MirH_981209.html.

Rahimieh, Nasrin. 1990. *Oriental Responses to the West: Comparative Essays in Select Writers from the Muslim World.* Leiden, N.Y.: E. J. Brill.

———. 2001. *Missing Persians: Discovering Voices in Iranian Cultural History.* Syracuse, N.Y.: Syracuse University Press.

Randal, Jonathan C. 1979. "Sexual Politics in Iran: Kate Millett Finds that Tehran's Feminists Are Not United." *Washington Post,* March 12, B1+.

Razack, Sherene H. 1998. *Looking White People in the Eye: Gender, Race, and Culture in Courtrooms and Classrooms.* Toronto: University of Toronto Press.

Rice, Clara Colliver. 1923. *Persian Women and Their Ways: The Experiences and Impressions of a Long Sojourn amongst the Women of the Land of the Shah with an Intimate Description of Their Characteristics, Customs, and Manner of Living.* London: Seeley, Service, and Co.

Rich, Adrienne. 1980. "Compulsory Heterosexuality and Lesbian Existence." *Signs: A Journal of Women in Culture and Society* 5, no. 4: 631–60.

Robbins, Bruce. 1995. "The Weird Heights: On Cosmopolitanism, Feeling, and Power." *Differences: A Journal of Feminist Cultural Studies* 7, no. 1: 165–87.

Rupp, Leila J. 1996. "Challenging Imperialism in International Women's Organizations, 1888–1945." *NWSA* 8, no. 1 (Spring): 8–27.

———. 1997. *Worlds of Women: The Making of an International Women's Movement.* Princeton, N.J.: Princeton University Press.

Said, Edward. *Orientalism.* [1978] 1979. New York: Vintage Books.

Al-Saltana, Taj. 1993. *Crowning Anguish: Memoirs of a Persian Princess from the Harem to Modernity, 1884–1914,* ed. Abbas Amanat, trans. Anna Vanzan and Amin Neshati. Washington, D.C.: Mage Publishers.

Sanasarian, Eliz. 1982. *The Women's Rights Movement in Iran: Mutiny, Appeasement, and Repression from 1900 to Khomeini.* New York: Praeger Publishers.

Savery, C. 1942. *She Went Alone: Mary Bird of Persia.* London: Edinburgh House Press.

Schreiber, Adele, and Margaret Mathieson. 1955. *Journey towards Freedom.* London: William Clowes and Sons.

Sciolino, Elaine. 1999. "Trip of Discoveries, Some Unhappy, in Iran." *New York Times,* February 28, sec. 5, 8+.

———. 2000. *Persian Mirrors: The Elusive Face of Iran.* New York: Free Press.

Scott, David. 1999. *Refashioning Futures: Criticism after Postcoloniality.* Princeton, N.J.: Princeton University Press.

Scott, Joan. 1995. "Universalism and the History of Feminism." *Differences: A Journal of Feminist Cultural Studies* 7, no. 1: 1–14.

Scott, Stephanie. 2001. "Tahmineh Milani Talks Back: A Feminist Filmmaker Forges Ahead and Fights for Freedom in Iran." December 11. http://www.newenglandfilm.com/news/archives/01december/Milani.htm.

Sedgwick, Eve Kosofsky. 1985. *Between Men: English Literature and Male Homosocial Desire.* New York: Columbia University Press.

Servan-Schreiber, Claude. 1979. "And Now a Word from the Male Leaders of the Islamic Republic." *Ms.,* June, 95.

Showalter, Elaine. 1990. *Sexual Anarchy: Gender and Culture at the Fin de Siècle.* New York: Viking Penguin.

Spivak, Gayatri Chakravorty. 1985. "Three Women's Texts and a Critique of Imperialism." *Critical Inquiry* 12, no. 1 (Autumn): 243–61.

————. 1986. "Imperialism and Sexual Difference." *Oxford Literary Review* 8, no. 1–2: 225–40.

————. 1988. "Can the Subaltern Speak?" In *Marxism and the Interpretation of Culture,* ed. C. Nelson and L. Grossberg, 271–313. Basingstoke: Macmillan Education.

————. 1989. "Who Claims Alterity?" In *Remaking History,* ed. Barbara Kruger and Phil Marian, 269–92. Seattle: Bay Press.

————. 1990. "Poststructuralism, Marginality, Postcoloniality, and Value." In *Literary Theory Today,* ed. Peter Collier and Helga Geyer-Ryan, 219–44. Ithaca, N.Y.: Cornell University Press.

————. 1993. "Woman in Difference." In *Outside in the Teaching Machine,* 77–95. New York: Routledge.

————. 1996a. "'Woman' as Theatre: United Nations Conference on Women, Beijing, 1995." *Radical Philosophy* 75 (January/February): 2–4.

————. 1996b. "Diasporas Old and New: Women in the Transnational World." *Textual Practice* 10, no. 2 : 245–69.

Stark, Freya. 1936. *The Valleys of the Assassins and Other Persian Travels.* London: Century Publishing.

Straayer, Chris. 1994. "The Hypothetical Lesbian Heroine." In *Multiple Voices in Feminist Film Criticism,* ed. Diane Carson, Linda Dittmar, and Janice R. Welsch, 343–57. Minneapolis: University of Minnesota Press.

————. 1996. *Deviant Eyes, Deviant Bodies: Sexual Re-Orientations in Film and Video.* New York: Columbia University Press.

Sullivan, Zohreh T. 1998. "Eluding the Feminist, Overthrowing the Modern? Transformations in Twentieth-Century Iran." In *Remaking Women: Feminism and Modernity in the Middle East,* ed. Lila Abu-Lughod, 215–42. Princeton, N.J.: Princeton University Press.

Sykes, Ella Constance. 1901. *Through Persia on a Side-Saddle.* London: John MacQueen.

————. 1910a. *Persia and Its People.* London: Methuen and Company.

————. 1910b. "A Talk about Persia and Its Women." *National Geographic Society* (October): 847–66.

Tabari, Azar. 1980. "The Enigma of Veiled Iranian Women." *Feminist Review* 5: 19–31.

Tavakoli-Targhi, Mohamad. 2001. *Refashioning Iran: Orientalism, Occidentalism, and Historiography.* New York: Palgrave.

Thorne, Susan. 1999. "Missionary-Imperial Feminism." In *Gendered Missions: Women and Men in Missionary Discourse and Practice,* ed. Mary Taylor Huber and Nancy C. Lutkehaus, 39–65. Ann Arbor: University of Michigan Press.

Thornham, Sue. 1999. "Second Wave Feminism." In *The Routledge Critical Dictionary of Feminism and Postfeminism*, ed. Sarah Gamble, 29–42. New York: Routledge.

Vander Werff, Lyle L. 1977. *Christian Mission to Muslims: The Record*. South Pasadena, Calif.: William Carey Library.

Van Sommer, Annie, and Rev. Samuel M. Zwemer, ed. 1907. *Our Moslem Sisters: A Cry of Need from Lands of Darkness Interpreted by Those Who Heard It*. New York: Fleming H. Revell.

———. 1911. *Daylight in the Harem: A New Era for Moslem Women*. Edinburgh: Oliphant, Anderson, and Ferrier.

Wallach, Janet. 1996. *Desert Queen: The Extraordinary Life of Gertrude Bell: Adventurer, Adviser to Kings, Ally of Lawrence of Arabia*. New York: Doubleday.

Ware, Vron. 1992. *Beyond the Pale: White Women, Racism, and History*. London: Verso.

Wearing, Alison. 2000. *Honeymoon in Purdah: An Iranian Journey*. Toronto: Alfred A. Knopf Canada.

Weber, Charlotte. 2001. "Unveiling Scheherazade: Feminist Orientalism in the International Alliance of Women, 1911–1950." *Feminist Studies* 27, no. 1 (Spring): 125–57.

Wells, Paul. 1996. "The Documentary Form: Personal and Social 'Realities.'" In *An Introduction to Film Studies*, ed. Jill Nelmes, 67–191. London: Routledge.

Wiegman, Robyn. 1999/2000. "Feminism, Institutionalism, and the Idiom of Failure." *Differences: A Journal of Feminist Cultural Studies* 11, no. 3 (Fall): 107–36.

———. 1999. "What Ails Feminist Criticism? A Second Opinion." *Critical Inquiry* 25, no. 2 (Winter): 362–79.

Whitlock, Gillian. 2005. "The Skin of the Burqa: Recent Life Narratives from Afghanistan." *Biography* 28, no. 1 (Winter): 54–76.

Wollstonecraft, Mary. 1997. *A Vindication of the Rights of Man and a Vindication of the Rights of Woman*, ed. D. L. Macdonald and Kathleen Scherf. Peterborough, Ontario: Broadview Press.

Woodsmall, Ruth Frances. 1936. *Moslem Women Enter a New World*. New York: RoundTable Press.

———. [1960] 1977. *Women and the New East*. Washington, D.C.: Middle East Institute.

Wright, Denis. 1977. *The English amongst the Persians: During the Qajar Period, 1787–1921*. London: Heinemann.

Yeğenoğlu, Meyda. 1998. *Colonial Fantasies: Towards a Feminist Reading of Orientalism*. Cambridge: Cambridge University Press.

———. 2002. "Sartorial Fabric-ations: Enlightenment and Western Feminism."

In *Postcolonialism, Feminism, and Religious Discourse,* ed. Laura E. Donaldson and Kwok Pui-Lan, 82–99. New York: Routledge.

Yonan, Rev. Isaac Malek. 1898. *Persian Women: A Sketch of Woman's Life from the Cradle to the Grave, and Missionary Work Among Them, with Illustrations.* Nashville, Tenn.: Cumberland Presbyterian House.

Zirinsky, Michael. 1992. "Harbingers of Change: Presbyterian Women in Iran 1883–1949." *American Presbyterians* 70, no. 3: 173–86.

———. 1994. "A Panacea for the Ills of the Country: American Presbyterian Education in Interwar Iran." *American Presbyterians* 72, no. 3: 187–201.

Index

Nima Naghibi is assistant professor of English at Ryerson
University in Toronto.